THE NEW CHINA PLAYBOOK

THE
NEW CHINA
PLAYBOOK

BEYOND SOCIALISM
AND CAPITALISM

Keyu Jin

VIKING

VIKING
An imprint of Penguin Random House LLC
penguinrandomhouse.com

Graphs on page 164 from "Demystifying the Chinese Housing Boom"
used with permission of Professor Wei Xiong.

LIBRARY OF CONGRESS CATALOGING-IN-PUBLICATION DATA
Names: Jin, Keyu, author.
Title: The new China playbook : beyond socialism
and capitalism / Keyu Jin.
Description: [New York] : Viking, [2023] |
Includes bibliographical references and index.
Identifiers: LCCN 2022015175 (print) | LCCN 2022015176 (ebook) |
ISBN 9781984878281 (hardcover) | ISBN 9781984878298 (ebook)
Subjects: LCSH: China—Economic conditions—2000– |
China—Economic policy—2000–
Classification: LCC HC427.95 .J54227 2022 (print) |
LCC HC427.95 (ebook) |
DDC 330.951—dc23/eng/20220602
LC record available at https://lccn.loc.gov/2022015175
LC ebook record available at https://lccn.loc.gov/2022015176

Printed in the United States of America
1st Printing

DESIGNED BY MEIGHAN CAVANAUGH

To my parents

CONTENTS

ONE

THE CHINA PUZZLE

his book is about reading China in the original, coming to understand its people, economy, and government in such a way that the truth is not lost in translation, as is far too often the case. I first realized this fresh perspective was sorely needed way back in 1997, when, as a teenager, I came to the US as a Chinese exchange student. Dr. Lawrence Weiss, visionary headmaster of the Horace Mann School's upper division, in New York City, anticipated China's future significance in the world, despite its much smaller economic and political heft at that time. He believed it was important to introduce an authentically Chinese perspective to the school's intellectual and social life. I was selected to help fill those gaps, eager in return to learn from the America that so impressed all of us back home.

Having parachuted in from a geographically and ideologically far-flung land, I seemed exotic to my classmates. Outside of school, anytime I mentioned that I was from mainland China, a blizzard of questions followed. When will China become a democracy? Do you feel oppressed? How do you wake up in the morning knowing that you can't elect your own president? When will the Chinese economy stop growing? I was fortunate enough to live with a hospitable American host family who brought me directly into American political life. Fresh from Communist China, I plunged straight into democratic campaigns for high office in New York State, handing out leaflets and attending fundraisers. I met lots of well-informed, politically savvy people, but they surprised me by posing the same questions as my fellow students. It was becoming clear to me that even sophisticated Americans possessed only a simplistic understanding of life in China. Between the lines I sensed sympathy for my having grown up in what seemed to them a backward country, with limited freedom of expression or political choice.

But the China they imagined was far from the one that I knew from my everyday life there—not to mention that by 1997 seismic shifts were already under way in my home country. People's excitement and hopes were bubbling over as we debated the value of new economic reforms, our bid to host the Olympics, joining the World Trade Organization, privatizing state-owned companies, and adopting the technology of the West—including its cars, infrastructure, and business models. In school, our Chinese political science textbooks were in a constant state of revision, as Marxist thought gradually morphed into "socialism with Chinese characteristics." People in China were living more comfortably than they had in many generations. And every summer when I went back to Beijing during my years as an undergraduate, and later as a graduate student at Harvard, the city's skyline astonished me with its latest transformation.

Fast-forward nearly three decades to the present. Today the backward homeland of my childhood has become the world's second-largest economy, its massive new cities animated by astonishing technological wonders. Yet so much of the world is still asking the same questions, and still comparing China to former Communist countries with their autocratic and repressive regimes. Even when it comes to China's juggernaut economy, the world remains skeptical: China's economic model is running out of steam; the state is suppressing private entrepreneurs and stifling innovation; financial implosion looms on the horizon. However, in 2008 it was the US financial system that drove off a cliff, dragging with it a formidable array of European financial institutions and corporate giants. When so many other significant players in the global economy fell into the recession that followed, it was no longer clear that a one-size-fits-all economic system like conventional Western capitalism was necessarily destined to prevail.

Many people today still hold the deep-seated conviction that China's present course will end in disaster unless it converges with Western values, economic systems, and political persuasions; some of those who hold a more positive view of China's economic accomplishments also tend to see China as a threat. As an economist who grew up there but also works in the West—with one foot in each world, as it were—I believe neither of these perspectives accurately reflects what is truly going on in China. This book proposes an alternative view: more nuanced, more complex, and, hopefully, more helpful.

Understanding the Chinese system and its economy is essential to comprehending China more broadly. Those who wish to see China succeed will need to understand how its economy functions so they can better take advantage of the opportunities it presents. Those who don't trust China will be able to critique it with more relevance, to better distinguish the acts of the state from those of the people, and to separate macro appearances from micro realities. Between China and the West there are many areas of contention and differences in values, perspectives, and political approaches, so all too often immediate events and political dramas eclipse consideration of economics. In this book I will try not to succumb to these distractions, but will limit myself instead to orbiting the economic issues—and the political and cultural superstructure on which they depend.

In the decades that followed my high school studies in the Bronx, China has forged a unique economic model well suited to its purposes, aligned with its national conditions, and authentic to its culture. Despite regular predictions of its imminent collapse, China continues to defy conventional wisdom: far from acting with an invisible hand to manipulate the economy behind the scenes, the state has intervened often, heavily, and sometimes clumsily. The rule of law, sound corporate governance, and intellectual property protection—all long held up as essential to long-term growth—have been weak during much of China's economic upsurge. Yet somehow China's approach seems to have succeeded. A large segment of China's population has been lifted into the middle class. Twenty million private firms have sprung up like mushrooms, when only thirty years ago they couldn't even legally conduct normal business. In 2019, China had the world's largest number of unicorn companies (private firms valued at $1 billion or more). In a landscape where empty plains once reached to the horizon, now gleaming new smart cities feature separate driving lanes for autonomous vehicles, and robots serving Kentucky Fried Chicken. And for those who think that China's all-powerful political party and numerous state-owned enterprises (SOEs) point to a state-dominated economy, consider these facts: Today it is the *private sector* that accounts for more than 60 percent of national output, 70 percent of the nation's wealth, and 80 percent of urban employment. Thirty years ago, it was the other way around.[1]

To my European colleagues, exactly what role the Communist Party plays in a seemingly thriving capitalist economy has always been a mystery. To my American friends, China's dynamic entrepreneurialism seems wholly incompatible with its people's deference to authority. Resolving these paradoxes requires going beyond mere stereotypes. Only by fully grasping the new China model with its intricate and often contradictory dynamics can we truly appreciate how different it is from pure capitalism or socialism. Only then can we critique the China model intelligently—both recognizing its merits and identifying its challenges. As China's economy matures, this deeper understanding will help us anticipate which aspects of the model will endure and which are likely to change. As excited as I have been about China's mesmerizing economic surge, I am equally concerned about the long-term ramifications of its approach and the suitability of the system in the new era.

Demystifying China's meteoric ascent requires examining the fluid interplay between many elements, including households, business enterprises, and the state, along with the tidal pulls of history and culture. In subsequent chapters, we will explore the behaviors and incentives that drive each of these three basic economic agents, and how their interactions make up the colorful and often paradoxical Chinese economy. With a deeper understanding of their roles, we can then grapple with China's ambitions with regard to technology, trade, and finance, as well as China's impact on the global economy. Finally we take the key themes that have emerged—the role of the state, the importance of a new generation, and China's coming of age—and use them to consider how the nation's present will extend its reach into its future as it embarks on a new era.

Deng Xiaoping, China's supreme leader, who rose to power in 1978, once remarked that it does not matter whether a cat is black or white, so long as it catches mice. He shrewdly put an end to the febrile debate about the superiority of socialism and capitalism in an ideologically charged era. The idea that a market economy could be compatible not only with capitalism but also with socialism was a breakthrough that set the nation on a course of economic liberalization. Since then, China's economic system has begun to morph gradually into a unique form. Whether it is called "managed capitalism," the "mayor economy," or, more officially, "socialism with Chinese characteristics," its model does not neatly fit into any category. Instead, it embodies a unique blend of the state and the market economy, striking a balance between state and industry, coordination and market incentives, communalism and individualism.

The contrast between China's political economy model and the West's free market model is illustrated by Figure 1.1. The market economy of the West is made up of consumers and enterprises connected through a financial system, in which the state plays a minor role. In China, the confluence of consumers, enterprises, and the state (which exerts significant power over the financial system) results in a hybrid that contains elements of both market and "mayor" economies (about which we will learn more in chapter 5). The size and power of the Chinese state is greater than that of Western countries, as the figure shows, reflected in the fact that it has many more tools and instruments at its disposal as well as a wider range of mandates and objectives. The state in China is unique in its ability to mobilize collective action in service of the nation's goals. Not only can it allocate resources and create incentives, but it can also impose mandates and mete out punishment.

A second feature that makes the system different is that China's *political centralization* is paired with *economic decentralization*. The central government sets the strategic direction, but local officials deliver on the ground. The "mayors" are effective equity stakeholders of their jurisdiction. By supporting good private companies, they build an industrial cluster, and a thriving economy with multiplier effects: more GDP, jobs, and surging real estate prices. They collect more tax revenue and ascend the political ladder. This is why, contrary to our deep-seated assumptions about the state, local officials are more likely to lend a helping hand than to extend a grabbing hand. As we will see throughout this book, this unique marriage of local officials and intrepid entrepreneurs is how China reformed, industrialized, urbanized, and now innovates.

The third feature of China's growth model is that aspects of its economy are still nascent: its institutions, such as legal systems, regulatory bodies, and contractual rules, though improving, have been hitherto weak. In an economy with many institutional flaws and loopholes, the state holds the keys for any business looking to overcome a wide range of entry and operational barriers. As a result, in China, an intimacy between the state and the private sector has emerged unlike anything we see anywhere else in the world. There is a lot of good that the state *can* do in immature markets. The problem is that most developing countries have neither state capacity nor good institutions. China has strong state capacity and weak institutions, whereas advanced countries like the United States have strong formal institutions but state capacity is gradually eroding.

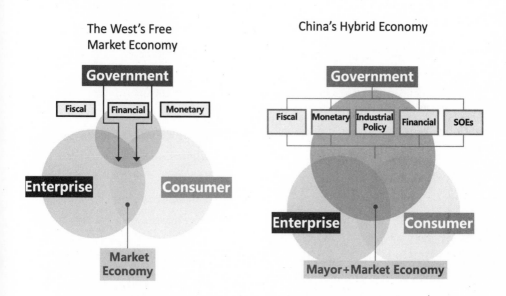

Figure 1.1: The left panel illustrates the free market economy of the West; the right panel illustrates the hybrid Chinese economy. Government in the West mainly influences the market through its fiscal, financial, and monetary policies, whereas the Chinese government also applies industrial policies and management of its state-owned enterprises. The size of government is much larger in China, and government is an active participant in a hybrid economy.

The biggest difference between socialism and capitalism is dynamic innovation—capitalism's most fundamental virtue, delivered by mechanisms such as property rights protection and competition, which are notably weak in socialist systems (Table 1.1). But in China, innovation and entrepreneurship have been defining features of the economy despite socialist characteristics of in-state coordination and resource allocation. It has found a way to combine private and state forces to suit its own circumstances.

TABLE 1.1

	CAPITALISM	SOCIALISM
Private Property Rights	Strong	Insecure
Research Initiatives and Decisions	Entrepreneurs/Firms	Government
Financial Reward for Entrepreneurs	Large	Insignificant
Competition (creative destruction)	Strong	Weak
Financing of Projects	Flexible and Market Based	Rigid and Allocated

Source: Modified version of Chenggang Xu, "Capitalism and Socialism: A Review of Kornai's *Dynamism, Rivalry, and the Surplus Economy*," *Journal of Economic Literature* 55, no. 1 (March 2017): 191–208.

Thus, it is easy to make the mistake, as many pundits do, of ascribing China's success either to the emergence of free market economics or to the power of a highly centralized Communist regime. But the truth lies somewhere in between. Yes, markets do work in China: goods and factor markets (capital and labor) operate on the basis of supply and demand, consumers shop freely, and firms innovate. Discovery, education, and sound financial investments lead to lucrative returns. But state planning and mobilization also have a starring role: How else is it possible, for example, that a developing country like China can become both the largest consumer and producer of electric vehicles in a matter of a few years? Mass adoption of a new-generation transport technology requires rapidly rolling out charging stations, organizing supply chains from battery makers to manufacturers, and even breaking old consumer habits. Western economies talk about "nudging" consumers to do the socially optimal thing—and have difficulty succeeding. In China, system-wide changes can be enacted quickly, with little political opposition. To some, this may sound both impressive and scary at the same time.

The combination of state guidance at the macro level and market mechanisms at the micro level, as we will see throughout this book, is what explains China's rapid growth spurts and its technological uptake in such a short span of time. It is also the approach taken toward achieving its new objective of shared prosperity. It explains many economic conundrums, such as the persistent undervaluation of China's exchange rate, sustained periods of low interest rates and suppressed wages, and large trade surpluses—all notable mysteries at various times in recent history. Contradictory mandates and the tension that arises when the state and markets pull in opposite directions are a recurrent feature of the hybrid economy. Although replicating China's successful economic formula may not be possible for third world countries looking for a model to follow, there are still many lessons to absorb from it as an alternative to full-fledged capitalism. And although our focus is on the Chinese economy today and tomorrow, I draw liberally from the nation's recent past in order to better comprehend both the present moment and those yet to come.

Making Sense of the Puzzle That Is China

Economists tend to focus on universal principles—a given set of fundamental rules established within a given framework that gives rise to predictable outcomes. But when we look at China, anomalies, paradoxes, and puzzles abound. Western economic thought is based on the premise that individuals seek to maximize their own welfare, and that companies are similarly motivated to maximize profit; markets establish their own equilibrium, while the state plays a largely passive role. But in the Chinese landscape, the state features far more prominently, a towering peak overlooking other imposing promontories like culture and history. In China's economy, those mechanisms identified by pioneers of economics like Adam Smith are not the only ones at work, nor always the most significant.

Consumers, entrepreneurs, and the state: in China none of them behaves like a conventional economic agent. Therefore, in our quest to learn more about China's present and prognosticate about its future, we will need to challenge Western assumptions, adjusting our lens so we can bring this global outlier into sharper focus. Chinese households tend to make decisions on a collective rather than individual basis, choices that take into account a rich network of intergenerational relationships and duties that often are placed above individual self-interest. Entrepreneurs decide not only what is optimal for their firm's profits, but also how to balance delicate relationships with local officials, align their goals with national policy directives, and manage symbolic and political responses to regulations that affect their business. The Chinese state is endowed with singular power, including an array of instruments that can be deployed to steer, manage, and push the economy in any direction. These tools of mass intervention are unparalleled. Policy directives, rules, and regulations can be set with little political obstruction. The state can scrap old rules and make new ones overnight, influencing when, how, and in what firms can invest overseas, granting or denying specific approvals and licenses, or leveraging the financial system to serve a national goal. But this power is not limitless. Internal controls and competition curb corruption. An increasingly demanding civic society holds the government more accountable on a wider range of issues. Social media—despite strict censorship—embodies a two-way monitoring platform between people and government.

If the first reason why the world so often misreads China is lack of a suitable perspective, the second is a shortage in the use of data; anecdotes are no substitute for hard evidence if we want to see the whole picture. While many are rightfully dubious about official Chinese figures, there is a plethora of good data available on the micro level, collected from households, firms, and industries. I will be drawing from this more granular information, including a wide range of internationally and privately commissioned data sets and surveys. These have the benefit of being far less prone to manipulation than national GDP figures or inflation rates, which are subject to political influence.

At the same time, data can be misleading without an appropriate framework for interpreting it. China's double-digit growth numbers for many decades may look staggering, but they're less impressive when benchmarked against the low base from which they started. Similarly, people have criticized China's investment in infrastructure as being far too high, based on its outsize 40 percent share of GDP, but for a country that is only a little more than halfway through its ambitious plan for urbanization, that number may not be high at all—if the money is efficiently used. With the right framework in mind and data for empirical validation, we can begin to see the Chinese economy for what it actually is.

A more accurate understanding of the Chinese economy also requires us to appreciate the impact of culture, values, and history. Only then can we come to explain its many paradoxes. Why does a Chinese household save 30 percent of its income on average, while its American counterpart saves on average 3 percent? How can a Chinese person with an income below the US poverty line afford Boston-tier housing prices? Why does China have the world's best-performing economy and the world's worst-performing stock market? How are government officials motivated to create massive wealth for private entrepreneurs without creating commensurate riches for themselves? How do we make sense of the fact that the fault lines in China's financial sector—its roller-coaster stock markets, exploding debt, shadow banking, and astronomical housing prices—have so far not led to a major financial implosion?

There are also many things that are difficult to reconcile with a Western orientation: highly centralized power with a government that is also attentive and responsive to its citizens; a new generation of strong-willed, hyper-educated (often in the West), and cosmopolitan Chinese that is still very oriented to what their parents want; a vast majority of China's citizens that willingly cooperates with the state, despite complaints and grievances over some of its stringent rules and impositions. What is acceptable behavior in some countries can induce quivers or distaste in others. According to the World Values Survey, which explores people's beliefs and values in more than one hundred countries, 93 percent of Chinese participants value security over freedom, as compared to only 28 percent of Americans.[2] Such differences can be fully understood only by taking culture and history into account.

In China, an interventionist state is rooted in paternalism, a hallmark of government in China since Confucian times, more than 2,500 years ago; it is based on the conviction that intervention by a senior person is justified if it benefits a junior person. This helps explain the urge of the Chinese government to steer the economy rather than just let the markets do all the work. This also offers up a reason for the state's aversion to economic and financial fluctuations, even when they reflect the natural cadences of a healthy market. And it provides a rationale for why the state prefers to liberalize slowly, treading carefully while avoiding certain risks, in contrast to the overnight overhaul of centralized economies we've seen in former Soviet bloc economies.

So far as the Chinese are concerned, there is little difference between state paternalism and authoritarian parenting. While those who grew up in Western cultures may balk at its intrusiveness, the Tiger Mom phenomenon of disciplining children and making decisions on their behalf is taken for granted by the Chinese people. Yet they do not see themselves as helpless pawns in the context of either family or society. Working around a social norm of strong tolerance, the Chinese constantly try to balance obligation and deference with free will. A longitudinal survey conducted by researchers at the Harvard Kennedy School—consistent with a range of surveys conducted internationally—reported strong satisfaction with the government, despite paternalism: 86 percent in 2003, 96 percent in 2009, and 93 percent in both 2015 and 2016.[3] The latest World Values Survey (2017–2020) indicates that 95 percent of Chinese participants had significant confidence in their government, compared to 33 percent in the US and 45 percent, on average, in the rest of the world.[4] As of 2022, that level of trust was at 91 percent, compared to 39 percent in the US.[5] Sentiments may fluctuate, and satisfaction levels tend to be lower for local government officials. But Chinese citizens *expect* the government to take on large roles in social and economic issues and do not see interventions as infringements on liberty.

The Good, the Bad, and the Future

China's economic story is by no means a narrative of unqualified triumph. It also serves as a cautionary tale. The Chinese economy in 1978, the year that it began to implement major reforms, was in shambles, and

China's people were mired in poverty. In the ensuing decades, hundreds of millions of people were lifted out of poverty, and the nation turned itself from an economic backwater into the most connected central component in the global economy. But China's economic ambitions have extracted a high price. In order to propel rapid industrialization and subsidize investment in production, households were weighted down with below-market wages and low rates of return on their savings. Imbalances deepened between trade exports and domestic consumption. Ancient towns with unique relics were flooded to build dams to power modernization. Grim, cheaply built housing projects sprang up, accompanied by widespread environmental degradation and wasted resources. China's economic development was based on a high-cost, high-growth model.

A poor nation with ambitions to catch up fast often ends up taking shortcuts. China was an archetypal country sprinting a marathon. Rules and regulations were bent as needed to foster GDP growth. Unfair competition widened the gap between a few insiders with good connections and the vast number of people without them. Unscrupulous businesspeople became billionaires overnight. And all of this was countenanced so long as capital flew in, investment grew, businesses boomed, and GDP surged.

The same approach applied to the drive to acquire technology. Chinese companies offered to swap big chunks of their domestic business to foreign firms in exchange for core technologies. Some were illegally appropriated. In its rush to modernize, China accepted substandard products, copying and counterfeiting, and investments made with little consideration for efficiency and consequence. I remember seeing new restaurants that looked like palaces, fancifully decorated with marble, mahogany, and Greek columns painted in gold, with elaborately dressed servers lined up at the entrance. But rarely did I see customers inside.

This shortcut approach left international controversy, excess, and waste in its wake.

So, were the cost and sacrifice worth it? Could a saner path to growth have achieved the same dramatic results? There is no way to evaluate the counterfactual; we just don't know. But we can become more aware of the forces that made those results possible and continue to exert their pull on the Chinese people today, for better and for worse. Sacrifice for the good of the family or community is a practice that conforms with social norms. It is neither good nor bad—just widely accepted. Recent debates on how to approach COVID-19 have given a new twist to the notion of sacrifice, but in early 2020 China chose to save lives and forsake economic output, and the West ended up with the pendulum swinging in the other direction.

For all its dramatic leaps forward, China's economy faces major challenges today, including some of its own making. Key aspects of the strategy that proved so effective during the economy's early development may not be well suited for its later stages. Catch-up growth is very different from innovation-based growth. When low-hanging fruit is abundant, the quality of the institutions supporting economic growth is less crucial. When markets are inchoate and disorderly, heavy-handed state interventions may be more effective than when markets are deeper and more mature. The apparatus that was so effective in mobilizing China to lead in new areas of technology like electric vehicles and clean energy has also produced excess production in steel and solar panels, causing them to flood domestic markets and international shores. A wise state needs to know when to recede into the background, and where it should loosen its control and let the economy ride its natural ebbs and flows. It needs to guide with a lighter hand on the reins and greater skill, especially in this new era of knowledge and information.

The New Playbook

The short-and-fast approach, with its febrile rush to boost GDP, is becoming a thing of the past as the Chinese economy comes of age. It is now running from a new playbook, powered by a new generation. Observers still fixated on Chinese imports displacing American workers, a Chinese economy based on cheap imitations, a growth model based on smokestack industries, an inflexible state crowding out the private sector, and sweeping corruption as the inevitable costs of doing business are not keeping pace with a rapidly evolving China. Its new playbook is based on innovation and technology, meant to be attained through self-reliance and mastery in an age marked by an unparalleled sense of national urgency and pride. Its rising middle-income group and new generation of consumers place high demands on civil society and standards of living. China's relentless pursuit of economic growth has been replaced with a burgeoning emphasis on improving the softer metrics of development—a cleaner environment, greater food security, and a higher quality of life. In China's old model, development was propelled by an ecosystem of loose regulations and subquality standards. Its new model is based on a slower but saner pursuit of growth—more orderly, regulated, and monitored. There is a growing consciousness that what is economically *efficient* may not be socially *desirable*, and that economic success does not necessarily guarantee a nation's overall well-being. In the new era, China will strive to move beyond socialism stained by shortages and capitalism stigmatized by inequality.

These changes are taking place against an important backdrop—the rise of a new generation. The generation of Chinese born in the 1980s, the 1990s, and the first decade of the 2000s marks a distinct break from the past. These cohorts, of which I am a member, seem different in virtually every respect from earlier generations, who were shaped by decades of shortages in a society that purged anything that smacked of capitalism, and by the Cultural Revolution and its impact on the public mindset. Most important, China's young people have been deeply affected—in both predictable and completely unanticipated ways—by the greatest social experiment in human history: China's one-child policy, enacted in the early 1980s. The generation molded by this policy is transforming the nation's spending and saving habits, innovation dynamics, competitiveness, and soft power.

As data reveals, these young people are big spenders, prodigious borrowers, and have a knack for lifestyle consumption. They have the potential to unleash trillions of dollars more into the global economy as they travel abroad, set global trends in fashion, and spend disproportionately more than their parents on culture and arts. Surveys indicate that they are substantially more open-minded and socially conscious than previous generations. However, despite much greater exposure to the West, younger people in China feel less suited to Western-style democracy than do older generations.[6] Although young Chinese may be wearing Adidas and watching the NBA, globalization will not displace what is already deeply layered in the national psyche, any more than replacing the Mao jacket with Western-style suits and ties signified a pivot toward a Western way of life. Deep down, China's people are steeped in their own culture, bound by their own traditions, and rooted in their own communities. They may be traveling the world in record numbers, but their reference points are overwhelmingly local. This younger cohort is ushering in an era of economic liberalization without political liberalization, although the situation is dynamic, and we still have much to learn about the new generation in China that is taking up the reins of power.[7]

But if miscommunication and misgivings have contributed to the deteriorating relationship between the US and China, there is the hope that the next generation of leaders in China, more educated and fluent with diverse cultures, are well equipped to bridge the gap between different worldviews. Even if an elite US education has failed to convert young Chinese students into avid promulgators of Western-style democracy and capitalism, it certainly has opened their eyes to the virtues of an open society, if not a wholly free society. Their desire to question, to challenge, to pursue the truth, and to push back against injustice will have important implications for the China they will shape.

There are major risks to the Chinese economy, but it will not likely be direct economic factors that will pose the greatest impediments to China's hugely successful economic upsurge since 1979. Some fear that ideology and politics will trump economic considerations in a way that will harm growth; others believe that it will be China's voluntary or involuntary withdrawal from global engagement. There is also the risk of politically charged technocratic errors. If not prudently calibrated, a hasty, hyper-charged implementation of well-intentioned policies to shift China's growth model may do more harm than good, as we will further discuss in the concluding chapter.

Extended skirmishes, export bans of semiconductors, and tariffs are reinforcing China's assertiveness and setting it on a course of national mobilization to attain self-reliance. There are those in the US who want to see China's rise contained; there are those in China who believe in the ancient saying "One thrives in adversity and perishes in prosperity." The mindset of self-sufficiency without continued global engagement is a dangerous one in a world where prosperity and technological proficiency are increasingly network based and interdependent. When economic interlinkages snap, everyone loses, especially the vulnerable.

It is a particularly gloomy time for the world economy, now more than a decade since the end of the Great Recession. The world's most important economies are all slowing down, the majority ravaged by heavy debt burdens and raging inflation. Disruptions to global supply chains, US-China standoffs in technology, and looming post-pandemic crises in developing countries do not augur well for the globalized economy. When major economies stood together in the spirit of collaboration to combat economic damage brought about by the 2008 global financial crisis, few would have predicted that the world was going down the route of bifurcation rather than of convergence. Few companies would have imagined that their fates could be sealed by geopolitical factors rather than their own strategic decisions or competitiveness. And few investors and multinationals could have envisaged China losing much of its appeal as the main destination of investment after years of travel restrictions.

The war in Ukraine only proves ever more forcefully the devastating consequences of war and its reverberations around the world. But it also highlights the power of the fusion of nations through economic and financial collaboration. If they behave rationally, the US and China will do their best to avoid confrontation, and while they might not work toward convergence, they will at least move peacefully in parallel. But that would lead to the creation of separate spheres for technological standards, models of globalization, management of domestic politics, and the economy. It would also mean a slower pace of innovation and a higher cost of doing business, product shortages, and inflation—all ultimately paid for by consumers. The theoretical case for maximizing economic efficiency through globalization turned out to be too idyllic for a world of great-power competition and shifting political landscapes increasingly shaped by post-liberal thinking, economic insecurity, and the rise of social media.

Two things need to happen before the China model can be vindicated. First, China must make the shift from being a $10,000 per capita income nation to a $30,000 per capita income nation. Getting there will not be as easy as reaching the first goalpost of $10,000 was. Second, it needs to demonstrate that it can do a better job than free market economies of addressing the most intractable problems of capitalism and globalization, such as rising inequality, displacement of jobs by technology, and the diminishing expectations of the younger generation, which in an age of unprecedented abundance is more disillusioned than generations that had much less. Hence, China's system is met with a challenge: a system that is powerful in mobilization and executing big industrial pushes may not be as effective in fostering breakthrough technologies and sustainable growth vital to becoming a rich nation; one that is expedient when a nation and its people are singularly focused on economic growth does not necessarily have the resilience and flexibility to manage a much more complex and pluralistic society. As material needs are fulfilled, the measurement of welfare extends beyond consumption and wealth accumulation; individuals will demand that their increasingly multifaceted preferences be respected and reflected in collective outcomes. There will need to be new mechanisms adopted to reflect choices from the bottom up rather than the top down; better processes to integrate debate, expertise, a diverse set of skills; and broad-based participation to cater to and balance society's various needs. Can China meet these challenges? The jury is still out, but we can come to keener conclusions and more insightful judgments about China. Analysis based on data and evidence can allay misgivings and dispel myths, help us forecast the future more accurately, and steer us away from decisions that are motivated by emotion, ideology, or politics.

Even natives cannot claim full knowledge of their countries. I have come to appreciate China's immense impact on the world economy as a professor based in London and a board member of some global firms. I have learned firsthand how business is often conducted in China in my role as an adviser to technology companies, whose young founders have constantly impressed me with their entrepreneurial spirit and skill at deftly navigating a highly complex business and political environment. Participating in government working groups and policy debates has led me to appreciate the wide range of considerations the government needs to take into account whenever it makes an important decision. The civil servants and leaders I have met are highly motivated and deeply committed to their mission. They want to do things the right way, which usually isn't the easy way. My background and experiences straddling East and West have allowed me to look at the Chinese economy from up close and also from afar, where things look a little clearer and differences are a bit easier to reconcile.

I believe that a better understanding of China's playbook can help reduce tensions and make the world a safer place. It was none other than John F. Kennedy who called for a world "safe for diversity." Politician, businessperson, student, or scholar: we can each do our best to rise above the morass of sensationalism, stereotypes, and biases. Only then can we engage with China in a measured and effective way, critique it with relevance, and ask good questions. Until we do so, we will continue to get China wrong more often than we get it right, at a time when a sense of common purpose has become crucial to addressing the existential threats that face humankind.

TWO

CHINA'S ECONOMIC MIRACLE

T he power of economic growth lies in its ability to change people's lives. In few places is this more evident than China, where during the period between 1978 and 2016 life expectancy increased by nearly ten years and infant mortality dropped by more than 80 percent. Over the past four decades, more than eight hundred million people in China have been lifted out of dire poverty—the largest global reduction in inequality in modern times. Statistically, we see the power of the rule of seventy-two at work here: given a 6 percent annual growth rate, an economy doubles in twelve years. Between 1978 and 2011, the average growth rate of China's GDP was an astounding 10 percent, and its tangible effects were visible everywhere: in new buildings springing up overnight, and in the flood of new tramways, cars, trucks, railway lines, bridges, highways, roads, and canals.

I was born into this era of China's modern economic transformation and experienced its life-changing effects firsthand. In the early 1980s, my family—and all the families I knew—were living on rationed food coupons. Eggs, cooking oil, sugar, meat, cloth, soap, and many other daily necessities were subject to strict monthly rations. Life in a twenty-square-meter apartment with a shared communal kitchen and lavatory was considered luxurious. We cooked our meals on coal-burning stoves. Electric power was so unreliable that blackouts were considered the rule rather than the exception, even in Beijing, the nation's wealthiest city. In those days, when you walked down Chang-an Avenue, Beijing's version of the Champs-Élysées, you saw only three posh hotels, and the handful of cars on the avenue were navigating an endless tide of bicycles that parted and rejoined as fluidly as a school of fish.

At that time, we were only a few years into the new era of Deng Xiaoping's economic reforms, and the Chinese people were poor but hopeful. As China's sputtering economic engine began roaring to life, what I noticed most as a child was the shift from scarcity to abundance. By 1985, coupon rationing was effectively a thing of the past, and decades later those coupons would be avidly sought after by collectors. By the time I reached middle school in the early 1990s, food was not just available in endless supply, but also in dazzling variety. Imported snacks like Coca-Cola, Korean cream cakes, and potato chips became wildly popular. When the first McDonald's opened at the corner of Wangfujing Street and Chang-an Avenue, the queue of eager customers extended for blocks, and as the golden arches expanded into other Chinese cities, Kentucky Fried Chicken and Burger King lost no time in following suit. Happy Meals were still enough of a luxury, however, that my parents used them to reward me for good academic performance at the end of the school term.

As China bade farewell to food rationing, its people also cast off the drab, gray clothes that for so long had served as the mainstay of Chinese couture. In the 1990s, the urge to find more colorful jobs inspired the first wave of adventurers to *xiahai*, "the plunge into the sea" of private business.

Some got rich overnight, proudly showing off their brick-shaped mobile phones and sporting about in new, domestically produced cars. As the nation's economy grew, the burdens of life eased further. Soon the privileged life of a ten-thousand-yuan-income family in Beijing was no longer a rarity. Having only known one day of rest from work each week, people now took two-day weekends—and not just to squeeze in more household chores, but also to enjoy new leisure activities like a walk in the city's many parks, or an evening of Peking opera. Fast-forward another ten years, and classmates of mine for whom a Popsicle had once been a rare treat now possessed white-collar jobs, one or more cars, and spacious apartments they didn't have to share with other families.

This extraordinary metamorphosis within China was matched by an equally momentous shift in the way China was viewed in the eyes of the world. In 1997, the same year that the British handed Hong Kong back to China, I left my family in Beijing to attend Horace Mann High School in the Bronx, the northernmost borough of New York City. It so happened that an American lobbyist in the education sector, to whom I will remain forever indebted, was looking for a mainland Chinese exchange student to recommend to Dr. Weiss, the headmaster of Horace Mann. That a proud Youth League member of the Communist Party could find herself immersed in an American family actively involved in democratic campaigns, conventions, and fundraising seemed utterly surreal.

These tectonic shifts in my own life opened my eyes to vast differences with regard to values that I had previously deemed universal. Whenever people learned where I was from, the same three topics came up: Tibet, Tiananmen Square, and human rights. To my great surprise, even cosmopolitan New Yorkers seemed to believe that all Chinese people lived in constant fear of an oppressive regime—when most of the Chinese were having the time of their lives embracing new opportunities. Fortunately, this narrow view of China was opening up thanks to a growing number of cultural exchange programs like mine. By the time I reached university in 2000, my friends were mesmerized by China and starting to learn Mandarin; by the time I graduated four years later, some of them had decided to move to China to embark on their careers. In the span of just fifteen years, China's image had radically shifted, not only because it had become a major new player on the global stage, but also because opportunities abounded for foreigners inside its borders. Soon China would be taking on a leadership role alongside the most advanced and prosperous countries in the world. All this has taken place during my own time as a student.

This transformation that I lived through—from food rationing to a vibrant global economy—is often described as an economic miracle. Because economists tend to prefer scientific rather than faith-based explanations, this chapter sets out to identify the various factors that contributed to China's economic metamorphosis. At first glance, two aspects of that change are particularly striking. The first is speed. Over the two-hundred-thousand-year arc of human history, the Industrial Revolution is considered pivotal because it improved the standard of living by 75 percent within a single lifetime. By comparison, growth rates in China mean that many Chinese will see living standards rise seventy-fivefold, or 7,500 percent.

History also tells us that periodic growth spurts do happen every so often. Brazil was a top economic performer in the 1960s and 1970s, as was Botswana. Latin American countries like Mexico and Peru, and such Asian economies as Malaysia, Indonesia, and Thailand, all experienced rapid growth during the same period. But sixty years later, not one of those countries has made it into the ranks of high-income nations. China's growth, however, has proven durable as well as swift. Its GDP has expanded at an astonishing average 9.5 percent per year *for the past four decades*. For context, GDP growth in the Western world from AD 1 to AD 1829 was 6 percent per *century*.[1] During the period of America's fastest economic growth, which took place between 1920 and 1970, its GDP grew an average of 4 percent per year.

Only a small handful of economies have come close to matching the pace and stamina of China's growth. These include Korea, Hong Kong, Singapore, and Japan,[2] but their economies are far smaller—comparable to that of a single Chinese city or province. Today China possesses the second-largest economic engine in the world, commanding about 16 percent of global GDP, and the gap with the global leader, the US, is narrowing fast. Based on current projections, by the early 2030s China will have recaptured its early nineteenth-century status as the world's largest economy.

So how did China become "the land that failed to fail"? When developing countries look at China today, they are less interested in debating the fine points of privatization versus nationalization and more eager to import China's model in its entirety. But what is that model, exactly? And to what extent can it be imitated? Nobel laureate Robert Lucas said, "Simply advising a society to follow the Korean model is a little like advising an aspiring basketball player to follow the Michael Jordan model."[3] He made this observation in 1993, before China had worked its own miracle, but it's even more appropriate for the Chinese model.

Many theories have been put forward to explain China's remarkable growth. Some scholars believe it was primarily a matter of "markets over Mao,"[4] a triumph of unfettered economics over ideology; some attribute it to the nation's outsize investment strategy; still others hold the view that China's enterprising people with their unusual predilection for saving was the key. Each of these factors certainly played a role, as we will explore, but they don't provide a first-order explanation for China's growth over the last forty years. The reason behind this surge can be summarized in one sentence: China was catching up to its own potential. In this sense, it was not a miracle, per se.

Just as a gifted athlete with poor training will fall behind the competition, China had been handicapped by its own flawed strategy during the years leading up to 1978, when plans based on the Soviet model shackled the economy. But when provided with top training, that athlete improves faster than any of his competitors, achieving what looks like "miracle growth." China's turbulent past obscured the fact that its underlying fundamentals were still sound. The nation's two-thousand-year history as a great power, the cultural values of Confucianism, and high levels of public education and bureaucratic competency lay waiting to contribute once China succeeded in moving beyond the devastating events of the first half of the twentieth century.

Intangible Fundamentals: Culture, Institutions, and History

The World Values Survey quantifies the way different countries express a wide array of cultural beliefs and values, including attitudes toward thrift, work and effort, individualism, innovation, trade, the role of women, openness toward other countries and other cultures, and political and legal institutions.[5] China ranks particularly high when it comes to frugality, hard work, and educating its children.[6] Many believe that these traits have been pivotal to China's economic success, but there is a fundamental confusion here between what drives *income levels* as opposed to *growth*. Culture and values change slowly, if at all, and thus cannot be considered first-order factors for growth; and as we have seen, an economy's growth can swing wildly up and down (unsound policies, political instability, or misguided ideology can easily knock an economy off its path or drive it to disaster). But over the long term, culture can play a major role in shaping an economy's income levels. (A country with a propensity for saving is more likely to become wealthier, for instance, although this outcome isn't guaranteed.) Culture can also serve as an "interaction variable" when it comes to determining growth. That is to say, cultural values do not necessarily contribute independently to growth but can jointly affect growth together with other factors.

Prominent among China's cultural advantages were the contributions of Confucius (551–479 BC), the famous Chinese philosopher whose teachings emerged from his search for pragmatic solutions to the problems of his day. In response to the rigors of life in an agrarian society, Confucius extolled the virtue of hard work, the value of a large family, and the honor of a long family lineage. Because having a big family meant stretching limited resources, the Confucian virtue of frugality became deeply embedded in China's psyche. According to *The Zuo Tradition*, a commentary written in the fifth century BC by one of Confucius's disciples, "Frugality is a feature shared by virtue of every description; extravagance is the worst of the evils."

For Confucius, alongside knowledge and learning, character and moral integrity were highly prized. The emperor held supreme power, yet the state's day-to-day affairs had to be managed by administrators who were competent, well educated, imbued with righteousness and self-restraint, and committed to discharging their duty. Political scientist Francis Fukuyama argued compellingly that good institutions required a merit-based bureaucracy. China, which has the world's oldest tradition of centralized bureaucracy, introduced a meritocratic system of selection for government officials in the third century BC.

To the surprise of many Westerners, upward mobility based on ability and character is still a hallmark of the Chinese system today. Where once the means of entry was the imperial examination system, today it takes the form of a grueling university entrance exam that has become a national fixation. For three days each year, millions of students around the country simultaneously sit down to a test for which they have been preparing for years. Outside the test centers, millions of parents line up, sweating under oppressive summer heat with lunch boxes and water bottles to get them through the day, anxious to find out what fortune awaits their children.

China's respect for order and governance also traces its origins to Confucianism. Confucius lived in a time when sovereign rulers had lost control over a dynasty, plunging the land into chaos as vassal states engaged in endless wars. He was therefore keenly aware of the vital importance of social stability and harmony, supported by citizens who knew their place in society, accepted it, and behaved accordingly. For a long time, modern economists held the view that Confucian aversion to individualism was antithetical to the enterprising spirit, and therefore limited innovation. But more recently, Confucian doctrine advocating social order, frugality, hard work, communalism, and merit-based bureaucracy has been credited with playing an important role in the astounding success of East Asian economies like Japan, Korea, Taiwan, and mainland China.[7]

These economies enjoy not only high rates of saving along with high rates of investment, rapid rates of industrialization, and a wealth of human capital, but also effective public institutions and well-trained technocratic bureaucracies. Singaporean economist Tan Kong Yam puts it this way: "Unlike the Euro-American model that traces its origin to the tradition of Adam Smith, which treats government as a necessary evil that should be confined to only law and order, Confucian values and tradition lead to a model of maximal government, with myriad responsibilities, duties, and obligations. The state is not just supervisory and regulatory in function, but plays a leadership role in development, education, and mobilization behind specific priorities. Government is not just made up of administrative functionaries: its members are often perceived as leaders, intellectuals, and teachers."[8] The emperor, apart from being the supreme sovereign, was morally obliged to *compassionate* ruling.

After the death of Confucius in 479 BC, China went on to create the earliest modern state, some eighteen centuries ahead of Europe. Four Chinese inventions—paper, printing, gunpowder, and the compass—

changed the world forever. By the time of the Song dynasty (960–1279), China had become the world's undisputed leader in science and technology, and its vast economy represented a quarter of the world's total GDP.[9] Political power had been consolidated under one emperor; an efficient bureaucracy managed the administration of the empire's vast territories, provisioned armies, and provided public goods; a sophisticated system of taxation based on household registration and land ownership was firmly in place; and competitive exams for official appointments supported a merit-based civil service.

China's isolationism made it miss out on the Industrial Revolution entirely. By the late nineteenth century, the Qing dynasty found itself at the mercy of Western powers. Its policy of isolationism had given way to foreign military incursions and war, political chaos, and poor policies. During the three decades after World War II, China's primary concerns became ideological purity and national security, its main goals to transform the economy into a socialist system and to build military muscle to safeguard China's sovereignty.

A historical fact that is often overlooked is that even in the difficult years running up to the turbulent Cultural Revolution in the nation's recent history, there were signs of forward movement. A governance structure based on economic decentralization was put in place, along with the practice of using local experimentation as a laboratory for major policy initiatives. Large strides took place in modernizing China: local and national power grids paved the way for new industries and technologies. The literacy rate rose along with life expectancy at birth, which increased from thirty-six to sixty-seven years. The majority of Chinese children became immunized. Despite misguided economic policies, the three decades prior to 1978 were not completely lost decades.[10]

These historical antecedents make China very different from other developing countries sitting on the tarmac waiting for economic takeoff. Most never before reached an advanced level of institutional and economic development, or they were once prosperous economies that at some point succumbed to colonial rule. In those countries, which include India, Bangladesh, and many Central African states, indigenous institutions were either completely uprooted and supplanted or permanently altered. China only narrowly escaped the fate of colonial servitude, clinging to political autonomy at the nadir of its fortunes, and even under Soviet influence in the 1950s and 1960s, its political and economic destiny lay in its own hands. Thus, culture and history laid the foundations for China's potential level of income, but the path to get there would require a radical overhaul of the economic system.

1978: A Watershed Year

The decades prior to 1978 were notable for two major political movements in China. The first was the Great Leap Forward, Mao Zedong's campaign from 1958 to 1960 to shift China's economy from agrarian to industrial and fulfill Mao's ambition of surpassing the US and the USSR in steel production. Government financing came from squeezing modest surpluses from other parts of the economy, while households did their part by melting kitchen pots and scrap metal in their backyards. Tragically, the result was the Great Famine rather than the Great Leap Forward. A series of misplaced policies to accelerate agricultural output actually led to a 15 percent decline in grain output in 1959, and another 16 percent in the following two years, during which time the entire nation suffered from a severe famine.[11]

By the mid-1970s, China's economy was in shambles, devastated by inefficient Soviet-style central planning and economic stagnation during the Cultural Revolution, as well as by a disastrous earthquake in Tangshan that killed more than 240,000 people and severely injured 160,000 more. Although China had become a nuclear power in 1964, and just the fifth nation to successfully launch an orbital satellite in 1970, it was still mired in poverty. Then Mao Zedong, founding father of the Communist People's Republic of China, died.

Against this backdrop, Deng Xiaoping stepped onto center stage as China's new supreme leader, applauded by those who remembered him as a pragmatist keen on economic progress, before being stripped of power shortly before Mao's death (after which he came back to power). Despite their high hopes for Deng in his new role, few Chinese could have imagined the historical reforms he would initiate as he paved the way for China's future. The challenges he faced were daunting—and not just economic, but also ideological. Until this point, the nation's leaders had been guided by a political mindset based on class struggle. Hard-liners among the old guard would resist change that deviated from orthodox Marxism-Leninism. But if one pocket of the nation could demonstrate visible success from a particular reform, then even those voices most strenuously opposed to reform could be drowned out by a chorus of supporters.

Deng Xiaoping rose to the occasion by focusing on two issues. The first was creating party consensus by assessing Mao's historical performance in order to avoid a long, drawn-out controversy over the Cultural Revolution; this would help unify the party rather than divide it. Deng made the case for this political reorientation by arguing that Mao Zedong Thought should be interpreted "holistically, correctly, and comprehensively," easing the bonds of ideological orthodoxy enough to open a path to economic reform. The second issue was how to implement new economic policies, and here Deng Xiaoping was both flexible and patient. Recognizing the dangers of uprooting China's Soviet-style economy overnight through massive privatization programs, Deng took the approach of "crossing the river by groping for the stepping-stones." This gradualism was an ingenious way of deferring some thorny issues, such as how private ownership could be reconciled with the ideals of a socialist state, or free exchange with Marxist theories of value.

So 1978, the year that Deng Xiaoping was resurrected for a third time from political banishment to become undisputed leader of the People's Republic, marked a crucial turning point in contemporary Chinese history. This was the year China began to move away from a playbook based on strict Communist doctrine and embarked on a series of transformational reforms. The bottle containing the genie of rapid growth had been uncorked, although there were still some major hurdles to overcome before its powers could be unleashed.

China's twentieth-century transition from poverty to economic prosperity was both swift and sustained, but as the graph below indicates, a closer look at the nation's year-by-year growth reveals that the upward climb was not a smooth sail. In some years the annual growth rate soared to 14 percent, while in others it sank below 3 percent.

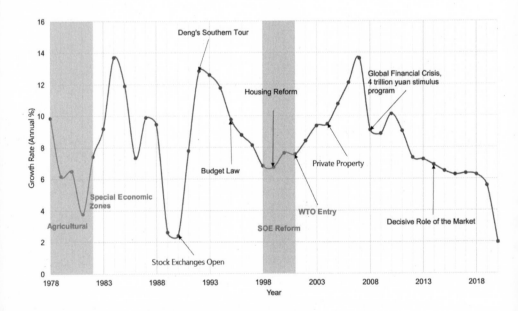

Figure 2.1: GDP Per Capita Growth of China, 1978–2020

Source: World Bank Dataset

No one momentous change propelled the economy forward in a continuous climb. Instead, growth came in surges that turned out to be linked to specific waves of reform, each directed at a particular structural weakness in the economic system. When the positive effect of one particular reform eventually began to ebb, it was replaced by a new wave of reforms leading to another surge, until that, too, had run its course. "Reform is China's second revolution," Deng Xiaoping famously stated, and between 1978 and 2008 four major tides of reform triggered major surges of growth.

The former Soviet Union and Eastern bloc countries also turned to reform as an economic lifeboat, but with one important difference: they tried to address all the inadequacies of a central planning system in one fell swoop, applying the economic equivalent of shock therapy. Unprepared for the shock of sudden privatization and liberalization of their markets, these societies didn't enjoy the therapeutic benefit. China, by contrast, waded through the river stone by stone. This gradualism allowed the country's leaders to experiment with change—even when it was risky or ideologically problematic—without leading to destabilizing disruptions. The transition from central planning to a market-based economy was choppy, as we see above, but each improvement made it a little easier for the Chinese people to cope.

Underlying China's reforms was an effort to address the fundamental limitations of a planned economy. For one thing, prices in China were not determined by the same forces of supply and demand that establish value in a free market economy; instead, for both ideological and political reasons, prices were established by the government. Keeping prices low was important because it allowed essential consumer goods to be affordable for everyone, ensuring social stability. Production was set according to quotas established by the government in a process largely patterned on the Soviet model. Farmers and other producers could not use price as a guide to expand or scale back production; instead, everyone produced to their particular government quota. Because price had lost its ability to function as a signal of underlying scarcity or excess, and quotas were a hit-or-miss proposition, the result was severe shortages of some basic goods and massive stockpiles of others.

Reform-Driven Growth

China's four major economic waves of reform began with the agricultural sector. When Deng Xiaoping came to power, 80 percent of China's people lived in the countryside. The nation had adopted a utopian system of centralized agricultural production and equal distribution administered by the people's communes. This tethered most of China's vast labor force to the countryside, where families worked together on plots of land in exchange for tiny but equal shares of whatever they produced. All other commercial activities were considered capitalist and therefore strictly forbidden. Surplus food from the People's Commune was turned over to the government at artificially suppressed prices and used to support heavy industry, considered the ultimate symbol of Chinese economic prowess.

This collective farming system provided little incentive to increase productivity. As a result, even though most of the Chinese people were working in the fields, agricultural production failed to put enough food on the table to feed everyone. By way of reform, the government formally introduced a dual system of pricing in the early 1980s, replacing collective farming with a "household responsibility" system that allowed farmers to work individual tracts of land and claim some of the fruits of their own labors: after turning over a portion to the government at state-level prices, farmers could then sell the rest at market prices and keep the profit.[12]

Based on its early success, this new system was officially endorsed, and its effects were dramatic. Between 1978 and 1984, grain yield per unit of land increased by 43 percent, and real agricultural output increased by more than 50 percent, despite an overall reduction in the agricultural workforce as people moved to urban areas. Productivity in agriculture grew so quickly that many fieldworkers who remained in the countryside were freed up to engage in activities unrelated to farming. In six years, the number of rural people living in extreme poverty fell by half, from 250 million to 128 million.[13] For consumers, food prices did rise somewhat when the state stopped artificially suppressing them, but this increase was kept tolerable by the rapid increase in food supply.

Here I'd like to mention an interesting caveat. Although many of the economic forces that provide incentives in a free market had been suppressed, the Communist Party of China tried to make up for this by encouraging revolutionary spirit, patriotism, and pride in national rejuvenation. Top performers were honored with the highest possible award, National Model Worker. This recognition was directed not only to the working class, but also to intellectuals, engineers, scientists, teachers, and medical doctors. People were also appointed to prestigious positions as deputies of the National People's Congress in recognition of extraordinary achievement in their fields of endeavor. Such incentives inspired many workers to contribute to national reconstruction at the expense of their own personal interests, and even their lives, earning them canonization as revolutionary martyrs.

In the early to mid-1980s, the government implemented a second wave of reforms, creating special economic zones (SEZs) that mimicked the effects of open, export-oriented market economies. The privileges extended to SEZs were both extensive and exceptional; they included tax exemptions, reduced custom duties, cheaper land prices, and greater flexibility to negotiate labor and financial contracts. This experiment with SEZs turned out to be a huge success. Foreign firms brought in technology, equipment, and know-how while benefiting from China's cheap labor, business-friendly environment, sound infrastructure, and huge domestic market. Foreign investment poured into China. The success of the first four SEZs—established in Shenzhen, Zhuhai, and Shantou in Guangdong Province, and Xiamen in Fujian Province—boosted the government's confidence enough so that by 1984 similar opening-up programs were rolled out in fourteen cities. Eventually, China would become a global center for processing exports—essentially, assembling intermediate goods imported from abroad before reexporting them as final products.

By the late 1980s, the terrific pace of this new economic surge had eased. The decade marked its lowest point of growth in 1989, when the events around Tiananmen Square ground the national economy to a halt. Taking advantage of the politically fragile situation, opponents of the reform were starting to gain ground, but Deng Xiaoping doubled down on his commitment to boost the momentum of reforms in his 1992 Southern Tour. He encouraged local officials to be enterprising and entrepreneurial, and to continue to open up markets. He also pledged his unwavering support to private enterprises, which experienced a burst of growth in the subsequent years. As private companies started to surpass many of their state-owned counterparts, the government turned to reforming these lagging SOEs. Historically, these state companies had served as the economic backbone of the nation, enjoying monopoly status by purchasing materials and equipment at reduced cost and selling finished products at artificially elevated prices. However, after decades of playing a key role in a system devoted to socialist entitlement, many state firms were now becoming a drag on the overall economy.

Following the same phased-in strategy it had taken with agriculture and SEZs, the government cautiously granted more and more autonomy to company managers, particularly when it came to decisions on production, marketing, financing, investment, expansion, and upgrading technology. State-owned enterprises started to incorporate and file for listings on public stock exchanges. Unprofitable companies were selectively allowed to fail, or were sold to employees. By 1994, only a decade after the term "privatization" was taboo, the private sector was generating 40 percent of China's urban employment. Today, the private sector employs around 80 percent of the urban labor force.[14]

This third set of reforms addressed another deep flaw in the Soviet-style socialist system China had adopted: the absence of competition. Until the mid-1980s SOEs had neither the incentive to expand through their own initiative nor the need to compete or adopt new technologies. Inefficient laggards were indulged, and more productive and innovative newcomers had little chance of obtaining the government's blessing. In a nutshell, the cleansing effect of market mechanisms was absent under the centrally administered plan; without competition, there was little incentive for progress or innovation. By subjecting SOEs to higher standards of performance and opening markets to privately owned competitors, the government gave these subsidized entities a healthy dose of market discipline.

The last high tide of economic reforms came with China's entrance into the World Trade Organization (WTO) in 2001, flinging open its doors to global trade. The government aggressively liberalized exports, removing major barriers to trade and slashing tariffs in half. Of China's 160 service sectors, 100 were opened to foreigners in the subsequent years. Rules and regulations were rewritten to meet international standards. With the exception of a few state monopoly sectors considered essential to national security, Chinese businesses were encouraged to trade with foreign companies directly, instead of having to work through an SOE as they had in the past.

Membership in the WTO heralded a new wave of growth between 2000 and 2007, when China's real GDP per capita nearly doubled. Within a few years of joining the WTO, China amassed a large trade surplus, accumulated a massive pile of foreign exchange reserves, and owned a significant portion of US Treasuries. Foreign capital continued to rush in, flowing to export companies, the industrial sector, hotels, and construction. In 1978 China had been ranked thirty-third in global trade, with total imports and exports valued at US$206 billion. By 2009—less than a decade after joining the WTO—China had become the unequivocal global export leader. In 2017 China's total imports and exports hit US$4.1 trillion.

The consequences of China's rigid economic planning prior to 1978 did have the benefit of providing new leadership with lots of low-hanging fruit, and Deng Xiaoping found a way to harvest it. Begin with an economy performing way below its potential; restore the link between effort and reward, releasing an avalanche of incentives, mobility, competition, price flexibility, and innovation; and open the economy up to experimentation with international trade and investment while maintaining political and social stability: now you have an economy primed for an explosive burst. This massive surge took place in China even in the absence of the typical prerequisites of economic growth: rule of law, secure property rights, and an easy business environment. In other words, conditions in China were far from ideal, yet this did not slow the frenetic pace of growth once reform became the order of the day.

Labor, Capital, and the Importance of Productivity

One common mistake people make when they consider China's boom between 1978 and 2008 is ascribing it to massive infusions of capital by the central government. This is understandable, given the fact that China's investment rate has averaged twice that of the US over the years. This view is further bolstered by China's historical emphasis on smokestack industries, and by more recent images on the internet of a building craze that created suburban ghost towns and gleaming bridges to nowhere. However, as we've learned from observing the effects of China's four waves of reform, the truth is more nuanced—and more interesting.

A plethora of research studies supports the idea that although capital investment played an important part in China's success, total factor productivity (TFP)—the measure of how efficiently inputs like labor and capital are used—played an even more significant role. This is important for us to consider, because as a strategy, massive investment is unsustainable in the long run. After all, how many machines and workers can you keep adding? Eventually, when the economy reaches full employment, providing workers with more machines becomes less effective. Economists commonly refer to this as the "curse of diminishing returns." Productivity growth, however, is different. With a rising level of total TFP, the same number of machines and workers can continue to generate greater and greater output.

To clarify this concept let's consider Figure 2.2, which depicts an economy's growth trajectory. The vertical axis indicates output per person (y), and the horizontal axis represents capital per person (k). An economy at point b can grow its output along the curve as it accumulates capital per capita, but at some point that pace of growth slows down. Karl Marx predicted that capitalist greed would eventually drive the return on capital to zero, and reduced incentives to save and invest would bring about the demise of capitalism.

However, growth can overcome the curse of diminishing returns *so long as it can count on continual rises in TFP*. More effective allocation of resources and technological advances are two ways to raise total factor productivity. By raising TFP, the economy can now jump from a lower path onto a higher one. Observe that at point c (top), the economy achieves a higher level of output y than point b (middle), even with the

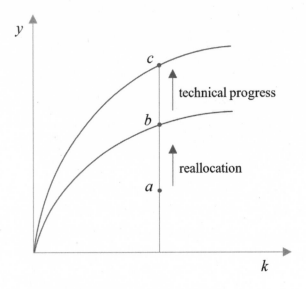

Figure 2.2: Economic Growth and Two Ways of Improving Efficiency

same input k. In this way developing countries can continue to grow if they can constantly improve productivity and expand the production frontier.

So just how much of China's GDP growth was based on increasing inputs, labor and capital, and how much of it was based on increasing TFP? Scholarly analysis of Chinese data leads to the general consensus that productivity accounted for about *half* of China's growth in output over the period of its fastest growth, the thirty years or so after 1978: despite deriving different data sets and measurement schemes, the calculations yield very similar results. Researchers Barry Bosworth and Susan M. Collins found that increases in productivity contributed 49.3 percent of the growth to China's overall GDP[15]; Dwight H. Perkins and Thomas G. Rawski came up with 45.2 percent[16]; Jinghai Zheng, Arne Bigsten, and Angang Hu arrived at 49 percent[17]; Loren Brandt and

Xiaodong Zhu calculated 51.3 percent;[18] and an IMF study came up with more than 50 percent.[19] If instead of GDP, we look at GDP per capita, TFP accounts for a striking 78 percent of China's growth.[20] The decade since 2009, as we will see later in chapter 6, is a different story. The quality of firm-level data unfortunately deteriorates from 2013, but broad estimates suggest that TFP growth declined substantially over the last decade.[21]

When we focus our gaze specifically on TFP, its overall annual growth rate in China between 1978 and 2007 averaged 3.92 percent, and in the years between 1998 and 2007, it reached 4.58 percent.[22] To put that into perspective, TFP growth, which is the main driver of US economic growth, averaged 1.6 percent to 1.8 percent in the US between 1870 and 2010, and 0.4 percent between 2010 and 2018.[23] Europe's TFP growth rate has been below 1 percent. During comparable stages of development, Korea averaged 3 percent (1960–1990). In sum, contrary to popular belief, *productivity* was an important contributor to growth in China.

What drives TFP growth, making an economy more productive overall? The first thing that comes to mind is innovation and technical progress. For instance, the discovery of electricity and the invention of the steam engine, internal combustion engine, telegraph, and computer chip substantially elevated productivity for decades. We can also do more work with air-conditioning that keeps us cool in hot weather, and with modern medicine to keep us healthy. Today's office workers can generate ten times what they used to thanks to telephones, printers, computers, and software.

Fundamental technological advancements like these, however, are few and far between. Luckily, they are not the only stimulus for productivity. In the early stages of its growth boom, China did not have to wait for the emergence of the Chinese equivalent of Bill Gates, Steve Jobs, Sergey Brin, or Larry Page. The process was far simpler than that: reducing waste and inefficiency by reallocating resources made an enormous difference. For developing countries in particular, this way of improving TFP—reducing the misallocation of resources—is far more relevant.

To illustrate this, let's return to the growth figure. A possibility we did not consider is this: What if an economy starts out not *on* the frontier at point *b*, but *inside* it—at point *a*? This possibility arises when resources are used ineffectively—they're wasted or misallocated—in such a way that the economy is kept below its potential.

There are lots of examples of misallocation in real life: it is not always the best firms that get the best workers; despite merit exams, it is not necessarily the best students who get the best jobs; nor do the most productive farmers get the largest pieces of land. Private entrepreneurs struggle to find financing for their innovative companies, while behemoth SOEs flush with funds buy soccer clubs or SeaWorld. Some firms with political connections get abundant subsidies, while other more productive firms have to fight through a sea of bureaucratic red tape. All these problems point to large-scale inefficiency. As Nobel laureates Abhijit V. Banerjee and Esther Duflo put it in their book *Good Economics for Hard Times*, describing the challenges of developing economies, "It is not so much that profitable technologies are not available and accessible, but that the economy does not appear to make the best use of available resources."[24]

In China particularly, this is a recurrent theme. In post-reform China, the biggest and most important source of growth was reaching its own potential—that is, getting from point *a* to point *b*. This was accomplished by significant shifts in the way resources were directed during the period from 1978 to 2005, when some four hundred million workers moved out of low-productivity pockets of the economy into high-productivity ones. This involved two major exoduses. The first was a migration out of agriculture and into industry, which took place gradually from 1978 to 2005, when the share of labor devoted to agriculture declined from 70 percent to 30 percent. The second exodus took the form of a massive reallocation of labor from the state sector into the private sector, when the state share of employment plunged from 52 percent to 13 percent over the same period.[25] A big "diversion program" for SOE employees sent some back to school for retraining, mostly funded by the government; others joined private firms or became entrepreneurs. As the saying goes in China, trees wither from uprooting whereas humans thrive by moving. In both cases, government policies broke down barriers to mobility that they had previously erected.

These major efforts helped redress a massive imbalance of human resources, but China faced similar issues with regard to capital and land. Market economies typically deal with these through a process of creative destruction, whereby the innovative replaces the obsolete. Competition leads to natural selection, driving out poorly performing companies and redirecting resources toward those that are succeeding. But such forces can weaken under central direction, where very often less productive enterprises take up more resources and crowd out more competitive ones. Only when the "grasp the large and let go of the small" policies were implemented in the midnineties did unproductive firms face the culling effect of market forces. This huge rise in efficiency gains through reallocation accounted for almost three quarters of the productivity growth experienced in the manufacturing sector.[26]

Clearly, policy changes were enormously important to China, but they would not have been so effective were it not for the heavy hand of the state. The state mobilized resources, connected and coordinated different actors into a nationwide network, and pushed through tough reforms that would have been met with resistance or taken much longer to implement elsewhere. Of course, not all countries have strong states, and not all citizens are happy to have an outsize government. As we've seen, the effects of the Confucian tradition, with its emphasis on communalism, social order, and respect for government leadership, have rippled throughout Chinese society for more than two thousand years. In contemporary China, people have gotten used to omnipresent state intervention and simply assume it.

State intervention on a massive scale is certainly tricky. It's good for some things, like jump-starting development, building infrastructure, filling in missing markets, providing public goods and services, and developing ground-breaking new technologies, as we will see in chapter 7. But it is less beneficial for others—like picking industrial and technological winners and attempting to subsidize them to success. It is difficult to generalize lessons from China for developing countries. China is still feeling its way through trial and error. Sometimes, it involves painful experiences when the state is seen to have overstepped its role, resulting in a severe loss in confidence in 2021 and 2022. Because there is no universal formula for growth, no single set of ideal economic and political conditions, no model is universally applicable. Those wedded to faith in unfettered markets will be baffled by the Chinese, Japanese, Singaporean, and Korean experiences; those who believe in the heavy hand of the state have a host of economic disasters, historic and current, to choose from. Even if we know what is definitely bad for economic development, we do not know the full spectrum of what is good or effective. Unsatisfying as it is, developing economies will have to tailor their own policies to befit their environment, suit their stage of development, and address their own unique set of cultural and historical elements.

The Perils of Rapid Industrialization

China was able to achieve astounding rates of growth, but this does not mean that its growth model between 1978 and 2008 was a paragon of success. Household share of income in China steadily declined from 70 percent of GDP to below 60 percent of GDP over that period; in the US and other advanced economies, the household income share has remained at roughly 80 percent. The return on Chinese households' savings was (and still is) exceedingly low, with household deposits earning on average 1–2 percent in real terms during a period when the economy grew at 10 percent per year, and when the economy-wide average return to capital registered 24 percent per year.[27] At the same time, housing prices climbed at staggering double-digit growth rates, making housing less and less affordable to the average household. In the industrial sector, subsidies ran rampant, leading to oversupplies in steel, mining, and solar panels, to the point where some local officials suggested bombing the factories to cut back their supply. Cheap credit became a drug supporting the industrial sector, and at one point served as a lifeline for the entire economy.

These economic malaises are not disparate phenomena. They are interlinked and interwoven by a root cause: the impatient desire of a nation to industrialize *fast*. For a long period of time, the state's mentality was that industrialization was tantamount to modernization and had to be China's economic focus. For a country that had suffered half a century of humiliation for its "backwardness," modernization was an absolute objective. Industrialization is a good thing, of course, and particularly beneficial to developing countries, but the cost of rapid development in China was high: to subsidize industrialization, interest rates were capped at an artificially low rate that did not reflect the economy's productivity growth. This "financial repression" was made possible by the fact that China's financial system was dominated by state banks. Low interest rates reduce the cost of borrowing but hurt households striving to earn a decent return on their savings. This led to an economy with too little consumption, too much investment in the wrong places, and high net exports. These imbalances, as we will see in chapter 8, would spark international controversy.

Low interest rates produce high equilibrium asset prices for housing and stocks while at the same time encouraging vast amounts of borrowing throughout the economy, threatening financial stability. In essence, although reforms weeded out some of the distortions that brought about rapid TFP growth in the last forty years, new distortions were created in the wake of China's big push toward heavyweight industrialization. Weaning China off steroidal industrial policies that feel good in the short run but are toxic in the long run is the key to sustained, high-quality growth and reconciliation of international disputes.[28] The old model of growth must give way to a new model, one that is centered not on industrialization but on innovation and continued improvements in productivity.

The Case for Future Growth

Decades ago, if you had to predict China's economic fortunes based on established economic principles, you would never have dreamed that China would land where it is today. Whether measured in terms of rule of law, ease of doing business, or corporate governance—factors deemed essential for economic growth—China has fared poorly, consistently hovering around or below average world rankings.[29] China placed 82 out of 126 countries for rule of law; in 2018 China was ranked 78 in terms of ease of doing business, behind Azerbaijan and Rwanda; in corporate governance, it is ranked 72 out of 141 countries surveyed. In addition, China is Communist—and fervently red; after all, no Communist country except China has yet escaped the fate of either outright collapse or economic destitution.

So, given the obvious difficulty of prognosticating for China, what can we expect with regard to future growth? In the decade that followed the global financial crisis in 2009, things took a different turn. Total factor productivity dropped following a large fiscal stimulus aimed at saving the economy from a deep plunge, which resulted in a substantial misdirection of resources. As we will see in chapter 6, resources flowed to large SOEs, to shadow banking, and to countless numbers of infra-structure projects. The three steps forward taken in the first three de-cades following 1978 were followed by one step back. Growth maintained its pace not by improving efficiency, but through large amounts of credit and state-led investment; in the decade since 2009, the economy experi-enced low, or even negative, TFP growth, relying on investment to sus-tain overall expansion.

As we've seen, Latin American countries such as Mexico and Peru, and Asian economies such as Malaysia, Indonesia, and Thailand, have all experienced rapid growth, but as of this moment none of these devel-oping nations has graduated into the ranks of high-income countries. Data shows that the main reason is that they suffered from a significant slowdown in productivity. Of course, the numbers don't show *why* that productivity slowdown occurred; it could have been due to corruption, political instability, poor infrastructure, or inadequate investment in re-search and development, among other things. This phenomenon is what economists call "the middle-income trap." Since 1960, only 13 out of 101 middle-income economies have managed to escape it. South Korea and Israel made it, but can a gargantuan country like China do it? This is perhaps the single biggest question concerning its economic future.

If China gets stuck in the middle-income trap, it may follow in the footsteps of Japan, which experienced a lost decade of no growth in the 1990s. If, however, China can keep growing at 5 percent on average, and assuming that the US continues to grow at a 1.5 percent annual rate, then the Chinese economy will overtake the US economy by about 2030. China would not be as rich as the US for several more decades, but by then more than a billion Chinese would enjoy the same living standards as the average American. However, in order to follow the trajectory of its East Asian neighbors, rather than those of Brazil and Mexico, China will need a new model of growth.

As of this writing, the growth rate of the Chinese economy is slowing down and is currently at its lowest level in the last forty years. A projection of 5 percent annual growth rate seems overly optimistic at this point. Apart from "cyclical factors," such as shocks to the global economy and supply chains or COVID-19 lockdowns, lingering distortions and structural deficiencies are weighing down the economy. For one, China's record level of 275 percent overall debt to GDP ratio as of 2022 points to a painful path of deleveraging. Stimulants like cheap credit to save the economy from a slump no longer work as potently. The economy has turned from "seldom cool and frequently hot" to the other way around. And threats of deglobalization make an export-oriented economy particularly fragile.

Prolonged economic downturns make it difficult to see China's considerable untapped potential going forward. But the truth is that there are still around 870 million people with a monthly income below RMB 2000 (about US$300). They have yet to join the four hundred million in the middle-income group, which by Chinese standards have a qualifying monthly income of RMB 2000–5000—far below the advanced-economy average.[30] Having an enlarged middle-income group, which has the highest marginal propensity to consume, is the only way to truly bolster China's consumption engine.

There is also room for convergence. China's productivity level is currently only a fraction of the US level; China's share of labor force with a college degree is even smaller than that in South Africa and Brazil, and way below rich countries.[31] New government reforms could further free up the economy. Despite more open policies in general, the floodgates have yet to be flung open for private enterprise to compete in the service sector, including entertainment, education, and health. Currently, this service segment of the economy accounts for about 50 percent of China's GDP, a level far below the 70–80 percent found in other industrialized countries. Because services are more labor intensive than manufacturing, expanding them will offer more opportunities for employment. The prospect of private insurance companies, hospitals, schools, and cultural agencies is not only a boon for society, but also fertile ground for domestic and foreign enterprise to participate and invest.

Although there is still plenty of room for catching up to wealthy nations, delivering incremental prosperity also depends on the political ability to fully implement unfinished reforms. In that regard, the recent growth slowdown is more a symptom of a reform stalemate than it is of diminished potential. As we've seen, reform has served as a powerful economic impetus, and there are still many areas that can reduce distortions and raise efficiency: improving the financial sector would improve the allocation of capital and provide stable and long-term financing critical for innovation. Reforming the hukou system (the household registration system), which tethers a person's labor to their birthplace, would allow the flow of talent across regions and improve the allocation of labor as well as reduce regional disparities.[32] Fiscal reforms can help resolve the local government's high levels of debt, as we will discuss further in chapter 6. Reform is an important ingredient in the mix for China, yet as time goes on, this model of reform-driven growth is losing momentum and potency. Many items in the comprehensive reform package ambitiously laid out by the Eighteenth Party Congress in 2012, when Xi Jinping became president, are still in process.

China has made the first quantum leap—going from US$380 to US$10,000 of per capita income over a span of four decades. The second quantum leap is to go from US$10,000 to US$30,000 of income. Only then can the economic miracle be fully realized. To this point, much of the speed of China's achievement can be ascribed to *catching up*. But unqualified success for China will be achieved when a country with 1.4 billion people reaches high-income status, particularly when this occurs in a political environment completely antithetical to the Western conventional wisdom. If that happens, half of the most prosperous people in the world may be living under Communist rule—not a situation anyone would have predicted in 1989 when the Berlin Wall fell.

The new generation that would be responsible for a wave of new technology is more likely to shift the economy in this direction than away from it. China's young people do not share the appetite for industrialization of previous generations, a perspective that so far has shaped the nation's economic identity and steered the process of its economic growth. But the new generation is proud of the nation's growing innovative capacity and confident in its ability to contribute to it. This generation is market savvy, innovative, and entrepreneurial. Its dreams include a higher living standard, a more sustainable environment, more balance between work and leisure, a broader space for creation and innovation, and citizenship in a country leading the world in sustainable, intentional economic growth.

If I had to pick one theme from Confucianism that runs most prominently through the veins of the Chinese people, it would be this: "To be a credit to one's ancestors." The achievements in a career should serve as a way to honor one's ancestry. The new generation stepping into leadership roles in China can make their families proud through a wide range of endeavors, but trailblazing innovation has now become the one of the highest forms of such glory. And it is only through innovation that China has a hope of becoming the foremost economic power of the twenty-first century.

THREE

CHINA'S CONSUMERS AND THE NEW GENERATION

n China, November 11 is known as Singles Day; the 1s in 11/11 look like bare branches, which signify being single. Singles Day began as an anti–Valentine's Day conceived by students at Nanjing University. Born into a one-child policy era, these students belong to a generation of lonely, highly pressured, and superbly educated young people. Singles Day may have started as a form of social subversion, a way of expressing frustration and discontent—but with a push from large e-commerce companies, the holiday quickly morphed into the biggest online shopping event of the year—for everyone. On November 11, 2021, $140 billion worth of goods were sold on two e-commerce sites alone, Alibaba and JD.com. This is more than US sales on Black Friday, Thanksgiving, and Cyber Monday combined.

The disposable income of these snappily dressed young men and women—and their willingness to spend it—poses a stark contrast to the frugality and thrift of the Chinese people as we usually think of them, the biggest savers in the world. These young consumers are part of an assertive new elite, zipping around busily with their appointments and travel plans, enjoying material goods and leisure as a way of life. This barrier-breaking younger generation was born in the 1980s, 1990s, and the first decade of the 2000s. Its members are confident, privileged, prosperous, and highly educated, but above all their life trajectories have been defined by the most radical act of social engineering in human history: China's one-child policy, introduced in the late 1970s. Its primary objective was to address the population explosion of the previous decades, but its socioeconomic consequences were far-reaching and in many ways unintended. As we will come to see in this chapter, it has profoundly affected not only China's demographics, but also family relations, gender equality, saving behavior, and human capital in the form of education and skills.

The consumer is the first of three primary agents in any economy, followed by firms and the state. By burrowing deep into what drives Chinese households, by mining their incentives and preferences, we can better understand their spending habits and investment proclivities, and how these go on to shape various aspects of the macro economy, from saving rates and stock and property markets to trade imbalances and disputes between nations. We will be exploring these larger topics throughout the book, but we begin with the first of the three basic agents that fundamentally shape China's vast economic landscape: the individual and the household.

China's 1.4 billion consumers have long fired the imagination of businesses around the world. Apple, which sells twice as many iPhones in China as it does in the US, earns more than $100 million in China *every day*. Starbucks derives more than a fifth of its sales from China. Tesla is making significant investments in China, building the first wholly owned foreign car plant in China. It expects its sales there to match and then outstrip those in the US. Nike and Estée Lauder thrive globally due in large part to their popularity with Chinese consumers, whom they access through WeChat, the most popular social media platform in China, with one billion active monthly users. Most recently, the "influencer economy" in China has doubled every year and has become as large as the restaurant industry, approaching US$1 trillion. And Chinese consumers also spend abundantly beyond China's borders, helping prop up prices of Bordeaux wine, buying shoreline residential properties in Sydney, and paying tuition for their children to schools around the world.

Yet for all the treasure they offer, the waters of China's vast consumer market can be treacherous to navigate. Rapidly shifting consumer trends render popular products unfashionable or obsolete, and unexpected shifts in policy can wreak havoc—in the blink of an eye. When President Xi administered his "Eight Rules" in 2012 to rein in gift giving to government officials, one unintended consequence was a massive blow to the luxury industry. Overnight, the frenzy of lavish gifts that had been smoothing the way with government officials evaporated, and sales of expensive wines and luxury watches plunged.

Given the kaleidoscope of variables, the single most important lens for viewing China's consumers is the generational changing of the guard. Increasingly, China's new leaders are those born under the one-child policy. To understand who they are, let's begin with a closer look at the policy's social and economic impact while striving to make sense of an enduring paradox: over the course of four decades of rapid income growth, the Chinese have been the world's most assiduous savers.

The New Generation:
Little Emperors and Empresses

"LITTLE EMPERORS AND EMPRESSES"

You, my little emperor and empress!
You take a fancy to rain or shine,
And they will come at your beck and call.
You're fed and you're attired,
without lifting a single finger.
O, how can I hold you?
What if you melt should I take you in my mouth?
And what if you fall should I try to hold you tight in my arms?

—*Author's translation of a popular verse*

Throughout all of history, no country has adopted so draconian a measure to control population growth as China did, for thirty-odd years starting in 1978. The new regulation imposed a limit on the number of births for all families of Han ethnicity, China's primary ethnic group: at most they could have one child. Within a few years, the vast majority of urban families was abiding by the rule, which was a sharp departure from the government's previous position: in the early days of Chairman Mao, women were encouraged to have as many children as possible and were often rewarded for having big families with public accolades like "heroine mom." For Mao, more people meant more power: his newly founded nation needed a big army and a large labor force. His strategy worked. The result was a steep rise in China's fertility rate, which climbed from a little more than four people per family in 1950 to more than seven by 1964. In fact, Mao's plan may have been too successful.

In 1957, the famous demographer Ma Yinchu warned of an imminent population explosion in his book *New Population Theory*. He cautioned that China's population was growing at an economically unsustainable level, and he recommended active steps to stem the tide. But Ma's advice went unheeded, and it was not until the early 1970s that the gravity of the situation became apparent to the country's leadership. By this time, with 80 percent of China's eight hundred million people below the poverty line, feeding the nation had become a major challenge. According to an ancient Chinese saying, "The emperor regards his people as heaven, people regard food as their heaven." China's leadership was well versed in the history of revolutions, which were often triggered by an underfed population.

A series of restrictive policies followed, but in the beginning they were more like moral suasion. The government came up with the slogan "Late, sparse, and few," which encouraged men to marry no earlier than age twenty-five and women no earlier than age twenty-three, a minimum of three-year spacing between the first and second child, and fewer children ("Three is too many, and two is just right"). Despite being voluntary, these guidelines did have some effect. In the 1970s China's total fertility rate dropped significantly. The average fertility rate for urban households fell from three children in the early part of the 1970s to two children by the middle of that decade.

But for Deng Xiaoping, who stepped into power two years after Mao died in 1976, this was not enough. Aware that a large populace slowed the growth of GDP per capita, Deng wanted "quality over quantity" when it came to his people. Deng's instruction to the state population council was blunt and forceful: "Bring the population down. I don't care how you do it." This led to the imposition of the one-child policy in 1978, and, according to the Urban Household Survey, within four years 96 percent of urban families were having just one child. Exemptions were granted to rural families that needed helping hands on the farm; to ethnic minorities, who could have two or more children; and to twins, whom families were (thankfully) allowed to keep.

Growing up in Beijing in the 1980s, I was in the vanguard of the one-child policy generation. I did not know of any Han families like my own with more than one child. Of the 120 peers I came to know closely during my grade school and middle school years, only a Uighur student had a sibling.

Implementation of the new law was enforced at the community level. Birth planning enforcers in each residential compound kept detailed records of contraceptive use and even menstrual cycles, detecting out-of-quota pregnancies early.[1] Enforcement led to many horror stories. Still, the vast majority of people went along with the new one-child policy, aware of the need to manage China's exploding population. For most families, the cost of breaking the rule—a large financial penalty, job loss from state-owned companies, or the loss of social benefits like education, healthcare, and residence permits—was simply too high to bear.

Socioeconomic Consequences of the One-Child Policy

Under normal circumstances we usually choose how many children we're going to have. That choice is not just a matter of preference, but it also reflects levels of income and education. On average, higher-income households have fewer children, much the way richer countries have lower fertility rates. If we observe that a family with one child saved more than another family with three kids, it may be just because that family is richer, not because it had fewer children.

What makes the one-child policy in China so remarkable and potentially informative about the *causal* effects of fertility is that it was an exogenous event, something imposed by the government and not a matter of personal choice. Every urban household was constrained by the policy, which is what makes this massive social experiment so fascinating as a case study. This "natural experiment" can help us understand fundamentally how fertility changes affect household behavior. To do so, we simply need to compare these only-child families to the lucky ones who happened to have given birth to twins. As we'll see, the "twin test" reveals some striking patterns.

The basic message is that fertility does matter, and it has broad—and sometimes unexpected—implications. The one-child policy can help account for China's high urban household saving rate, the extraordinarily rapid rise of higher-education attainment, and even the large gender-ratio disparity that we see in China today. But in a surprising twist, having fewer children dramatically elevated the status of women. Numerous studies have explored the negative impacts of the policy, but to give a different perspective, the chapter will focus on the policy's unexpected economic consequences.

A NEW INCENTIVE TO SAVE

The world has always been struck by how much Chinese people save. In China the average net household saving rate as a share of disposable income is more than 30 percent over the last two decades. By contrast, in the thirty-seven industrialized nations in the Organisation for Economic Co-operation and Development (OECD), this same rate is below 10 percent, and in many cases, below 5 percent. If the Chinese would save a little less, then global companies can reap more profits from their greater spending power, China's growth would need to rely less on investing and exporting, and there would be fewer disputes over trade imbalances between China and other countries. We will grapple with this phenomenon later in this chapter and explore a range of explanations, but it turns out that the one-child policy has a prominent place in the mix. If you're a parent, you know that economies of scale come into play when you have children; items like clothing and toys can be shared, for instance. But even if the total spent on two children is less than twice the cost of one, the overall cost still rises with the number of children, since things like food and education are consumed individually and cannot be shared. Indeed, the data shows that a family with two children in China spends significantly more than a family with one, even controlling for such variables as income and the age of the parents.

I f parents spend less, their saving rate naturally increases. But there are additional reasons for this increase in saving. Why the one-child policy raised the saving rate also had to do with a Confucian tradition, which we'll explore in chapter 5. Throughout history, parents have expected children to help support the family, even at a young age, and to display *xiao shun*, filial piety, a basic sign of moral character. Filial loyalty is not just a virtue according to Confucian philosophy, but part of the nation's cultural bedrock. Respecting elders, heeding their advice, and taking care of them in old age: these are powerful social norms. They are also enshrined in China's legal system. In the data, there is overwhelming evidence that the elderly rely on family for old-age support, whether it is financial subsidies or co-residence with children. In the past, a big family with many children was considered a blessing. As the saying goes, "The more the children, the greater the happiness." And those with more children were financially better off than those who had fewer.[2]

Let's take my father's family as an example. He was born in 1949, before any fertility policy was put in place. His mother was a heroine who had five children. It seemed sensible that having a big family would ease my grandparents' concerns about their old age, and that proved to be the case. After they retired, my father bought them an apartment. Regular financial support came in from my father's siblings, and on top of that a daughter and son living nearby looked after them and kept them company. They were well cared for by a large group of children working together to meet their various needs. My father and his four brothers and sisters, however, were in a very different position. They were all limited to having only one child. As a result, they needed to rely more on themselves in their old age. One child's support—no matter how prosperous that child becomes—cannot replace what could be provided by three or four, as this might also include living nearby or offering daily care. To offset this gap, my parents' generation felt compelled to save more during their income-earning years.

Greater risk and uncertainty also provide additional incentives to save. The earthquake in Wenchuan in 2008 that killed many young students in flimsily built schools highlights the potential tragedies that are even more horrific for only-child families. Typically, in a country with a well-functioning social security system, the current working population supports retired elders through this form of intergenerational transfer. But in China, government pensions and social security have covered only a portion of the population, often modestly, and sometimes fail to meet their obligations altogether. In urban households, pensions make up for less than a quarter of retirement income. In 2014, the largest strike in recent history took place in Dongguan, Guangdong Province, where as many as sixty thousand workers walked off the job for two weeks. Their employer had been underpaying social insurance contributions for years, leaving employees who had spent their lives working at the company with a much smaller pension than they were entitled to receive.

This is not uncommon in China, where enforcement of social insurance law—even the most basic provisions—has been lax. So, wherever institutionalized intergenerational transfers in the forms of pensions have fallen short, families fill the gap. Some important social security reforms have taken place, starting in 1997, and then again a decade later, and it is likely that older generations may be better protected in the future.[3] But for current generations of old people, pensions have never been a reliable source of income.

THE TWIN TEST

A lot has happened in China during the period that witnessed the sharpest increase in household savings, between 1990 and 2010. Rapid growth, market reforms, and privatization all affect saving, making it difficult to tease out just how significant the one-child policy has been. One can't simply compare Chinese saving rate "before" and "after" the one-child policy was initiated and attribute the differences to the policy itself. And as we have mentioned, one also can't compare across families—say between a Han family who had only one child and a minority or rural family who had two children, given their intrinsic differences. But a good test is to compare Han families who had one child with Han families who happened to have had twins (1 percent of urban families). There is nothing noticeably different about families with twins—except their good luck—so they present us with an unusual research opportunity to study the effect of having two children instead of one during the same time period.

Data on households informs us that on average, between 1990 and 2010, families with twins did have much lower saving rates than only-child families. The difference is as large as 9 percentage points. This means that if only-child families saved an average of 30 percent of their disposable income, families with twins might have saved only 21 percent. Across different income groups, this same pattern still holds. Families with twins spend more on education and consumer goods. These parents also spent more on themselves once the kids left home, reinforcing the notion that parents with more children have a weaker motive for saving than those with just one child. We estimate that if the nation had implemented a two-child policy instead of a one-child policy, the saving rate would be closer to 20 percent than 30 percent, a significant difference.

A SUPER-EDUCATED GENERATION

The twin test is also helpful in examining another effect of the one-child policy: how families whose children were born in the three decades between 1980 and 2010 approach education. Nobel laureate Gary Becker and his coauthor Gregg Lewis famously studied the trade-off between quantity and quality when it came to raising children in the 1970s. They found that the fewer children there were, the bigger the education investment per child;[4] by reducing the number of children in a family, the one-child policy was likely to raise their "quality," just as Deng Xiaoping intended.

To begin to see how directly the one-child policy led to the rise in human capital in China, we refer back to the twin test. The results are quite striking. Figure 3.1 shows spending on education for an only child (the solid line), and for a twin (the dotted line), according to the age of the child. For younger children, the difference is negligible; these are the mandatory education years, when public education is basically free in China. But as children become older, we see that the only child gets a much larger allocation of family spending than a twin, and at one point nearly twice as much.

The second noteworthy feature of the data is that Chinese households spend a lot on their children's education. On average they devote

25 percent of their annual spending to educating one child. This is an enormous sum. To put this in perspective, the average American household earmarks about 5 percent of its annual spending to educating one child. American families have more children, and differ from Chinese families in many ways, but the large discrepancy in per capita education spending suggests that the one-child policy significantly raised parental focus on education. The motive may be partly pragmatic—if we have only one child, let's make sure that child is highly educated and can earn a higher wage to offset the lack of other children—or it may be driven by a desire to make sure our child can go further than the neighbor's child. It is no secret that Chinese people are fiercely competitive.

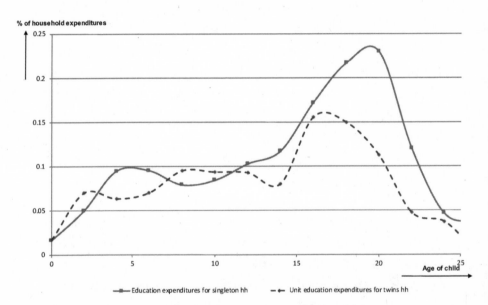

Figure 3.1: Spending on Education for an Only Child and for a Twin

Source: Taha Choukhmane, Nicolas Coeurdacier, and Keyu Jin, "The One-Child Policy and Household Saving," Working paper, July 2017.

The question that logically follows is this: Does more education investment per capita necessarily translate into better education outcomes?

The answer is a resounding yes. In the sample that covers young people aged eighteen to twenty-two during the period between 2002 and 2009 (my peers, born in the 1980s), twins are 40 percent less likely to pursue an academic secondary school that prepares them for college compared with only children. Twins are also 30 percent more likely to attend a vocational high school that provides specialized training. Anyone familiar with China today knows that filling children's schedules and fretting over their education and achievements has become a national pastime. In the new social landscape in China, parents rush around after school and on weekends, bringing their children to tutoring classes and extracurriculars, carefully planning every second of their children's lives, and making nice to teachers (no matter how much rank or wealth the parents enjoy).

Public education in China is free from primary school to middle school. Until recently, private schools were virtually nonexistent. But because the one-child policy generation triggered a higher education arms race (or, more precisely, because the parents did), discretionary education costs have climbed sharply. Today it has become enormously expensive for families to pay for tutors and extra prep classes for important academic subjects, not to mention extensive lessons in English, Math Olympiad courses, all kinds of study-abroad and travel-abroad programs, summer camps, and internships.

Why all these expenses? The overarching objective is to ensure that the child can successfully compete; as the popular saying puts it, "Don't let your child fall behind right from the starting line." Because other kids get tutoring for five subjects outside of school, yours are under pressure to do the same. Urban households spend inordinate sums of money educating their only children—costs that even include buying or renting apartments in highly coveted school districts. My graduate school classmate, now a senior government official in China, left a spacious apartment he owned in central Beijing for a much smaller rented apartment so that his family could be close to a good elementary school. His driver's son, who is only eight, is already taking three supplementary classes outside of school—which still isn't enough to keep up with his peers. When the kindergarten headmaster found out that my cousin's son did not already know his multiplication tables by age four, he roundly scolded my cousin and his wife for their negligence.

In 2019 the internet giant Tencent conducted a survey of students living in cities ranging from the fourth tier, with a population one hundred fifty thousand, to first-tier cities of more than fifteen million residents.[5] According to the survey, 88.7 percent of students in these cities took supplemental classes outside of school. The national average was 2.1 classes per student. Of course, spending is greater in first- and second-tier cities, and the children significantly busier. But households in a fourth-tier city, where average incomes are roughly half of those in a first-tier city, still send their children to supplementary education. This means that virtually every student not coming from a poverty-stricken area is getting tutored outside of the classroom.

As we see, Chinese parents are doing everything humanly possible to boost the quality of their children's education. On the face of it you might think that shrinking the school-age population for three decades had a negative impact on China's education system. Instead, there was a vast expansion in the number of schools and teachers, educational services, school uniforms, and textbooks, as well as a rich smorgasbord of educational experiences. A huge new market has been created by this national obsession, and businesses have flocked to it. Foreign schools and programs tap into this unprecedented pool of cash. International schools are opening campuses all across the country. The opportunity has been not just domestic, but global. Headmasters of the best high schools in the UK and the US were relocating to China before the onset of the 2020 pandemic. In addition, millions of Chinese students attend foreign high schools, universities, and summer programs.

The education arms race has its dark side. It has induced parents to pay whatever it takes to get the best services, often interpreted as the most expensive. Endless demand has allowed tutorial companies to charge ever higher prices. This, in turn, has led to another dramatic unintended consequence of the one-child policy: The astronomical cost of education in China is making people less inclined to have children. When the government relaxed the one-child policy in 2013, people did not rush to have more children. Since then, the government has begun to actively push childbearing couples to have more children, with little success. China's birth rate fell to a record low in 2021, with no signs of an upward trend. An insidious cycle had been set in motion, with significant implications for the future: the one-child policy led to a noteworthy increase in human capital investment, which hiked the cost of education, and in turned weakened the inclination to have more children.

Education competition is a common source of national angst. A telling fact is that the country's most popular TV series at one point was a family drama about getting their kids into the right schools. The distress around education is wholly antithetical to "common prosperity," President Xi's signature agenda of maximizing inclusive prosperity. Ordinary parents cite education and property costs as major impediments to raising a big family, even in the absence of the birth limits imposed on them. Thus, in the summer of 2021, the government mandated a complete shutdown of tutorial classes for school-age children. The move caused a historic drop in the market value (and even a wipeout in some) of China's largest education companies. It is also seen to be a driver behind the property market clampdown, intended to slow down the rise of housing prices so as to render housing more affordable for middle-income families.

A GOLDEN AGE FOR CHINESE WOMEN

Twenty-five million women are missing in China, girls who should have been born between 1980 and 2010 but were not.[6] According to the

National Bureau of Statistics, as many as 118 boys were born for every 100 girls in some years; to put this in perspective, prior to 1982 the ratio was 108 to 100. The larger root cause for all these skewed gender numbers lies in a historical preference for sons over daughters. This bias is easy to fathom given the filial obligations we've been discussing; historically, sons have been better positioned to take care of their parents financially than daughters. When ultrasound technologies were introduced in China to implement the population control policies of the 1980s, they were frequently used for sex selection. This is no longer legal in China, but in the past the practice was quite widespread, and nowhere was this more true than in rural China.

In China's countryside, families need sons to help with physical labor. Although fertility restrictions were relaxed in rural regions, in part because they were more challenging to enforce, families still had a profound interest in knowing the gender of their unborn child. Studies show that parents who had a daughter first were more likely to have sons on the second and third try, strongly suggesting that sex selection was taking place.[7] Another piece of suggestive evidence comes from the fact that since the one-child policy was relaxed in 2013, the gender ratio has come down somewhat; in 2017, it fell to about 111 boys born for every 100 girls.

The "missing women" phenomenon reflects an egregious bias against women in China back in the day (we also see this in places like India, Pakistan, and Qatar, but China's gender-ratio imbalance is among the largest in the world), yet the one-child policy had the unanticipated effect of reversing the fortunes of the girls who *were* born. In fact, it launched a golden era for Chinese women that is still transforming the face of China today. The reason may be as simple as "daughters are raised as sons." The legendary heroine in the film *Mulan* stepped into her old father's place as the head of his army because she did not have a brother, and in the generations shaped by the one-child policy there are many such families. Although daughters may not literally be raised as sons, they no longer need to compete with their brothers for resources, particularly in education.

Today, daughters are even better educated than sons. A number of studies confirm that, on average, girls receive more years of schooling thanks to the one-child policy.[8] This stands in stark contrast to larger families of the past, where in the case of two children, a boy and a girl, the daughter would receive 0.4 years less schooling than the boy; in families with five children, daughters received on average 2.1 years less of schooling. Some fascinating studies find that financial returns on education are also higher for women than for men. For the years between 2000 and 2009, economists estimate an 11–12 percent return per year of schooling for women, compared to 6–7 percent for men.[9]

When it comes to higher education, China's census supports the premise that the gender gap has basically closed for my cohort and for those that followed. In 1978, the share of women in college was 24.2 percent, but by 2009, half of all college students were women. In my parents' generation, the rate of college completion was twice as high for men as it was for women; by the time my cohort finished college, those rates were roughly the same—and 47 percent of graduate degree students were female. Of course, a reduction in the gender gap usually comes with economic development, as is the case in most countries. However, China is an outlier—the rate of increase in its degree of female higher-education attainment (relative to male) is substantially higher than countries with similar or even much higher levels of income.[10]

Beyond the fact that fertility policies meant a larger allocation of a family's education money for girls, there are some less obvious reasons why having one child would close the performance gap between genders. For one thing, knowing that they are in high demand gives women more say in the timing of marriage and child-rearing. They can choose to delay those choices,[11] and when they don't marry young, those long years of education become even more valuable. Having fewer children also frees up women to enter the labor force, and to reenter it sooner after having a child. All this gives parents even more incentive to invest in their daughters' education, knowing they're more likely to find a job, stay in it longer, return to it faster, and keep putting that education to work.[12]

Today, daughters contribute financially to the care of their parents just as much as sons. It's not only that they're equipped with more education and higher-paying jobs. According to convention, when young people marry it is often the man who is tasked with the job of buying an apartment, setting up the nest, and bearing the brunt of that cost. Knowing this makes it easier for the parents of a daughter to invest their savings into her education. Ironically, now that girls have so many more options, urban families are becoming more interested in having daughters than in having sons!

Empowerment for women and the narrowing of various gender disparities is one of the great stories of the last half century. In the United States, the birth control pill liberated women.[13] Access to contraceptives allowed them to take more control of childbearing, devote more time to education, and increase their participation in the labor force. In China, the one-child policy had been even more transformative: it is estimated to have had ten times the impact compared with the pill in raising girls' college attainment.[14] According to China Stock Market and Accounting Research Database (CSMAR), which provides information on companies listed on the domestic stock exchange, more and more leaders in every field in China are female. In 2017, a snapshot of public company executives who were born in the 1950s showed 12 percent were women. For the cohort born in the 1970s, that number rose to 23 percent, and for those born in 1980s, to 35 percent. For executives born in the 1990s, the percentage of women has risen to 42 percent.

We see this trend even in the political arena, which is particularly difficult for women to break into. According to the same data set, 5 percent of women born in the 1950s became city-level mayors and party secretaries, whereas 21 percent of women born in the 1970s have done so. Women make up less than 10 percent of the total membership of the Central Committee (the political body of the Communist Party comprising its top few hundred leaders). There is at most one member in the Politburo (the top twenty-five officials who oversee the party), and none at all in the Standing Committee (the seven to nine most senior leaders). Women born in the 1980s are only just reaching forty, which is the minimum age for taking on senior government roles in China, but we will likely see each successive generation feature more female political leaders, much the way we see this in business. And women in politics tend to have higher levels of education than their male colleagues: 75 percent of female leaders have graduate-level degrees, compared with 56 percent of their male peers.

If the one-child policy raised Chinese women's status in the family and in society, the recent relaxation of the policy has caused some erosion of women's status. Employers are wary of women of childbearing age, especially those who have had no children or have had only one child. The possibility that they will take maternity leave and need maternity health coverage provokes serious discrimination against women. Unfortunately, China's laws do not do a good job of protecting their interests and rights, at least not so far. A close friend of mine from middle school told me it was impossible to get an interview with any major companies once they learned she had only one child; the possibility that she might have another in a few years has put her at a significant disadvantage in the workplace, which would not have been the case when the one-child policy was still in effect.

THE SCRAMBLE FOR WIVES

In the marketplace for domestic partners, however, women are in the dominant position. Jane Austen famously opened her novel *Pride and Prejudice* with the statement "It is a truth universally acknowledged, that a single man in possession of a good fortune, must be in want of a wife." Two centuries later, this social principle has made its way to China, with some slight modifications: "It is a truth acknowledged in China that a single man in want of a wife must be in possession of a property and a car."

Given the gender imbalance we explored earlier, marriageable Chinese women are in short supply, which means that a lot of bachelors will have difficulty finding wives. Like it or not, a bachelor's eligibility is firmly tied to the sum of his material possessions. This provides a powerful motive to rapidly accumulate wealth—and yet another reason to save. In fact, saving has become a competitive national sport among parents with one child, along with education. Because family lineage (and, by extension, offspring) is so important in Chinese culture, families will chip in to help a son save money so that he can find a wife. Having no grandchildren is the worst possible nightmare for a traditional family.

All this is particularly true in rural China, where the gender imbalance is even more pronounced and family traditions stronger. Also, men in rural China tend to have less mobility and are therefore less able to move to places where there are more women. In the past there was no tradition of a dowry in China, but today it is families with a son who are saving up for marriage and even making payments to the family of the bride. Two Chinese economists, Shang-Jin Wei and Xiaobo Zhang, find that families with sons saved more on average than families with daughters, controlling for factors such as income and other household characteristics; those living in places with more skewed gender ratios saved even more. These patterns are also consistent at the macro level: provinces in China that experienced a faster increase in the gender-ratio gap experienced a greater surge in saving rates. And as the gender gap increased, the national saving rate also surged.[15]

You might assume that if families with sons were compelled to save more, then families with daughters could relax and save less, which would lessen the impact of gender imbalance on aggregate savings. But what the two economists find is that families with daughters also save in order to raise the bargaining power of their daughters even further—investing more in their education, and generally hoping to raise the quality of their daughters' prospective matches.

There is an unusual secondary development in this tale of the scramble for wives in China. To redress the large gender imbalance, especially in some of China's underprivileged areas, the solution has been to import wives from abroad. Why pay for a local Chinese bride who can cost up to ten thousand dollars when you can import one from Vietnam for much less? In a new wrinkle on outsourcing and globalization, the mail-order bride phenomenon has swept across rural China, offering psychological as well as financial relief from the stresses of finding a wife inside a country where relatively few families have eligible daughters.

Advertisements in newspapers in Vietnam and other Southeast Asian countries offer different package deals at different price points. A more expensive package may include a round-trip ticket to visit the parents and the bride in Vietnam, visas and permits, and even guarantees! If the bride runs away within the first year, for example, the groom is entitled to a replacement bride. But other sides of the story broach serious moral concerns. Some women are exploited or abused. Many never learn to speak Chinese or get along with their mothers-in-law. In 2016 an entire group of Vietnamese women fled from a Chinese village. The somber stories of bride trafficking caused social media uproar, setting in motion a recent nationwide campaign to crack down on trafficking of women and children.

SOLVING THE SAVINGS PUZZLE

The one-child policy, with its pressure on retirement, and the competition for marriageable women are by no means the only explanations for why the Chinese save so much. Needless to say, this question is important as it relates to the overall economy. If we understand why the Chinese save—and what might induce them to save more or less—we can predict the future with greater accuracy. If Chinese households saved 20 percent of their disposable income instead of 30 percent, hundreds of billions of dollars of extra spending could be unleashed on goods and services. This would be good not only for China's economy, but also for the world. As we've seen, Chinese tourists, millennials, and general consumers provide an important anchor for global demand.

The high saving propensity of a Chinese household stands in sharp contrast to that of an American household, which saves about 7 percent (before the 2008 crisis that number was closer to 2 percent). This leads to popular stereotypes of frugal Chinese and profligate Americans, but these differences in saving rates have consequences beyond personal behavior. They contribute directly to the large trade imbalance between the two countries, and therefore lie at the heart of the fierce political and economic debate on trade policy that led to a full-blown trade war between the US and China. The essence of the problem is America's hyper-consumption and China's underconsumption. When China produces more than it is able to absorb domestically, it will run a trade surplus. When America consumes more than it produces, it will run a trade deficit. Punitive tariffs to redress the imbalance will prove insufficient to the task.

Understanding the reasons for China's high saving rate is therefore crucial. But there are many myths surrounding it. One prominent one is that Chinese people are inherently frugal. That has some cultural validity, but it doesn't solve the puzzle of why, in a growing economy where everyone is getting richer and richer, China's households are saving *more*, not only in the absolute amount, but also as a percentage of income. Despite seeing their disposable incomes increase sixfold over the last few decades,[16] Chinese people still set aside more and more of it over time!

Another misplaced explanation is culture. Cultural norms tend to change slowly, and so there's little here to explain why Chinese consumers are saving more and more over time—unless they are becoming more and more frugal—an unlikely scenario. Japan and Korea are also culturally influenced by Confucian values, but their households saved on average about 2.5 percent and 6 percent of their disposable income, respectively, before the onset of the 2020 global pandemic. Yet another common explanation is China's weak social safety net, which encourages people to save a lot during their prime working years in order to pay for retirement. However, if an inadequate social security system was the culprit, we would expect people to save less as the social security system improved. But despite substantial progress in China's pension system, that saving rate keeps on climbing.

One plausible explanation for the saving puzzle is rising property prices. As we will see in chapter 6, when we explore the financial system, the cost of property in China has been taking off at runaway speed. Urban Chinese households would need to save in order to afford an apartment, which they typically like to own, and so property prices rise higher and higher, and buyers are compelled to save more and more. Rising income inequality may also play a role, because rich people have a higher saving rate than poorer people. Some experts focus on China's corporations to help explain the rising national saving rate, but data shows that the Chinese household's contribution is just as important: household saving accounts for a third of the rise in saving between 1990 and 2009, equal to the contribution of corporate saving. Nor is rising corporate saving a uniquely Chinese phenomenon; it has risen in many countries around the world. Household saving behavior in China, however, is truly a global outlier.

THE GRAYING OF CHINA ACCELERATES

We have learned how the one-child policy can affect household behavior at the micro level, but one of the most profound changes it has brought to the economy at the macro level is the acceleration of aging in China. The reason is obvious: the young cohorts have gotten dramatically smaller over time. According to UN world population prospects, about half of the Chinese population was under the age of twenty before 1980. By 2015, that share has fallen to 24 percent. And by 2050, more than a third of the population will be above sixty. Demographic transitions like this happen naturally when a country becomes richer and its people have fewer children: the population ages in a slow but sure trend. But in China, the much faster transition has led many to pose the question: Will China grow old before it grows rich?

There are a number of economic risks associated with an aging population, such as huge fiscal pressure emanating from overburdened pension programs, and a reduction in the labor force—and therefore growth. I am among the minority who is a bit more sanguine about the situation. For sure, it is worrying that the Chinese young generation is not having more kids—even now that they can—and this may not be just because of higher education costs and property prices. Habits and preferences may have changed—permanently. Still, I believe that China's low fertility rate and aging population are not a harbinger of a looming disaster. Rather than headcounts in the labor force, what matters is the amount of *productive* labor force. To give an extreme example, even if the labor force halves, a labor force that is four times more productive than before will more than make up for the reduction in the number of people actually working. In addition, automation is making many jobs obsolete. The rise of artificial intelligence has sparked speculation over which kind of skilled jobs would even be relevant in the future. The problem in China today and in the near future is not the labor shortage, as some would expect, but a serious skill *mismatch*. The nation's top graduates are increasingly without appropriate jobs and left in the lurch, while enterprises are bereft of the vocational and technical labor they require. In 2022, the highly educated youth had a record-high unemployment rate of 20 percent.[17] A story that caught the nation's attention is that a cigarette manufacturing company's new production line workers in 2021 consisted of one third master's graduates, and two thirds undergraduates from high-ranking universities.

If the demographic dividend—the economic growth potential that can result from having a young population—did not explain China's GDP *on its way up*, a tapering dividend should not explain its GDP *on its way down*. As we have seen in chapter 2, the first-order factors contributing to China's growth are specific reforms that include opening up markets, sharing the benefits of production, and more efficient use of capital and labor, with emphasis on improved technology. What may cause a significant slowdown in economic growth are economic policy overcorrections, hitting the panic button in face of aggressive private-sector development, or, worse, a dramatic reversal of reforms. Aging doesn't make it to the top of the list.

Rather than demographics, I see shifting paradigms within generations as making the biggest difference to China's economy. Every generation distinguishes itself in terms productivity, consumption and saving patterns, appetite for risk, life-work balance, and political preferences, which we turn to next. One thing is clear: the current young generation today like to spend and borrow. On the Alibaba e-commerce platform, one can purchase a lipstick with one click, and with another click, take out a loan to finance it. The function Huabei in Alipay is a word that means "just spend," and is highly popular among the young. As the only-child cohorts enter middle age and replace their high-saving parents as the main economic agents in the economy, they will likely turn China from a saving nation to a spending nation, and from surpluses to deficits.

Toward a New Vision of the Future

The one-child policy was a unique intervention that shaped the course of China's modern development in ways that few could have predicted. Few even understood its sustained and unexpected consequences for the economy, gender imbalance, human capital, saving, and the family fabric. Along with the drastic changes that have taken place since 1978 in China, it produced a special feature of present-day Chinese society: the coexistence of generations with radically different characteristics, including attitude, ethos, aspirations, and overall ways of life.

This wholly unprecedented generational gap constitutes a social revolution in its own right, a profound break from the past. The new generation has never experienced poverty and psychological hardship the way their parents did. The new generation grew up in the comfort of their parents' modest prosperity and basked in the indefatigable attention of their teachers. They did not have to save for a rainy day. They had no siblings to compete with, nor any with whom to share burdens and responsibilities, including the heavy weight of parental expectations. Equipped with modern tools and skills, exposed to Western ideas and thoughts, and comfortable in a changing world whose economy is underpinned by technology, they are a group capable of imagining—and realizing—a new vision of the future.

It is the unintended consequences of a social policy on ordinary Chinese households, as well as the dramatic shifts in attitude from one generation to the next, that I find most fascinating. The new generation shaped by the one-child policy embodies unprecedented spending power, consumerism, and prosperity as a way of life; what was once an "American dream" the Chinese people only fantasized about can now be materialized in China. This generation has vaulted into consumerism with surprising ease. A taste for pleasure, a creative sartorial sensibility, and a high degree of comfort with spending have made them both targets and subjects of advertisements and news stories. Optimistic about China's economic prospects, they are not nearly as risk averse as their parents. The haunting memory of economic depression and expropriation so firmly embedded in the minds of previous generations play no part in their consciousness. Their outlook on the economy and their own prospects is a rosy one, which makes them different from millennials around the world.

They are also a socially conscious group—indignant about societal injustice, passionate about environmental sustainability, and sensitive to things as remote and far-flung as African wildlife protection. They have purpose, drive, and an appetite for hard work that goes beyond material pursuit and personal gain. They are the first generation in China to seek happiness more than wealth. They are proud of their nation's growing power and influence, a sentiment that is only accentuated by alarm from the West over China's rise. All this draws them closer to things Chinese, to events that take place internally rather than externally. Previous generations that once looked up to Western standards, foreign brands, American jobs, and foreign ways of being are giving way to a new generation convinced that their own education, goods, and services are as good as any, if not better. The confidence of a new generation will define China's future.

The one-child policy no doubt curbed the explosive population growth, but the policy probably outstayed its proper duration. It has left a lot of side effects in its wake, far beyond the scope of this economics-oriented analysis. But from my own experience and those of the many Chinese students I have taught over the years, I can relate to the many burdens of an only child. A strong sense of responsibility to their parents and teachers, loneliness, and a life of endless competitive pressure are all complications that cannot easily be articulated or quantified. Over years of teaching many Chinese students at the London School of Economics and Political Science, as well as at Tsinghua University as a visiting professor, I can see that, for all their accomplishments, these students struggle over the tension between fulfilling their obligations to their parents and meeting their own expectations of personal life and career.

When they come into my office and I ask what they would like to do after graduation, the first words out of their mouths are "My parents would like me to . . . [pursue a master's, go home to China, go get a job, etc.]." In some important sense, their education and experience of the West have not liberated them from their mindset of obeisance—at least not the majority of them, at least not yet. According to a survey of 1.2 million people conducted by Wonder Technology, a tech start-up helping millennials find their ideals mates and careers, more than 82 percent of young people born in the 1990s or later would choose a job different to the one they now have if they could. As a popular saying goes, "Can't die! Can't travel far! Really want to make money because my parents have only me." For all their new sense of empowerment, this generation's "onliness" has become a shackle both mental and physical, and from which they may never break free. They carry a heavy burden of expectation, from both their parents and their society. So it is not surprising that they are a lonely group, the creators of the first Singles Day holiday in the world.

FOUR

PARADISE AND JUNGLE, THE STORY OF CHINESE FIRMS

T he emergence and evolution of Chinese enterprises has been every bit as dramatic as the modern history of China itself. How twenty million private firms could have sprung up within just thirty years remains one of the most fascinating questions in China's economic landscape, especially when you consider modern China's origins as a nation steeped in anti-capitalist doctrine.

Firms are a principal actor in any economy. They hire workers and invest in order to create goods and services. Consumers purchase those goods and services with income they earn either from firms or directly from the state. Whatever consumers don't spend, they save, allowing financial institutions to lend those savings to firms in order to fund new investments. In these ways, consumers and firms are tightly intertwined. In the next chapter we will see how a third actor, the state, interacts with these two agents to provide the third pillar of an economy.

Unlike most countries, China's corporate sector contains two distinct types of firms: state-owned enterprises (SOEs) and private firms. Their perspectives—and their prospects—could not look more different. If you are a large state-owned enterprise, the gates of paradise swing open: guarantees, loans, and contracts effortlessly come your way. And if you're lucky enough to be an SOE operating in a strategic industry like telecom or energy, you enjoy the kind of monopolistic power that could catapult you into the ranks of global giants. On the other hand, if you happen to be a small or medium-size private company, the world looks like a jungle full of threats to your survival, including high entry barriers, the exorbitant cost of capital, and endless bureaucratic red tape. If you want to set up shop or break ground on an office building, you need to obtain hundreds of approvals from a byzantine network of district, municipal, and provincial governments.

The outcome of this differential treatment, however, defies all logic. Despite the overwhelming advantages of state-owned enterprises, not only have private firms in China managed to take root, expand, and catch up to their state counterparts in most sectors, they have *surpassed* them. And with startling speed. In 1990, private enterprises accounted for a negligible share of China's economic output; twenty years later, they accounted for more than half, largely a result of their much more rapid productivity growth. And since then they have become the driving force of the Chinese economy, accounting for 50 percent of tax revenue, 60 percent of GDP, 70 percent of innovation, and 80 percent of urban jobs.[1]

These numbers encourage stereotypes—the inefficient, unwieldy SOE versus the nimble, highly motivated entrepreneur—that make it tempting for Westerners to view this dynamic solely as a triumph of free market forces. But the truth is more complex, as is so often the case in China. For one thing, the boundary between state and private enterprise turns out to be anything but a straight line. It's more like the curve in a yin-yang symbol, where seemingly opposed elements turn out to be complementary. As we'll see, SOEs and private firms in China have found ways to collaborate, compete, and coexist, thereby reaping the benefits of many possible interactions between them.

In China, private businesses need the government to provide resources and overcome a plethora of barriers, but the government needs good private firms every bit as much. Well-run businesses create more jobs, generate more tax revenue, boost local GDP, and score political points for local government officials. When Chinese economists Chong-En Bai, Chang-Tai Hsieh, and Zheng Song wrote about the rise of Chinese firms after visiting southern cities in China, they found that the primary focus of local governments was to attract and support private businesses, even when officially their work had nothing to do with business development. Nine vice mayors in one city spent most of their time prospecting for new businesses, each being the point person for about thirty private firms.[2]

Symbiosis between the state and the private sector can be especially useful in an economy with immature institutions and imperfect free markets, a theme that runs throughout this book. Even in the rough-and-tumble early days of private industry, it was not uncommon for hard-charging entrepreneurs and officials in local government to share the fruits of these new, market-driven entities, skirting or bending regulations to the snapping point as they wined, dined, and sang karaoke together. "Reforms start with breaking rules," as the famous Chinese saying goes.

From this unlikely brew of informal, and sometimes illegal, collaboration, millions of private corporations were born during the 1990s and early 2000s. But once that era had fulfilled its role as incubator, President Xi launched a major anti-corruption drive in 2013, cutting deeply into the illicit relationship between private firms and those who held political power, curbing graft, and checking the prairie fire of corruption. Since then, the firm-state nexus in China has evolved into new, ever more sophisticated—and legal—forms. The story of China's corporate world is a narrative of the divergence and convergence of public and private enterprise, and of a Chinese entrepreneurial spirit that overcame massive historical roadblocks to infuse the nation's economy with a vitality whose evidence is everywhere to be seen in today's China. We'll also take a look at the way a new generation of Chinese entrepreneurs is reshaping the way the country does business.

China's SOEs: A Brief History

When the People's Republic of China came into being in 1949, state enterprises served as bedrock for a Chinese economy struggling to hold its ground. At the time, SOEs played nearly every role vital to a fledgling nation. In a country with few economic structures, limited industrial capacity, and very little private wealth, SOEs were tasked with rebuilding infrastructure devastated by war, meeting national output targets, and providing regular wages, medical care, and pensions to employees, while turning virtually all profits over to the state. Workers were given jobs for life, the famous "iron rice bowl"; they could even pass these jobs on to their children. No one was fired, and hardly anyone ever quit. In short, SOEs met the cradle-to-grave needs of China's population, particularly in cities.

From the outset, financial performance was not considered all-important for SOEs. They were the agents to maintain stability in society and to carry out important national goals. The state had endowed them with all kinds of advantages, and assumed this would be enough to keep them viable, at the very least. And for a time it was. Eventually, however, troubled by inefficiencies and financial losses, SOEs failed to provide enough jobs and tax revenue to meet the central government's national economic goals. Many attribute this to the lack of incentive for managers working in state enterprises, particularly the absence of a profit motive and profit sharing. But the story is not so simple. As we'll learn more about in the following chapter, those executives were less driven by compensation than they were by knowing that their achievements would serve as stepping-stones, either in the party organization or the government. Many saw the success or failure of the state-owned enterprise as a reflection of their own dignity and self-worth.

A more significant obstacle to the success of SOEs arose from the fact that special privileges can sometimes be too much of a good thing. Easy access to capital, cheap costs of borrowing, and an implicit understanding that debts would be extended and even forgiven encouraged some SOEs to indulge in reckless behavior. With growth as the primary measure of success, many SOEs heedlessly gathered assets of all kinds and ventured into areas far removed from their core business or expertise. A customer walking into one defense contractor's office tower could buy a painting on the third floor and a missile system on the twenty-seventh; that same company also sold sports cars and operated national theaters, opera houses, and the third-largest art auction house in the world. AVIC, a Chinese aviation company, invested in Hollywood films, while Anbang, an insurance company, became the highest bidder for the Waldorf Astoria Hotel. Many SOEs expanded into real estate, regardless of whether or not those property holdings contributed to their business objectives. China was home to the largest number of Fortune 500 companies in 2020, the largest companies measured by revenue in the world, and out of the 135 companies, the vast majority are SOEs.

Just as size is often seen as the most important measure of power and prestige in the corporate world, executives are drawn to the perks that come with running a world-class conglomerate; some may want to wield political clout; others may want bragging rights to impress relatives, friends, paramours, and those with political connections who might be interested in patronage. The director of a large SOE enjoys vice-ministerial-level political treatment, and may well have the chance to climb even higher rungs of the political ladder. When there is easy access to capital and size becomes paramount—when the goal becomes growing until you're "too big to fail"—these perverse incentives can become the order of the day.

But by far the biggest challenge faced by state-operated enterprises is rooted in their original reason for being. Profitability was never the most important objective for SOEs. As we have seen, right from the inception of modern China, SOEs had to bear the full burden of social responsibility. Today, more than seven decades after SOEs first took up the task of rebuilding China's war-torn economy, the social responsibilities placed on them have been eased significantly, but SOEs are still the foot soldiers, firefighters, and essential implementers of national strategic planning. In times of economic need, they are asked to invest in or build infrastructure, absorbing whatever hefty price needs to be paid. In 2008, when Chinese policy makers wanted to rescue the economy from havoc wrought by the global financial crisis, they called on SOEs, which spent massive sums to spur employment and took on countless stimulus projects regardless of their commercial viability. And when China's economy was overheating and creating a surfeit of goods without ready buyers, it was SOEs that cut supply and closed down factories.

Their numbers have dramatically reduced, but in the eyes of the government, SOEs are still considered the backbone of the economy. They are still the agents that carry out the government's momentous national plans. Need to build an Olympic stadium in record time? Call on SOEs. When it comes to implementing the Belt and Road Initiative, China's ambitious plan to connect Asia to Europe and the rest of the world through an infrastructure network including airports, seaports, and railroads, it is SOEs that have taken the lead. The majority of them, and the largest of them all, are in what are known as "strategic and pillar industries," such as energy, defense, telecom, and infrastructure.

Created with the understanding that profit would always take a back seat to national strategic interests, SOEs came into the economic game with a considerable handicap, despite the many advantages showered on them. But when they consistently failed to provide enough jobs and tax revenue to meet China's national economic objectives, some of the state's top leaders began to consider an alternative that had long been unthinkable: removing their opposition to private enterprise.

The Rise of the Chinese Entrepreneur

For decades, private enterprise had no place in Chinese society at all. There were virtually no private firms in China following the Socialist Reform of Industrial and Commercial Companies in the period of 1952–1956. State-owned entities completely dominated the Chinese economy, both at the central and local levels. In the course of time, small family businesses would spring into being, but in a socialist state, mom-and-pop stores were often made to feel embarrassed, if not downright ashamed, about the "shady" way they earned a living. Small-business owners certainly did not enjoy the same sense of honor, status, or job security as workers associated with state-owned institutions. In this social climate few in their right mind aspired to become private entrepreneurs, and authorities concerned about the spontaneous growth of capitalism kept a tight leash on those individual or family businesses that did pop up.

China's first significant nonstate enterprises emerged in the countryside. At first these township and village enterprises (or TVEs) were collectively owned by local residents and often controlled, managed, and supported by local governments. Although they gave every appearance of being public rather than private endeavors, they were decidedly market oriented. These TVEs were permitted to borrow from state banks and enjoy local government support, yet their ownership was neither state nor private in the strictest sense; they functioned in a gray area somewhere between the two. Given their ability to take advantage of market opportunities instead of blindly striving to meet the latest central mandate, TVEs flourished first during the period from 1978 to 1989 (and then again between 1992 and 1998), especially in regions that had been suffering from severe shortages or unwanted surpluses, places where SOEs guided by central planning had been particularly ineffective.

By 1990, 14 percent of China's labor force, some ninety-three million people, were employed by TVEs, many of which specialized in labor-intensive or resource-intensive sectors including textiles, clothing, food processing, and toys.[3] At a time when ideology was a major obstacle to privatization (Karl Marx's theory that surplus value led to capitalist exploitation was followed with religious fervor in Chinese government circles), the trademark "collective" affixed to those companies served as a mask to cover what was really going on, and was the best defense against forced closure. With no legal framework in place for private businesses, entrepreneurs began registering them as TVEs.[4] In this sense, these township and village enterprises served as transitional institutions; in the ensuing years, many would become fully private.

Unlike rural TVEs, which enjoyed the protective coloration of being "collectives," private family and small-scale businesses in China's cities faced formidable barriers. For one thing, their size was strictly limited by law: they could employ at most eight workers. This issue famously came to a head when Nian Guangjiu, creator of Fool's Melon Seeds, was found to be employing a dozen people, significantly exceeding the limit beyond which a businessman was considered a capitalist, triggering the wrath of the state.

NIAN GUANGJIU AND HIS FOOL'S MELON SEEDS

Chinese people love melon seeds. They enjoy cracking them open with their teeth and teasing out the soft inner kernels with their nutty sweet taste. This pastime, long a popular part of any social gathering, also became a vehicle for one pioneering young man from poor, rural beginnings to feed his family, and eventually to open the floodgates for China's first generation of post-1949 entrepreneurs. At age seven, Nian Guangjiu started collecting cigarette butts to make money. By age nine he was helping his parents sell fruit. As an adult with no formal education, Nian Guangjiu turned to various odd jobs to earn a living. In the 1960s, he was arrested and sentenced to a one-year prison term for making money as a middleman; considered financial speculation, this was strictly forbidden at the time.

China began gradually opening up to private enterprise as a way of offsetting the failings of its SOEs, but even then private vendors and middlemen had to be nimble enough to stay one step ahead of law enforcement. And sometimes their best efforts were not enough. Nian Guangjiu was thrown in prison again for selling fish and chestnuts. After his release, he was hired by his neighbor to help prepare and sell melon seeds, a skill he quickly picked up. At that time melon seeds fell into the category of rationed goods, so their private sale was illegal; Nian Guangjiu was caught and his goods confiscated on a regular basis, yet he persisted.

In 1981, the government decided to make it legal to set up businesses and create jobs, under tight restrictions. Nian Guangjiu was poised to make the most of the moment. Now that his carts didn't have to pack up and leave at the first sign of a police officer, he was able to set up vendor stands at fixed locations, selling melon seeds with a unique flavor that he had developed over time. He had also earned a reputation for giving his customers more seeds than he charged them for, which had led to the nickname "fool." Taking this as a compliment, he adopted the term in his brand name. Fool's Melon Seeds became so well known that people stood in long lines in front of Nian Guangjiu's stands, waiting for their generous portion of his delicious seeds. Before long he earned his first RMB 1 million, a dizzying sum in those days. A humble melon seed vendor had become a millionaire!

Nian Guangjiu was in the vanguard of a new emerging group of self-employed people with no legitimate history of working for a state firm or institution. His enterprise may have been frowned upon, but Nian Guangjiu's success was undeniable—and intensely desirable given the hardship so many of China's rural workers were forced to endure at the time. Despite that success—or perhaps because of it—Nian Guangjiu ran into trouble yet again. (As the saying goes in China, "Humans should avoid getting famous, and pigs should avoid getting chubby.") He hired young people to work his growing number of melon seed stands, and when his employees mushroomed to twelve, this set off the trip wire of "capitalist exploitation."

A nearly illiterate vendor of melon seeds, Nian Guangjiu had become a major headache for the state, which was now forced to reconcile Marxist orthodoxy with the new Chinese reality of underperforming SOEs and the public success of an entrepreneurial venture. Yes, some restrictions were easing, but just how far were China's leaders willing to go in their support of private enterprise? And who was going to make the call?

The case of Fool's Melon Seeds became such a political hot potato that it eventually made its way to the very pinnacle of power—the desk of China's paramount leader, Deng Xiaoping. In a high-level meeting of the Central Advisory Committee in October 1984, Deng arrived at a momentous decision: Fool's Melon Seeds would be allowed to stay in business. The implications were clear for anyone reading the economic tea leaves: the issue of worker exploitation was not going to be invoked as a form of control; for the moment at least, individual businesses in China would be allowed to expand unhindered.

Grasping this opportunity with both hands, fledgling entrepreneurs worked feverishly to grow their businesses in the wake of Deng's ruling. As private enterprises surged to fill the vacuum created by less efficient SOEs, they delivered an economic windfall to the nation as a whole. Deng's unorthodox ruling paid off. There were a few notable milestones along the way. Two years after Deng's Southern Tour in 1992, which re-affirmed his commitment to reforms and opening up the economy to private enterprise, the Company Law legalized channels of financing for the private sector that included the formal banking system. And finally, the amendment of the constitution in 2004 made it clear beyond any vestige of doubt that the state supported the private sector, providing legal protections for private property.

THE SECOND AND THIRD WAVE OF ENTREPRENEURS

When Deng's decision to permit Fool's Melon Seeds to exceed the eight-employee limit signaled that Marxist ideology would no longer suppress the growth of private firms, China's entrepreneurs embarked on a period of extraordinary expansion. Adventurers, risk takers, and iconoclasts by nature, they had little to lose and everything to gain. They understood in their bones that they would have to work harder and take more punishment—possibly even a jail sentence—if they were going to succeed, and they turned this handicap into a wellspring of motivation. Familiar with the landscape for private enterprise, they were quick to spot loopholes in policies and regulations, identify arbitrage opportunities, and circumvent restrictions and legal requirements. If they had been commuters driving to work, their strategy would have been to speed through green lights, run the yellow, and drive around any that had already turned red. Their guts to bend or break the rules—and their skill at doing so—lured a broad swath of lucrative economic opportunities that would have eluded more scrupulous enterprises owned by the state.

Before long, other entrepreneurs proved that the phenomenal success of Fool's Melon Seeds was no fluke. Lu Guanqiu was born into a poor peasant family in Xiaoshan, Zhejiang Province. After the country was hit by three successive years of natural disasters and economic catastrophes in the late 1950s and early 1960s, he lost his job as a blacksmith's apprentice. After he started a rice and flour mill, his business was shut down, and in order to pay off his debts, he was forced to sell the three-room farmhouse left to him by his grandfather. But Lu did not give up. In 1969 he began repairing farm machinery, and with six helpers he started to produce automotive products. By continuing to emphasize high quality and low prices, he became the first private businessman in China to sell his products in the US. Despite his success, Lu Guanqiu remained humble; he never moved his offices out of the unassuming two-story gray brick house where he started his journey.

As time went on, the profile of China's private business owners began to expand. The first wave that poured through the opening created by Nian Guangjiu was largely cast in his mold; having grown up in poverty with little time for formal education, these entrepreneurs had never tasted the privileges of life inside the Chinese bureaucracy, making them truly proletarian. The second wave differed from the first in that many were either former senior government officials or other well-connected elites in Chinese society. Well educated and groomed for lifetime job security and high social status, they were willing to give up their iron rice bowl and opted to *xiahai*—plunge into the turbulent seas of business. Fully aware of the challenge of navigating the rough and tumble of private business, they embraced the chance to make a fortune. With the help of their social connections, these entrepreneurs aimed to start high-end businesses rather than seek out just any opportunity to bring in money.

Liu Yonghao embodied this second wave of Chinese entrepreneurs. In 1982 he and his three brothers all quit state-sector jobs to launch a business together. Within eight years they owned the biggest livestock feed producer in China. In 1995, their diversifying business led to the creation of four separate companies, each managed independently by one of the four brothers. As a newly elected member of the National People's Political Consultative Conference, a powerful political advisory body, Liu Yonghao proposed the establishment of a state-sanctioned bank that would mobilize private resources to promote private-sector development. The result was Minsheng Bank, which was listed on the Shanghai Stock Exchange in 2000.

SOEs and Private Firms Converge

As we've seen, state enterprises and private businesses were treated differently right from the very beginning. While state enterprises were being granted monopoly rights, priority access to stock markets, and easy access to permits and licenses, private firms had to rely on family, friends, trade credits, and pawnshops to obtain financing.[5] If SOEs were borrowing at 5 percent interest, private firms were borrowing at three times that rate. Even when the weakened state sector would contribute less than half of national GDP, it claimed more than half of the bank lending and investment in the country. All these advantages did not lead to superior economic performance for SOEs, however, nor sound the death knell of private enterprise. As Figure 4.1 indicates, within several decades the overall share of assets, profits, and jobs contributed by SOEs was steadily declining. In short, the two breeds of firms, one living in paradise and one struggling in the jungle, were now beginning to look as if their conditions at birth had been totally reversed.

Private businesses had a notable advantage over SOEs: flexibility. They could make quick decisions and adapt to changing circumstances without checking in for approval from a byzantine bureaucracy. They could also enter a market when they wanted to and exit when it looked

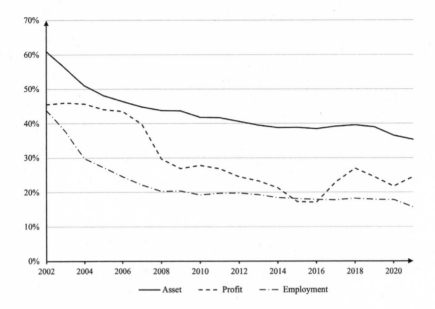

Figure 4.1: State-Owned Enterprises' Share in Industrial Enterprises

Source: CEIC China Premium data set.

the better part of wisdom. SOEs, however, could not simply scale back or close down when they were submerged in red ink or when future prospects grew dim. They had restrictions on firing workers and commitments to national policy goals. They could downsize by selling assets, or restructure by merging with another SOE, but they didn't have the option to just bail out. Nor were unproductive SOEs forced to give way to more efficient ones, as was the case in the ultracompetitive private sector. But all this changed after 1995.

FROM IRON RICE BOWL TO PUBLIC SPRINGBOARD

Determined to address the long-overdue problems of China's bloated, inefficient SOEs and get them standing on their own feet, Premier Zhu Rongji implemented a series of measures in the midnineties that few could ever have imagined, initiating the third wave of reforms discussed in chapter 2. It began with "grasping the big and letting go of the small"; big SOEs were drastically overhauled, while smaller ones were left to sink or swim. Major SOEs embarked on a period of fundamental restructuring, inviting strategic investors to take over a portion of equity, selling off minority interests to the public, or becoming listed on the domestic stock exchange. The result for state-owned firms was massive shrinkage.[6]

More than 80 percent of the state-owned firms operating in 1998 were shut down or privatized by 2007, particularly the smaller and less efficient ones. The annual exit rate of the smallest SOEs (in the bottom tenth percentile) exceeded 30 percent, which was much higher than the exit rate of private firms of comparable size. Employment in the state sector fell by forty-four million as the number of SOEs declined from 118,000 to 34,000, and the national share of state assets fell from 70 percent to below 50 percent. Even highly protected strategic industries felt the dwindling presence of SOEs as their share of the mining, petroleum, chemical, and metals sectors almost halved.

As a consequence, the overall performance of state enterprises improved. Back in 1998, 60 percent of SOEs had been operating in the red; unprofitable SOEs accounted for nearly half of state jobs and 23 percent of the employment in manufacturing. By the end of 2003 the tide had turned. For the largest, profitability soared threefold in just seven years. Larger SOEs were becoming more profitable and productive. Between 2001 and 2007 the gap between the productivity of state companies and private firms rapidly narrowed. The improvement was staggering; the tide had completely reversed.

The goal of "grasping the large" was to boost the profitability of large SOEs while still keeping them under state control. In 2018, half of China's central SOEs were listed among the five hundred largest companies in the world. Some large state-owned industrial conglomerates merged to become even larger. In the steel sector, state-owned manufacturers were consolidated into five large industrial groups. In the automobile industry, state-owned companies were merged into six state-owned conglomerates, the largest of which is owned by the Shanghai municipal government (SAIC). In this way, the larger SOEs that emerged from the purge of the midnineties turned out to be bigger than ever. The average asset size of industrial SOEs increased sevenfold between 1999 and 2008.[7]

The state business sector was radically transformed. Many state companies were dismembered or dissolved, but those that survived took on even greater prominence. The reforms of the late 1990s also spawned a period of rapid productivity growth. Mergers eliminated unprofitable SOEs without sacrificing jobs, and price wars between competing SOEs were brought to a halt. Less was more. And SOEs showed that they could become profitable enterprises almost as competitive as private firms.

This transformation also rendered obsolete the conventional wisdom that all-out privatization was the inevitable future for the command portion of China's economy. The big bang approach of massive overnight privatization applied in Russia and Eastern European economies, with its oligarchy, corruption, and social problems, turned out not to be the only option. It seemed that China could successfully create a dual-track system where SOEs and the private sector could coexist, once the former was gradually reformed. This way, the messy transfer of assets from the state to an elite group of political moguls was averted, along with mass layoffs, high unemployment, and social instability.

China's gradual but steady reforms had successfully revitalized the state sector: their productivity gap with the private sector narrowed, and returns on assets quickly doubled after 1998. For a time SOE productivity growth outpaced that of the private enterprises, and they became worthy competitors. The surgical operation that the government conducted on themselves had worked, and the Chinese economy thrived for the decade that followed. As we will see in chapter 6, when we explore the workings of China's financial system, this progress halted in the wake of the economic crisis of 2009, when SOEs were called on to salvage the economy. In the decade that followed, the financial performance of SOEs and private enterprises would diverge again.

THE BUSINESS-GOVERNMENT NEXUS

You may have heard the Chinese term *guanxi*, which means "relationships." In the past, *guanxi* referred to that special connection and trust that formed the basis of strong business relationships. It took time to establish, but once it was formed, things moved along more quickly and effectively. Entrepreneurs relied on *guanxi* more than contracts to expand their businesses. Eventually, *guanxi* began to characterize the interplay between private businesses and local governments. It's easy to understand why local governments would want to aid their local SOEs, but in a country that historically heaped favor on its state firms and obstacles on its entrepreneurs, why would government offer a helping hand to private enterprises? Why would a local government in Jiangsu block unflattering internet stories about a private apparel company? Why would another local government build an extra runway at its airport to accommodate cargo jets for a single private company? In one case the government of a small city even blew up a mountain to make space for a private factory. And it was common practice to help the wives of entrepreneurs to find jobs, and to place their children into the best schools. Why?

By way of explanation, let's consider a scenario. In the past few years, top local government officials in Beijing, Shanghai, and other major cities and provinces have turbo-charged their efforts to build all-electric vehicles. Why? For one thing, the Chinese government has expressed its support for a green vehicle produced in China; for another, such an enterprise could also make a huge contribution to local GDP and employment, especially given the large network of additional suppliers required to make automobiles. A local chief could derive two kinds of direct benefit from a booming new auto sector. He could enjoy personal financial gain by sharing in the profits of companies he decides to back. He also stands to gain politically; by boosting local growth, and meeting the central government's mandate for auto production, he is more likely to be promoted within the government and the Communist Party. The link between local growth and political promotion is what makes China's case unique.

At this point, a local government faces various choices. It could back a local SOE that has started making EVs, or it could choose to support an innovative private company. Alternatively, it could throw its support behind any number of less productive firms willing to bribe their way to success. Expropriation is always a last-ditch possibility: the local government could choose to take over a desirable private company, but if the local government cannot run it as capably as its market-savvy entrepreneurial management, the company's returns will make it much less desirable.

Let's consider the trade-offs here. The SOE would be the easiest of all to help because it requires few additional resources, if any, and politically it's uncontroversial. But the downside is that it might not make a stellar electric vehicle, meaning it's less likely to generate big profits and abundant jobs. The innovative private company might require more resources, but with help it could become a star. Less productive firms offering all kinds of perks have become far less tempting in today's environment, when the central government is cracking down on corruption.

So what's the likely outcome in this scenario? Backing the private entrepreneur looks like the best bet. And this is exactly what happened when the local government of Hefei, the capital of Anhui Province, succeeded in persuading Nio—a smart, successful Chinese EV manufacturer with great potential—to locate its headquarters there. It injected cash in return for a stake in the company, provided it with cheap land, and offered all kinds of services to ease Nio's journey. Not only did Nio, as a global company listed on the New York Stock Exchange, earn the Hefei government a great reputation and a huge financial payoff as its stock price soared, it also fostered a thriving local industry. The local government of Guangzhou is playing a similar role for another private EV company, XPeng.

This logic behind the alternative scenario helps explain why local governments were motivated to break with China's history of antagonism toward private enterprises and encourage productive private firms in their region. This form of economic natural selection may not have been as efficient as one based on market mechanisms, but it worked well enough under the circumstances. And it continues to work today.

The kinds of support that can be deployed by state governments are numerous. Local governments can give out licenses, contracts, cheap land, and direct loans from local banks to the firms they preferred. They can make new laws or sidestep the old,[8] give out permits, and lobby the central government for exemptions. *Guanxi* translates into real monetary value. One study shows that party elites who entered the private sector after the constitutional amendment of 2004 (which encouraged party members to embrace entrepreneurship so as to have better party representation in the private sector)[9] gained regular access to bank loans and state subsidies. The sprawling real estate giant that became one of the world's largest companies, Evergrande, grew from a small operation thanks to elite political connections it cultivated early on.

As we've seen, support provided by local government officials to private firms was not altruistic. In addition to increased political clout, there were private benefits, which in the past often took the form of gray income or illegal bribes. The former might include high-end trips, accommodations at resort hotels, or defraying the overseas tuition of an official's children. And of course, there were also outright cash transfers or equity stakes in private businesses given to family members of powerful state officials. Even though there was no shortage of corruption cases among state enterprises, striking a deal was still easier with private companies.

This was the old model of state-private collusion. Call it cronyism, corruption, or the grease that lubricates the wheels of the machine of the local economy, but whatever the label, the idea is the same: take a cut from firms in return for offering a helping hand. Whether the motivation was kickbacks, better chances of being promoted, or a combination of the two, local government embraced the feverish rush for growth and expansion with open arms, and were especially receptive to large and productive private firms. But discrimination against the smaller ones still existed. Still, there is one notable downside of the model: local governments have an incentive to protect their own firms and block competition coming from other regions, and in turn hurt innovation and competition. The Shanghainese government protected GM's monopoly, while the local government of Wuhu backed its own local private company, Chery. Even though Chery had a license to sell all around the country, it was met with resistance in Shanghai and other places where there was a local car company.[10]

A New Model Changes the Economic Landscape

The old model was struck a significant blow after the Chinese government clamped down on corruption in 2013. More regulations, more control, and much tighter surveillance on corporate as well as government officials meant that private corporations had to stand on their own feet. Cut off from easy financing and political favors, both private and state firms found new paths to prosperity—by forming conglomerates and becoming each other's mutual owner.

Let's come back to the story of Nio, the electric car company. In April 2020, its share price had fallen 62 percent from its initial public offering in 2018, and the company teetered on the brink of bankruptcy, with its financing cut off. At this point, the Hefei government of Anhui Province stepped in, successfully outbidding its competitors with an offer of RMB 7 billion (the equivalent of about US$1 billion) in exchange for a 25 percent stake in the company.[11] Nio moved its headquarters to Hefei, where the local government helped it secure loans from six large state banks, in addition to helping create, organize, and coordinate a supply chain for batteries, engines, and control systems (encouraging other productive businesses to establish themselves in the region). Over the next year, Nio's car production grew by 81 percent. Its total valuation, which had been roughly US$3 billion in April 2020, increased to about US$100 billion eight months later. By being a stakeholder, the local government benefited handsomely in many ways: it was able to attract a high-quality enterprise to its high-tech park, create employment and a name for itself, and make a handsome profit from owning Nio stock.

Governments, through their SOEs, have become important equity owners of prominent private businesses. In 2016, Shenzhen Metro Group, a local state enterprise of the Shenzhen government, became the largest shareholder of Vanke, formerly a fully private real estate company in China and a Fortune 500 company. Vanke benefited by getting cheaper land and numerous construction projects, while the Metro Group profited by monetizing its resources through its delegated manager—Vanke. Another famous example is the East Hope Group, the huge conglomerate founded by the four brothers I mentioned earlier, whose business runs the gamut from animal feed to chemicals. Whenever they ventured outside their home turf of Sichuan to start a new business, they formed a joint venture with a local SOE. To date, this company has joint ventures with fifteen state owners and eleven private owners. Its successful formula has been widely replicated: in agriculture and heavy industry, 90 percent of joint ventures are formed with state governments outside the company's home province.

Today, it's even more evident in the technology sector. When China's STAR market, the Chinese equivalent of the tech-heavy Nasdaq stock market, first opened, half of the companies listed had state-owned investors. It is fair to say that local governments have transformed themselves into not only Silicon Valley–type venture capitalists (investing directly in risky technology companies), but also Wall Street–like fund-of-fund managers—picking fund managers to do the selection and investing of companies on their behalf.

Many private enterprises welcome state stakeholders. After all, engaging a local government or a connected SOE in this way has many advantages: it can use its connections to tap local resources, link distribution networks, obtain hard-to-get licenses, and get some political protection, etc. All of this would require substantial time and resources for a private company, assuming it weren't utterly impossible. And some believed that they would become "too connected to fail." For state agencies, working with highly capable private managers in a joint venture or becoming an investor makes good economic sense—the most productive utilization of state resources. But the collaboration is successful only when the state is a minority shareholder—letting managers and entrepreneurs make key business decisions free of political interference.

Thus, the Western view of China's so-called state capitalism—where subsidies are lavished onto giant SOEs to carry out state mandates and industrial policy—is outdated. This characterization may be true for a small set of strategic industries, but a much subtler and more prevalent state-private collaboration model has emerged to benefit from China's fundamental characteristic: strong state capacity coupled with weak institutions.

The pervasiveness and depth of these interlinkages is shown in a fascinating study by economists Chong-En Bai, Chang-Tai Hsieh, Zheng Song, and Xin Wang, drawing from data that includes every registered Chinese firm,[12] thirty-seven million of them as of 2019. The universe of firm data provides information on the entire complex network of ownership—with owners comprising sixty-two million private "capitalists" and sixty thousand state agencies, including local and central governments. When an SOE forms a joint venture with private firm A, then A is directly linked to the state. But if firm A forms a joint venture with private firm B, then B is *indirectly* linked to the SOE. Private firm B might then go on to become a shareholder of private firm C, making C also indirectly connected to the original SOE. These different layers of equity relationship form a megacorporate conglomerate. SOEs form major nodes in this network, often the very largest.

The number of active firms doing business in China increased ninefold in between 2000 and 2019. But a more striking fact is that private owners with state connections owned about a third of the capital registered by these companies, which shows just how pervasive equity linkages between state and private businesses have become in China's corporate sector. By 2019, there were more than a hundred thousand private owners who had joint ventures with state owners, a fivefold increase compared with 2000. In 2019, sixty-three out of the one hundred largest corporate owners (measured by registered capital) are state players. But the surprise lies in the fact that every single one of these state owners has a joint venture with a private company. The same is true in reverse for the largest private owners—the majority of them have a joint venture with a state owner.

Such tight linkages between government and business are not unique to China, but the pervasiveness of it *is*. Its conglomerate model may remind us of Japan's *keiretsu* network and the Korean *chaebol* system, but nowhere are equity links as intricate and commonplace. The fact that a third of registered private capital is connected to the state significantly eclipses other economies with notable state ownership, such as France, Brazil, or Russia. In the US, state governments can compete to attract successful companies, as they did in the massive bidding war for Amazon's second headquarters, but they do not provide financing for these companies, nor do their dealings include taking a stake in them.

MIXED BLESSINGS

In a country with less-than-sophisticated institutions and markets yet to mature, cooperation between government and business can be very helpful, especially when incentives on both sides are clear and aligned. Still, bad actors are a problem whenever and wherever large sums of money are involved without proper oversight. In China some state and private companies started using the easy access to money from state backing to invest in some highly risky areas. When those investments soured, the debt they generated was covered by the state enterprises involved, sometimes dragging them down along with sinking private businesses.

The collaborative model also works less well when it's flipped around—when private owners become minority shareholders of large SOEs. In 2013, the government encouraged private companies to take large stakes in state enterprises, with the goal of improving the profitability, governance, and productivity of SOEs. But these marriages were often unhappy. The private enterprises made efficiency their priority, while the ability of state enterprises to pursue this goal was limited by the tight leash of government control. Private owners had little say in the SOE's management or strategic direction. They turned out to be not active participants but passive financial investors, diluting the effects of their best qualities—fast decision making, tight cost controls, and first-rate management. The results were mixed at best: the private sector did not improve state performance, not were the private owners noticeably better off.

Government participation can be both a blessing and a nuisance. The model of state-private collaboration can be particularly helpful at certain stages of a country's development—when formal institutions are weak. It has proven to be useful for China by condensing the hundreds of years it took for the West to transform its agrarian economies into industrial and information economies into just forty years. But it comes with significant downsides. For firms, the collaboration can amplify volatility; private companies are subject to changes in management, but not nearly as unpredictably as the SOE managers or local officials with whom they often collaborate or share ownership, where a promotion or demotion can easily lead to relocation.

Local leaders who succeed often leave their districts to pursue bigger political opportunities elsewhere. Their vision of the future may have led them to expend considerable resources in aid of particular firms that can help realize that vision, but when their successors take over, they have their own visions to pursue. They may stop implementing their predecessor's plans simply to differentiate themselves, or to benefit from a shift in the political tide. In this process, firms can suffer. The darlings of one local government leader can tumble from favor under a subsequent leader. And the central government can also amp up the level of uncertainty. If one year the central directive is to focus on the environment, local officials may lavish preferential treatment on businesses related to waste management. But if the next year the central government is all about cultivating domestic competitiveness in semiconductors, local governments will follow suit.

When government and private firms collaborate, the phenomenon of too much success can pose a particular danger all its own. As the Chinese saying goes, "Tall trees bear the brunt of high winds." The government can help firms grow, but when these companies start to wield influence over public institutions, or become so ruthless in their treatment of competitors that they stir up public grievances, the government will rein them in. This means that the largest Chinese firms are never truly independent. High-profile companies like Alibaba and the property giant Evergrande that have already drawn the attention of government monitors are only a decision away from also incurring the government's wrath.

The benefit of being big in China is that its vast market brings with it hefty profits. But at the same time, successful private companies have responsibilities and duties reminiscent of the old SOEs, such as providing services and creating technologies to aid the government during the pandemic, or pledging funds to help recovery from natural disasters. When China needed to catch up with the rest of the world in technology, it allowed the tech sector free rein, creating many billionaires and catapulting China's digital economy to the forefront of the global frontier. Twenty years on, after creating nearly one hundred companies worth more than US$10 billion each, the government decided that the time for allowing them to run loose should come to an end. Many of the largest tech companies were accused of exploiting their monopoly power, using their data to manipulate consumer preferences, and even illegally selling data to third parties. After numerous cases of data abuse, the government made a dramatic move in 2021 by introducing new restrictions on certain big tech, education, and gaming companies. These include fines for the most well-known internet companies in China: the e-commerce giant Alibaba, delivery and shopping platform Meituan, and ride-sharing company Didi. Even the loss of US$1 trillion in stock value for Chinese internet companies seemed to have left the government unfazed.

As governments around the world have recognized, regulations and anti-monopoly policies are justified and especially pertinent in a country where disorderly growth has been the rule of the day. If designed and implemented well, they could lead to fairer outcomes and more innovation and efficiency. If the opposite occurs, they can hurt dynamic entrepreneurialism and disincentivize the most talented. But the "balancing act" between regulation and innovation, fairness and efficiency—the new objective in China's playbook—requires ever greater skill on the part of the government. Transparent and clear guidelines, good communication, and predictable policy are critical for harnessing confidence and ensuring the continued virtuous circle of investment and innovation. Few governments have managed to do it well so far.

Foreign Firms

Foreign firms started to enter China in the late 1970s.[13] Japan's Panasonic was the first, in 1978. A year later, Coca-Cola became the first consumer brand to sell its product in China. That same year, IBM came to China. While many survived and thrived, like General Electric, Apple, and Microsoft, others stumbled, or packed up and left, like Motorola. The fortunes of foreign firms in China are so variable that one cannot paint the full picture with a few simple brushstrokes. The government displayed a certain amount of ambivalence toward foreign direct investment (FDI) in the early days. On one hand, the state welcomed FDI, which brought with it much-coveted technology and know-how, but at the same time the state was concerned that foreign competitiveness would hamper the development of some local infant industries. So while some companies faced all kinds of hurdles and restrictions, others enjoyed special treatment. The general picture is different from what is typically depicted: data shows that in the period between 1998 to 2007, foreign companies in the manufacturing sector were the *most* subsidized of all, on average a few times more than SOEs.[14] Foreign firms also bore lower value-added taxes than domestic firms, on average, and rather enjoyed a foreign-ownership bias.[15] Some of this is attributable to the government's strong support for exports, which many foreign firms were helping China to ramp up.

There is no single yardstick for measuring the foreign investment climate in China. There are sectors where foreign investment is restricted, like mining, education, media, telecom, and certain information-related internet companies, or where joint ventures with Chinese companies are the only option. Many foreign companies also complain about requisite technology transfers that go along with setting up a joint venture with a domestic company and getting access to the Chinese market, unfair competition from state-owned enterprises, or outright government protectionism. These factors were particularly relevant historically (for instance, the Foreign Investment Law passed in 2019 prohibits forced technology transfers), as we will see in chapter 8. But it's also true, as many studies and experts have argued, that blaming the economic failure of foreign firms on discrimination is overly simplistic.[16]

In any given industry, one can point to both successful foreign firms and distinct failures. In the automotive sector Volkswagen and Toyota have done very well, while Ford and Hyundai have not. Audi, BMW, and Lincoln succeeded while Citroën and Peugeot did not appeal to the Chinese consumer, despite their early entry into the Chinese market. In the consumer industry, Procter & Gamble, Yum! Brands, and Starbucks were hugely successful. Mattel did not succeed in selling Chinese girls Barbie dolls that looked like them, simply because the company did not understand that Chinese girls preferred blue-eyed blondes. The fact that virtually every Fortune Global 500 company is doing business in China speaks volumes to its appeal as a market, as does the fact that it was the second-largest recipient of FDI in 2019, and the largest recipient in 2020. Foreign financial institutions such as BlackRock and Fidelity are rushing to establish wholly owned subsidiaries in China to offer a gamut of products, from savings to retirement. Their enthusiasm has increased despite trade wars and geopolitical antagonism. These economic developments and financial linkages between the US and China seem not to reflect mounting tensions, at least not so far. All of this is happening despite the many challenges and frustrations that foreign firms experience.

The opportunities for foreign firms were always there—in manufacturing, IT, software, finance, consumer goods, real estate, etc.—but their mindset and approach determined their fate. Some companies, like Google, chose not to comply with regulatory restrictions and pulled out of the market. Some were bested by local players: eBay's, Amazon's, and Walmart's online business lost out to Alibaba, for example. Uber lost the battle to Didi, although the two companies then reached a mutually beneficial agreement. And many other foreign companies, like Apple and Samsung, flourished.

One advantage that domestic companies have over foreign competitors is that they are better able to handle the political intricacies of dealing with government. As we have seen, this is not easy. Foreign firms that recognized this issue and adjusted their strategies accordingly fared better than those that didn't. Local teams authorized to make decisions were more successful than those forced to wait on decisions from headquarters abroad. Foreign companies that build and maintain congenial relations with local governments, adapt to local customs, and carefully study local demand for products have sometimes been able to get the better of domestic companies. A popular business motto in China is *"Jie di qi"*—keep your feet on the ground, or stay embedded in local conditions. Many firms tried to replicate in China business models that had proved successful elsewhere in the world. But by now it comes as no surprise that this approach rarely turns out well.

Another instance of a discrepancy between anecdotes and systematic evidence relates to the effectiveness of joint ventures in China. Anecdotes often point to their failures, while data reveals that, on average, joint ventures perform better in China than both wholly owned foreign firms and domestic ones.[17] Joint ventures are required in industries where full foreign ownership is not allowed, but they also make sense more broadly. The domestic partner can navigate the Chinese market and its laws, capitalize on political connections, and manage a fluid regulatory environment, while the foreign partner can provide new technologies, infusions of capital, strong corporate governance, and established international trade networks. McDonald's recently formed a joint venture with an SOE in order to grow its footprint in China. In the auto industry, joint ventures predominate. Mercedes, Audi, and BMW have all enjoyed successful business expansion through joint ventures with local partners in China. The ones that don't work out so well could be due to a mismatch of management skills, approaches, and disagreements over control. Cultural differences and different visions of how to achieve growth are still common obstacles.

A thorough treatment of foreign firms in China would require a full-length book to justify their importance. It is also difficult to fit them into a single framework, as they are as diverse as any group of enterprises are. But they do point to some of China's most attractive facets at the same time as they bring into sharper relief the fallacies about the business environment. As we discuss further in chapter 8, many of them are holding back their expansionary plans in China, and some have exited altogether—whether as a function of geopolitical tensions, pandemic controls, or difficulties of doing business. But the reality is that the majority stay, and there are more who plan to enter and expand than who seek to downsize. A more confident China and a more resilient corporate sector have led to a country that is more open to foreign entry and competition. The latest government policies underscore the importance of further opening up to foreign enterprises. In recent years the list of industries or sectors where foreign investment is prohibited has shrunk precipitously. Today the challenge for foreign firms is less about policy restrictions and more a matter of fierce domestic competition. As we've already seen, the productivity of domestic firms has risen substantially, and as we'll see in chapter 7, Chinese firms are becoming more and more innovative, both in the products they bring to market and the business models that support them.

In 2018, Tesla was welcomed by China with open arms and established the first wholly foreign-owned auto plant there. The government of Shanghai gave the company cash, subsidies, and cheap land. But to succeed, Tesla will have to compete with fierce domestic rivals like BYD and Nio, and many other rapidly emerging EV companies. It will have to adapt to the changing taste of a new generation. It will have to effectively manage relations with local suppliers and the government. It will have to be culturally sensitive and steer clear of the inappropriate advertising that has tripped up foreign brands in the past. It will have to abide by the domestic laws on data protection. And it will have to set its course in keeping with the general policy direction set out by the central government.

This is a lot to ask of a foreign company. Firms looking for growth opportunities cannot afford to ignore the vast Chinese market, but both risks and rewards have always been high. And they keep changing. Domestic companies are rising up the value chain, even in sectors like fashion and cosmetics, which so far are still dominated by foreign brands. This formidable local competition is emerging against the backdrop of a proud new generation intent on building its own identity around reinvented Chinese tradition and style. All this means that even with the right approach and mindset, foreign companies will find success more difficult, although still possible.

The New Generation

In this era of intense competition on a global scale, where thousands of companies are pursuing market share or chasing the same group of customers, the requisite skills for success are speed, agility, awareness of local conditions, confidence balanced by humility, and the ability to adapt to changing circumstances. This is even more true in China, where today's entrepreneurs need to be innovative and creative in the quest for new ways to optimize and monetize their business models. Whatever short-term edge they may acquire early on will quickly dissipate if they do not grasp the opportunity to evolve, always staying ahead of the game. Many are socially conscious, with high moral standards, who hope to find ways to lift up those less fortunate than themselves and to address society's most fundamental problems.[18]

In an age where kickbacks, perks, cunning stratagems, subterfuge, maneuvers with regulatory loopholes, and outright bribery can no longer be the primary catalysts for business expansion, a new generation of entrepreneurs must be equipped with a clearer vision and sophisticated skills, and driven by more lofty motivations. I've come to know many of them over the years, and they are an impressive group. Servility toward government is no longer a necessary condition of success, nor a trait commonly found in this generation of only-child entrepreneurs. They are fueled by passion and a will to succeed—not by taking shortcuts, but by coming up with better products or services through ingenuity and good governance.

Many new generation entrepreneurs grew up neither poor nor underprivileged. Often they have first-class educations, with degrees from the best universities and work experience in top companies in the West. Wang Xing graduated from Tsinghua University's Department of Electrical Engineering in 2001 and went on to pursue his PhD in electrical and computer engineering at the University of Delaware in the United States. He dropped out two years later to start his first business back in China, at the age of twenty-five. Even though Wang Xing's early entrepreneurial journey was described as "copying to China" what he learned in the United States, his businesses were deeply embedded in the Chinese local context. His company, the technology giant Meituan, offers hundreds of services, including food and medicine delivery, taxis, bicycle rentals, hotels, travel, cinema, massage services, online prescriptions, and others.

Huang Zheng (or Colin Huang) studied at University of Wisconsin–Madison and worked for Google as an engineer before moving back to China to start Pinduoduo. His gift was finding ways to make bulk buying fun, creating a retail space where Costco meets Disney. Users participate in fun events such as group buys with family and friends, and raffles with great prizes, while conveniently getting access to a wide range of consumer goods at exceedingly cheap prices. Huang was equally astute when it came to politics. He steered clear of the media spotlight, avoiding the ostentatious behavior typical of megasuccessful entrepreneurs, quietly stepping down as CEO and chairman only a few years after founding of one of the most successful internet companies in China. On the other hand, his departure is not necessarily good news for his company, its investors, or a country trying to foster talent.

The new generation of entrepreneurs in China relies on persistence, innovation, and nimbleness to handle tremendous competition and navigate a much tougher regulatory environment than their predecessors faced. China's first generation of true innovators, they win based on the high quality of both their products and their ingenuity. Environmental, social, and corporate governance (ESG) is the new high standard for any company in the world to succeed in well-governed and reputable markets. This raises the bar for many Chinese companies, forcing some to go out of business. But the new generation embraces the challenge by adopting new technologies and practices, making rule bending and cozy relationships more a thing of the past.

In 2017, JD.com set up an anti-corruption coalition with other internet companies. If an employee engaged in illicit behavior, they would be blacklisted by the entire internet business community. Baidu, the Chinese search engine company, established a group to investigate serious offenses, and Meituan formed an ethics and conduct committee. Every year, they hand over dozens of cases directly to the police. The existence of such committees would have been unimaginable for the previous generation of companies associated with the old Chinese growth model. Every generation of Chinese entrepreneurs has needed to be mindful of the line between their business interests and the government's desire to maintain social stability. They have always needed to flexibly respond to sudden changes in policy and leadership. Even as the rules of the corporate game have evolved, the basic principles of being an entrepreneur in China have not. Though making huge sums in China is increasingly difficult in this more regulated and controlled environment, the optimism and confidence of its new generation of entrepreneurs continues to fuel corporate dynamism and dreams of success in fitting into niches of China's vast consumer market. For every billionaire unhappy about government intervention, there are many happy young millennials who believe they have a better shot at becoming multimillionaires or billionaires now that room has opened up for more players to compete.

FIVE

THE STATE AND
THE MAYOR ECONOMY

Today, hundreds of industrial parks are peppered across the full length and breadth of China's vast landscape. In recent years, more than one hundred fifty high-tech development zones have been built in small and medium-size cities around the country, with the aim of developing commercial hubs for electronics, biomedicine, and clean energy. Nearly all of China's twenty-three provinces and four municipalities have experimental commercial development projects under way: there is one in Guangdong for a maritime silk road, one in Fujian for connectivity investments with Taiwan, one in Shanghai to position the city as a center for international financial services, and many others. Within the city of Shanghai, individual districts choose a particular focus like trade logistics, shipping, high tech, finance, or industrial development. In addition to conventional power and steel plants, there is a plethora of cultural centers, museums, exhibition galleries, and tourism projects cropping up as China finds creative new ways to boost economic growth through regional and local initiatives.

This phenomenon is known as the mayor economy. In recent decades, pioneering local government officials have rushed at a frenetic pace to expand their local economies, transforming former fishing villages and farmland to technology hubs and industrial centers. These officials vie with each other for primacy in everything from economic growth to foreign investment, from the number of industrial, trade, and horticultural exhibitions to the size of cultural events like concerts and film festivals. Local governments busily commission landmark bridges, skyscrapers, opera houses, and gymnasiums with the latest avant-garde architecture. In 2019, more than three thousand exhibitions around the country showcased the latest environmental technology or new beauty product or breakthrough in gift wrapping—the focus of fifty-eight exhibits around the country. In Shanghai alone, a visitor would need to visit more than one new exhibition every day in order to see them all in any given year. Each expo aims to be larger than the next.

When foreign officials and business executives come to visit China, they are invariably impressed by the enthusiasm of provincial governors, municipal and county mayors, and even village chiefs as they rattle off awesome statistics about local industry, agriculture, services, import and export growth, and most especially the measures they are taking to improve their investment climate and ease of doing business. In China, the mayor economy rivals the market economy in importance.

Western countries often complain that there is too much state in China—that its inefficiencies, meddling, and rigidity combine to stifle private business development and create drag on the economy. It's certainly true that the Chinese state can sometimes throw obstacles in a business's way for its own reason, but much less known is the fact that it purposefully seeks to offset the rigidities of a central authority and its institutional deficiencies by giving tremendous economic authority and autonomy to local governments. In the mayor economy, local governments have strong incentives to help promising businesses overcome barriers and to foster innovation in their locality. Adam Smith's concept of invisible hands working behind the scenes is, in the case of China, replaced by the thousand-arm Buddha's extended and very visible hands.

The best term for describing China's developmental paradigm is "political economy": in China the state and the economy are deeply intertwined. Sometimes one moves to take the wheel, and at other times they switch seats, but rarely does either operate in isolation. When we consider the China model, it is this political economy that is truly distinctive. Complex and nuanced mechanisms embedded in the system—incentive schemes, competition, and a fluid system of checks and balances at work within various levels of government and business—make it one of the most fascinating subjects of study when it comes to understanding China.

There are three prominent features of the Chinese state. The first is its power: it has the resources and administrative skill to mobilize rapid collective action in service of the nation's goals. The second is its structure of political centralization paired with economic decentralization, which makes room for creative local business activity under central guidance. The third feature is its adaptability. It can adapt to the changing circumstances rapidly and flexibly, dialing back policy measures if they have gone too far and shifting between priorities when the situation warrants it.

In their seminal book *Why Nations Fail*, Daron Acemoglu and James A. Robinson argue that countries with narrow concentrations of political power give rise to institutions that allow the ruling elite to exploit the rest of the nation, instead of emphasizing growth, new technologies, education, and investment. China certainly fits the bill when it comes to power concentration, but it is far from being an extractive state. Instead of limiting growth by siphoning off the nation's wealth to a small elite, the state has encouraged twenty million private firms to spring up almost overnight; rather than inhibit new technologies, the government is fueling a national drive to make China the global leader in pioneering new technology, deploying trillions of dollars to support entrepreneurs, research centers, universities, and high-tech zones. As for the Chinese people, not only do they save and invest long term, they also spend huge sums to educate their children based on rosy expectations of the future. Clearly, something is working. Some would even argue that political concentration prevents political gridlock, while others believe that it was important for delivering China's stellar growth.[1] In this chapter we take a closer look at the role the state plays in this larger dynamic.

A Central Government and a Political Party Intertwine

The onset of the COVID-19 pandemic in March 2020 gave me firsthand experience of the reach of the state. I had returned to Beijing from London just before the outbreak engulfed the UK. The airport felt like a theater for military operations—hundreds of men and women in uniform were strategically placed at various checkpoints, questioning every passenger, accumulating detailed information before sorting visitors into various hotels. It took me about eight hours to clear all the checkpoints, and at the end of the process I was introduced to a member of the residential committee that would make sure that I honored my mandatory fourteen-day quarantine.

In nearly every Chinese town or city, large or small, residential neighborhoods include a residential committee comprised mostly of older volunteers; it's a Communist Party cell, tightly organized and charged with administering the locale. The chief of the committee, often an older woman, wields enormous power. Even ministerial-level officials in our compound defer to this woman, who enforces residential rules and regulations. For the next fourteen days a residential committee member checked on me twice a day to make sure that I had not sneaked out of my apartment. The door was sealed from the outside with a paper strip. When daily necessities were delivered, the strip was temporarily removed and then affixed again. I had to report on my health via a community online chat that was administered by a committee member. This system would be difficult to create or accept in many parts of the world, but Chinese citizens readily comply. They accept limitations on privacy in exchange for the sense of safety provided by a highly organized, capable, and paternalistic Chinese Communist Party. The party's network and organizational capacity proves helpful in times of crisis, like a global pandemic.

In China, the Communist Party and the government each function according to its respective mandate, but instead of working in parallel, they are intertwined. They function like a double helix, stabilized by cross-links between the two systems. Unlike the classic structure of DNA, however, the two systems merge at the top. China is a socialist republic run by a single political party, the Communist Party of China, or CPC. Its Politburo stands at the zenith of power and is directed by the Standing Committee, which makes decisions about major policies, legislation, and other important matters. At the next level down, power splits into two branches, with the party on one side, and the legislature and government on the other. The chairman of the National People's Congress heads up the legislature, while the premier directs the government; both are members of the Standing Committee, where the two strands of China's double helix converge. The secretary general of the party serves both as head of the state and as chairman of the Central Military Committee, assuring that the party maintains control over the military.

On the government side, there are a number of ministries under the State Council and provincial governments (see Figure 5.1 for a hierarchy of administrative divisions). The same parallel party/government structure is at work here. The highest-ranked leader in any organization at any level is invariably the party secretary. Likewise, in a municipal government, the municipal party secretary ranks above the mayor. One represents the party and the other represents the government, and both work closely together.

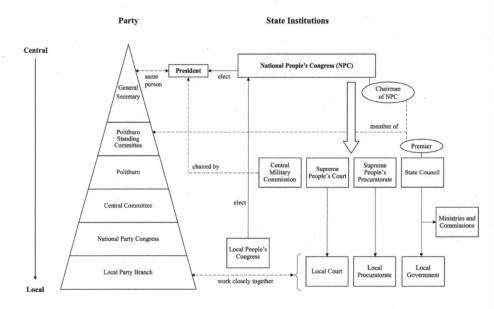

Figure 5.1: Hierarchy of Government Administrative Divisions

China's concentration of political power dates back to imperial times, when the emperor held supreme control. Today, it is exercised by the top leadership of the Communist Party, but this is not the case when it comes to day-to-day management of the economy; here, power emanates outward from the center to the local level. It is local officials in provinces, municipalities, counties, and towns who push for local development, meet growth targets, implement reforms, and attract foreign investment. These are the local cadres who have transformed fishing villages and rural backwaters into modern export hubs, manufacturing

	Division	2020
Province	Provincial Level	23
Municipality		4
Autonomous Region		5
Special Administrative Region		2
Prefecture-Level City	Prefectural Level	293
District	County Level	973
County-Level City		388
County		1,312
Town	Township Level	21,157
Township		7,693
Subdistrict		8,773

Figure 5.2

Data source: Statistical table of administrative divisions of the People's Republic of China (December 31, 2020), http://xzqh.mca.gov.cn/statistics/2020.html.

centers, and high-tech economic zones. Behind every economic success story stands a local government that has supported it at every step along the way.

This model of political concentration of power married with economic decentralization is unique to the Chinese state. It stands apart from wholly centralized states like the former Soviet Union, where all decisions were made at the top, and every major economic policy was coordinated and implemented by specialized central ministries. It also differs from American-style federalism, where the economic clout of state governors and city mayors elected by their constituents comes primarily in the form of fiscal allocations from state legislatures. Chinese local officials directly control vast resources, from land, energy, and raw materials to local banks. They can make and enforce regulations, build infrastructure, and undertake major commercial projects. In China the central government takes care of domestic and international politics and sets overall economic policy, while local governments tend to the economy itself.

CHINA INC.

China's unique governance structure became a turbocharged engine for economic development. But how, exactly, did this work? One way economists approach the Chinese state is by imagining it as a gargantuan corporation, China Inc., whose goal is to maximize both revenue and sustainability by motivating employees, ensuring that innovative ideas are not buried under layers of bureaucracy, and promoting healthy debate for every important decision. A fundamental challenge for China Inc. is how to align the best interests of its employees not just with the goals of management but also with its shareholders—the general public.

The Politburo's Standing Committee, which consists of the most important officials in the country, functions much like the senior management team of a giant corporation, with executives like a chief operating officer, head of human resources, and chief marketing officer, each in charge of a particular domain. Local government officials work much like department managers, finding ways to meet objectives set out by the central leadership. Power permeates the hierarchy layer by layer, from the province's boss to the municipal and city mayor, the county head, and the village chief.

As in any large corporation, designing an effective incentive structure is crucial. In China Inc., this is based on a governance system called *nomenclatura*, which appoints officials to key positions throughout the government and the party's own hierarchy. The Organizational Ministry of the Central Committee is responsible for screening cadres for promotion to senior positions in the party, the government, and major SOEs. This powerful ministry is effectively the largest human resources department in the world. All ambitious officials dream of rising through the party's ranks: city mayors set their sights on provincial governor or party secretary posts, and those who have already become province-level leaders aspire to the higher rungs of central government, even the supreme Politburo. Personnel management is the central government's mechanism for encouraging excellence and enforcing compliance. It decides which local officials are promoted, demoted, appointed to key positions, or thrown in jail on criminal charges.

In China Inc., economic achievement by local government officials translates into political capital. That is to say, those who can deliver economic growth in their region have a greater chance to be promoted in the party hierarchy. The official criteria for promotion include integrity, diligence, and competence, but performance—how well the local official manages the local economy—is essential. Historically, the primary yardstick in this regard has been GDP growth, although, as we'll see later, this is changing. Although imperfect as a measure of people's overall welfare, GDP does gauge how much the economy has expanded over a particular period, and how much employment has been created.

China Inc.'s ambitious annual growth target fosters competition among local governments to accelerate GDP growth in their respective regions, a phenomenon often referred to as GDP worship. Major media outlets play their part by publishing annual rankings of GDP growth rates across regions for everyone to peruse and gossip about. Why did the province of Jiangsu grow at only 10 percent this year versus 11 percent last year? And what's going on in the neighboring province of Anhui, with its 12 percent rate?

The Mayor Economy

The city of Kunshan offers a good example of how a local government single-handedly transformed an unremarkable agricultural town into a booming industrial and high-tech city. In 1978, its residents were saving an average of about US$12 per year. Sandwiched between two powerful neighboring cities, Shanghai and Suzhou, Kunshan had no chance of successfully vying for the attention of US and European multinationals. So its local government decided to reinvent itself as a niche market for wealthy Taiwanese investors. To do so, it initiated a wide range of business-friendly policies, including financial and fiscal support, land leases, one-stop license applications, and lower thresholds for capital. In addition, it adopted a tough no-tolerance policy on corruption. As a result, Taiwanese investors felt both sought after and safe. When several fell sick on one visit and were hospitalized, local leaders came to visit them and personally attended to their well-being and recovery. In the wake of this support and warmth, more than four thousand new companies sprang up in Kunshan.

Success stories like this also highlight the variety of motives that drive local authorities. Some are intrinsic: as we've seen, the importance of achievement is deeply embedded in Confucian culture. Other inspirations are external, including the possibility of greater responsibility at a higher level and popular acclaim. And, as is so often the case, success breeds success. Higher GDP generates more income, which local officials can then allocate as they see fit. These resources come in handy. Local government can spend the funds on building a subway system, the hallmark of a prestigious city. They can improve the environment, which has recently taken on more significance in the metrics of performance evaluation, cleaning up lakes and rivers and tackling air pollution and waste. They can finance social programs, including education, social welfare, and healthcare. A successful local government can also preen its tail feathers to attract new investment by constructing spectacular land-mark buildings, as well as organizing world-class exhibitions and festi-vals. When a town is upgraded to a city, or a county-level city becomes a prefecture-level city, these promotions bring local officials prestige, vis-ibility, and political clout.

This explains why local government officials not only are invested in promoting their own state enterprises but also actively support the pri-vate sector. This was not always the case. Until the 1990s, state-owned enterprises commanded wide swaths of the economy, including con-sumer products, from household appliances to bicycles to beer. Highly lucrative, SOEs drew local attention and resources because part of their profits went directly into local state coffers. But as many local SOEs be-came unprofitable or went bankrupt over time, local officials turned to promoting more innovative and resilient private enterprises, tending the seeds of their development.

Early on in this process, in the 1980s, when private-sector companies began to be politically countenanced but still bore the stigma of capi-talism, officials sometimes dressed them up as collective enterprises, giving them what became known as "red hats" to wear while carrying out their normal business. As the state became more tolerant of private enterprise—and it proved its effectiveness and value—local governments began to actively woo the best firms, engaging in beauty contests that included lavish tax breaks and flexible regulations.

Effectiveness is certainly a key factor in this process. As political sci-entist Francis Fukuyama notes in his book *Political Order and Political Decay*, a meritocratic bureaucracy is essential to the success of a mod-ern state. Luckily for China, this essential ingredient has been baked into its civics since the third century BC, as we've seen. But just as with any other system, patronage also matters. In Western countries, the winning political party lavishes government jobs on its supporters. In China, patrons are particularly important because they are associated with loyalty; senior leaders who promote their own protégés can count on their unfailing political support, particularly in times of crisis.[2] Political connections to senior party leaders are particularly important for senior-level promotions. Although officials with strong political connections would not be promoted if they were woefully incompetent or lacked valuable experience, a local leader who performs well but has no political connections is likely to hit a glass ceiling. Top-performing *and* well-connected provincial leaders have gone on to become the nation's highest-ranked cadres. In fact, all three general secretaries of the Chinese Communist Party since Deng Xiaoping were once provincial leaders: Jiang Zemin was the head of Shanghai, Hu Jintao was provincial head of Guizhou and Tibet, and Xi Jinping was the leader of Zhejiang and Fujian provinces.

As we've seen, a complex system of mechanisms and incentives is instrumental to China's economic growth. But the astute student of economics might ask why this extraordinary effort to engage local government participation was needed in the first place. Wouldn't the markets just do the work by themselves? The state is forced to take unusual measures because free market forces are still not in full swing in China. Some markets are still tightly controlled, the financial system is still adolescent, and inadequacies in the legal system make China's economy incapable of functioning as mature market economies do. It took hundreds of years for Western economies to develop markets that function relatively smoothly on their own, and they still contain many wrinkles that warrant government intervention. As we have seen, China's strong government coupled with weak formal institutions distinguishes it from other economies, and explains why China's hybrid market and mayor economy came into being and works so well under the circumstances.

In most countries, an ineffectual state underlies many major problems. China is not in this situation. When needed, the Chinese state has the capacity to intervene, providing money, logistics, and even the military, as I saw firsthand when China was faced with COVID-19. When it comes to the economy, China also provides a stabilizing political presence—the ability to stay the course when pursuing long-term goals and to resist pressure from short-term exigencies and special interest groups. For better and—sometimes, as we will see—for worse, China's is a political economy.

CHANGE, INNOVATION, AND RISK

One big factor in the success of China's economy is its ability to embrace change, innovation, and risk—qualities we do not typically associate with politically centralized regimes. As is so often the case, this tone was first established at the top. It was none other than Deng Xiaoping who threw his weight behind the local cadres when reform initiatives were being resisted by conservative party leaders clinging to ideology. Change is difficult, and in the late 1970s China's new economic landscape was terra incognita. At a time when nobody really understood how market economies worked, it required a giant leap of faith to grant so much economic power to the local officials. The stakes were high, but from the beginning, local chiefs were encouraged to try out bold ideas.

Importantly, there were few penalties meted out for trying and failing. Because these efforts were local, the fallout from failure was contained, but successful plans were lauded and emulated around the nation, their sponsors showered with recognition and praise. This high-risk, high-reward environment led to the development of an entrepreneurial state within a highly centralized one. Officials were encouraged to bend or even break rules and traditions, to come up with even the most outlandish original ideas, and to make creative or intuitive decisions even when the outcome was uncertain. They were both emboldened and empowered.

127

As it turned out, sharing power at the local level made sense in many ways. It was local officials, after all, who knew local conditions best, had the most extensive local networks, and knew how to collect local information and to make informed decisions on allocating resources. This put them in a far better position than a distant central government to develop their local economy. Indeed, a perennial dilemma for political centralization is that while it is good at establishing long-term goals for the greater good, it is often associated with distant bureaucracies insensitive to local needs. China's local officials enjoyed substantial autonomy to deviate from the norm, and they ran with it.

FLIES IN THE KITCHEN: CORRUPTION

For all its many benefits, a system that confers power and resources on local officials also comes with its downsides. One is that it creates ample opportunity for corruption. When development projects are up for grabs, there are many rent-seeking opportunities along the way: issuing licenses, channeling finances through local state banks, and auctioning land leases all offer local government officials many opportunities for profiteering. For some, the temptation to abuse the power and divert funds into private pockets can prove irresistible. Many of them think, *If I've been so instrumental in growing the economic pie, why shouldn't I have a slice?* Some economists even argue that in developing countries, a certain amount of graft is conducive to growth: it's the oil that greases the wheels when public institutions function poorly.

Throughout history Chinese rulers have struggled with the dilemma of how to provide incentives without letting the corrosive effect of corruption debilitate the system. In the feudal times, the emperor wore a crown that could block out whatever he chose not to see or hear. Literally. It included a small curtain of black gauze along with twelve tassels ornamented with jade beads, with a nugget of jade on each side that could serve as an earplug. Lowering the tassels or inserting the plugs allowed the emperor to see and hear only what he chose. The Chinese crown is symbolic of the ruling style of all Chinese emperors: because paramount importance is placed on keeping the overall situation under control, tasks that might prove impossible get ignored—like purging the kingdom of evil, corruption, political intrigues, or feuds. As the ancient Chinese saying goes, "No fish can survive in water that is too pure."

Today, China's central authority is well aware that corruption gnaws away at a system like termites, doing no apparent damage to the structure until it suddenly collapses. On taking power in 2013, President Xi lost no time in launching the most sweeping anti-graft campaign in the nation's modern history. Some 2.3 million officials at various levels have been punished for violating party rules or state laws. These officials run the gamut from elite "tigers" to common household "flies." In 2017, of the 527,000 officials who were punished, 58 were officials at the provincial or ministerial level or higher, 3,300 were at the bureau level, 21,000 were at the county level, 78,000 were at the town level, 97,000 were ordinary cadres, and the rest were from villages or local enterprises.[3] This highlights the inherent challenges of monitoring and controlling millions of local officials spread around the country. There may be political motivations behind the drive, but the scope, depth, and endurance of the program proves the seriousness of the intention to sever the corrosive links fostered in an era of rapid but disorderly growth.

When Zhao Zhengyong, the former party secretary of Shaanxi Province, left his post as provincial party secretary for a seat on the National People's Congress, a number of his business dealings that had led to huge personal gains were made public. The most notorious was a scheme with private developers to build expensive villas on the northern slope of Qinling Mountain, part of a protected area of enormous natural beauty and spiritual significance, known as the Alps of central China. After repeated warnings from top leaders, Zhao falsely reported that the villas had been demolished and the problem solved. When Zhao's various dealings finally came to light, he and a number of his accomplices were arrested and imprisoned.

As this example illustrates, corruption in China is no longer countenanced with a wink and a nod. The national cleanup has received wide public support and is an important contributor to satisfaction with the government, as evidenced in public surveys. But it also comes with its own set of risks for the economy. Without graft as an incentive, local officials may become less motivated to foster growth. They may become reluctant to commit themselves to major undertakings—including positive reforms—for fear they may draw unwanted attention. When the rules are changing, or being enforced differently, it's natural to err on the side of caution by choosing to do little or nothing. Anti-corruption programs can therefore create unintended inertia on the part of the cadres, leading to a slowdown in economic growth. For a party determined to shore up its image of good governance, the anti-corruption drive won't be aborted for fear of losing economic steam. To address this unintended consequence, the party is now increasingly monitoring the behavior of its cadres and punishing passive resistance to anti-corruption by apathy, inertia, sloth, or total inactivity.

Maintaining Control

In addition to corruption, a long-standing issue throughout Chinese history has been rebellious local chiefs in a vast country populated by diverse cultures and ethnicities. Granting autonomy is a good way to boost morale and get things done, but it also has the natural effect of shifting power away from the center. Consolidating and maintaining that power has always been a challenge for China's top leaders, and it is one of the reasons why Mao kicked off the Cultural Revolution in 1966. One way to keep regions from banding together to oppose mandates from the central government is by creating competition, which serves this valuable second purpose, in addition to providing an incentive to succeed.

To foster a competitive environment, the state has come up with all kinds of ways to quantify and reward achievement. A yardstick competition measures both absolute performance (such as GDP growth) and relative performance among officials. In a tournament-style competition, only relative performance matters. In a qualifying competition, local government officials have to meet basic criteria before even being allowed to join the challenge. In an elimination competition, government officials who don't meet a certain standard are no longer eligible for promotion regardless of their scorecards in other domains. What makes this competitive model work is the central government's tight grip on personnel decisions through its personnel ministry, and the fact that only a few cadres will gain appointment to highly coveted senior positions.

Competition, however, can be a double-edged sword. Intense competition between local government officials has contributed to local protectionism, as we have seen in the example of local automobile companies in chapter 4—despite the central government's sporadically successful efforts to encourage collaboration. Local governments can become so engrossed in creating unique economic identities that they work in silos, with little interest in cooperating with their neighbors even when economic synergies warrant it. Their primary goal becomes protecting their own industries and firms against outside competitors, and can extend to helping local enterprises dodge their responsibilities for quality control and meeting environmental standards. This local protectionism has a big impact on the aggregate economy. A 2019 study by economists Trevor Tombe and Xiaodong Zhu shows that removing *internal* trade barriers can result in much higher gains to productivity than boosting external trade via globalization.[4] These internal barriers not only reduce the nation's ability to take advantage of scale, synergy, and complementary strengths but also produce excessive administrative and jurisdictional constraints.

To prevent local intractability, the central government has another major tool at its disposal. No government official holding an important position is allowed to stay in any one place for too long. Cadre rotation is important because it limits the possibility of local officials building their own independent fiefdoms, where loyalty goes to the local boss rather than to the party's Central Committee. After most party secretaries and governors serve a five-year term, they move on to a new posting. Provincial bosses are brought in from other regions to prevent long-term consolidation of power.

Rotation plays other important roles. When capable, reform-minded local officials from more prosperous coastal provinces are transferred to the hinterlands, this fresh blood serves to strengthen local leadership and beef up local economies. Fresh transfusions of talent help lower-income regions broaden their horizons while promoting regional cooperation. And exposing officials to a variety of challenging situations that sharpen their leadership skills is also useful for grooming future leaders.

THE MIXED BLESSINGS OF GDP

As the jocular saying goes, "GDP figures produce the officials, and officials produce the GDP figures." Given China's all-important system of incentives and competitions, it is not surprising that local officials could be tempted to fudge their GDP numbers. Researchers have found that since 2004, the sum of China's provincial GDP—which should equal the national GDP—is consistently 5 percent higher, indicating that the provincial numbers are being inflated.[5] But massaging GDP figures is a minor problem compared with the creation of *empty* GDP—that is, GDP with no intrinsic value. When a colleague of mine joined an official trip visiting a county in northeast China, the local mayor led the visitors to an imposing bridge and pointed out that it had been built under his direction, going on and on about the grand scale and cost of this project. Finally, one of the guests could not help observing aloud that the bridge spanned a stretch of dry, flat land. "What is the bridge for, exactly?" the guest asked. The mayor chuckled and said, "Do not worry. The central government has agreed to dig a river underneath it."

Building bridges boosts GDP. So does digging rivers, for that matter. And bizarre behavior driven by GDP worship has been all too common in China. While visiting a resort city nestled in the scenic mountains of southern China, I noticed that we were driving on a wide road that was noticeably out of place. I asked the taxi driver, "Why do you need a street as wide as Beijing's Changan Avenue here at the foot of this mountain?" To which he replied, "We have a new mayor."

GDP worship has often led to excessive urban reconfiguration, sometimes at great cost to cultural and historical sites. Everything is seen through the lens of magnifying GDP—every square inch of redesignated land, every tree cut down or moved, every demolished historical site. The former mayor of the city of Nanjing, the capital of Jiangsu Province, lived up to the literal meaning of his name, Jianye (which in Chinese means "building or undertaking great enterprise"). He earned his sobriquet "Mayor Bulldozer" by launching into a massive wrecking and rebuilding spree that literally left no stone unturned. Enough of that money spent on generating empty GDP went directly into Jianye's pockets that he is currently serving prison time.

Feverish pursuit of GDP growth gave rise to too much of everything in China, an overkill of industrial parks and science parks, exhibition centers, steel factories, and coal mines. State-led, rather than market-led, allocation of resources led to excess capacity and also to a race to the bottom in prices: cheap steel, iron, and solar panels flooded the global markets and upset trading partners. Speed was the priority as the nation sought to sprint through a marathon. Everyone thought fast, acted fast, tried to make money fast, and moved on fast when they ran into obstacles. There was little time to take stock and learn lessons in order to adapt to a rapidly changing environment. The economy was running faster than the ecosystem's ability to renew itself, and faster than society could keep up.

China's New Playbook: Beyond GDP

Achieving high growth can be impressive, but the key question is, at what cost? China's excessive push for growth left hazardous environmental consequences in its wake: polluted rivers and lakes, cities blanketed in smog, topsoil turned toxic, and mountains denuded of vegetation, triggering landslides as the ecosystem lost its balance. Being the world's factory is an enviable position, but it has come with a high price tag. As advanced economies transferred polluting industries to low-income countries in order to reduce their own emissions, they have effectively passed on the environmental cost to others. China gladly took over a lot of such activities early on in order to industrialize, but it resulted in a much-ruined landscape across the country, beset with solid wastes and polluted water and overhung with a canopy of perpetual smog. For a long time local governments had little incentive to control and reverse environmental degradation at the expense of GDP growth, although today this is changing. Huge costs are being incurred to clean up lakes and rivers and to free cities from their Dickensian shrouds.

China has woken up to the urgent need to shift to a new developmental paradigm—from maximizing output to improving quality, from meeting hard growth targets to pursuing soft infrastructure, most notably education, healthcare, and other public services. This pivot reflects the new requirements of a nation with a rising middle class. A society attaining "modest prosperity," in China's terminology, requires more than a decent life, represented by a range of variables beyond material satisfaction. Hence, the state needs a new playbook. The Twentieth Party Congress, held in late 2022, made it clear that economic growth, which used to be a central fixture of the party's agenda, is no longer the only priority. It's a matter of quality over quantity, as well as security and common prosperity.

The wish list of citizens in a post-basic-needs society is a long one, and not always easy to satisfy. They enjoy driving to work, but cry out against smog; they appreciate the convenience of electric appliances, but prod the authorities to do more to stave off climate change; they buy higher-quality products that require more mining and resource extraction, but environmental protection is a priority. And the new generation is wondering, What is the point of having all this money if I can't make sure that what my children are eating and drinking is safe, plentiful, and of high quality?[6] The environmental Kuznets curve shows that pollution follows an inverted U shape: as income rises, pollution first increases and then falls.[7] Although there are various explanations for this, people's shifting preferences are prominent among them. In the beginning people are willing to trade environmental quality for a rapid rise in income, but after their income reaches a certain level, they prefer cleaner ways to grow, even though they are costlier. As a society becomes more prosperous, it also becomes more demanding about health and the environment.

Rising housing prices, horrendous traffic, and environmental degradation are all consequences of the rush to raise GDP, fueled by local governments that also pushed up land prices and encouraged consumerism. The emphasis was on speed and quantity. Today that emphasis is shifting away from creating as much GDP as possible and toward improving the quality of everyday life. A decade ago, foreigners visiting China were struck by "the spitting habit." People loudly hawked and spat, or blew their noses right onto the street, wherever they might be.

Littering seemed to be the national sport. Streets, rivers, lakes, and other public places were used as wastebaskets. Empty bottles, cans, and other trash were jettisoned by cars flashing by. Today, the streets of Beijing and Shanghai are spick-and-span, and residents have significantly changed their behavior. The government recently issued an elaborate trash-sorting ordinance, and the fact that there was more compliance than complaint speaks to the convergence of people's growing expectations and social norms.

Although the growing middle class in China has not formally been granted greater political participation, it is becoming an important political force. According to political theory, the rise of a middle class creates pressure on the political system, as increasing prosperity encourages people to feel they have a greater stake in that process. If political institutions fail to evolve along with socioeconomic progress, it can lead to social discontent. Some pundits believe that the Arab Spring may be a harbinger of things to come in China. But what makes China different is that the ruling party is acutely aware of the hazards of social discontent, and its political institutions evolve to keep up with the changing needs of the Chinese people. In the party's own words, "moving forward with the times" (*yu shi ju jin*) is critical. To that effect, it has strengthened people's power and held governments at all levels accountable. The National People's Congress, whose deputies are elected by local constituencies, is no longer expected to automatically ratify bills endorsed by the Standing Committee of the party's Politburo. The newly revised Administrative Procedure Law of 2015 expands the people's rights to sue the government, and cases have been won. Power is not taken for granted: if the legitimacy is not based on the ballot box, it critically depends on the party's ability to ensure an ever-improving living standard of the Chinese people, whose aspirations are still a political guarantee for their economic stability.

In Western societies, accountability is based on the rule of law, enforced by an independent judiciary and a free press. Although these systems are still underdeveloped in China, a combination of formal institutions and informal channels have come to fill in the gap. Because China does not practice Western-style, one-person-one-vote democracy, its best strategy going forward is to maintain popular support through accountability and responsiveness. Local officials are sacked summarily should they fail to respond to natural disasters or to outbreaks of epidemics, or if there are local coal mine blasts or serious accidents due to dereliction of duty.

Government responsiveness is not unique to democracies. Nor is a democracy always responsive. The US can be sluggish in meeting its people's needs, as it was in the aftermath of Hurricane Katrina and the outbreak of COVID-19. By contrast, Singapore, which is an authoritarian regime, is free of corruption and highly accountable to its citizens. In China, within three weeks of the first appearance of COVID-19 in Wuhan, the Chinese government built sixteen massive mobile hospitals in the city and dispatched forty thousand medical staff there. In addition, the Ministry of Finance allocated funds so that all medical expenses associated with COVID became free for everyone in the country. That said, sometimes *over*-mobilizing can be a problem; in many parts of China the direct costs of the COVID response were enormous.

An Attentive Power

The legitimacy of the Communist Party in China has always been an interesting question. As we have seen, numerous international surveys have shown a high level of satisfaction toward the government. It is, of course, due to the material prosperity and security delivered to a large swath of its citizens. But on a regular basis, satisfaction comes from the fact that the government remains an attentive and responsive power.

The system's accountability mechanisms can sometimes hold their own with those of democratic countries, particularly when it comes to confronting societal problems. For instance, the number of Chinese departments with investigatory powers has been rising in recent years, as they look into fire prevention, safety measures in the workplace, food safety, pharmaceutical standards, IP protection, pollution control, and anticorruption measures. A quarter million cadres are regularly dispatched to investigate private and public institutions at all levels. Between 2016 and 2017, environmental protection inspections resulted in more than seventeen thousand officials being disciplined, prosecuted, and convicted.[8] National and provincial tournament events for environmental protection have been held to award prizes to winners for their vigilance and tenacity. As a result, the air in Beijing has been cleaned up enough so that its citizens are now enjoying far more "blue-sky days." Largely in response to public sentiment, the government has taken tough actions like breaking up big oil companies such as PetroChina and Sinopec and shutting down factories in Hebei, the neighboring province to Beijing.

In addition to dispatching inspection teams, the government has instituted widespread use of complaint mailboxes, physical or virtual, encouraging whistleblowers to report all kinds of wrongdoing. Results indicate that this system is working, and that contrary to popular belief, a one-party state like China can successfully create and enforce a potent set of curbs and checks on public officials. Online public platforms where local citizens can post complaints and demands are closely monitored by the central government. Because local officials often prefer to be bearers of glad tidings rather than messengers of bad news, all too often covering up scandals or misrepresenting data, the central government has made citizen engagement a crucial source of information. Today more than three quarters of the three thousand counties all over the country have these public online platforms.

Social media can play a similar role. Despite tight government control of the internet, social media still offers a medley of diverse views on contemporary life in China and fosters a thriving civic debate on a wide range of issues. People of all generations spend hours online each day. With more than 1.2 billion monthly active users on the social media platform WeChat and half a billion microbloggers on Weibo (owned by Sina), the Chinese people are connected in real time. A study published in *The Journal of Economic Perspectives* looked at 13.2 billion blog posts on Weibo between 2009 and 2013. To their great surprise, American researchers found that many sensitive issues were openly discussed. Even the most contentious subjects—including ethnic conflict, scandals involving local government officials, anecdotes about top leadership, political protests, and most recently, US–China relations—were widely broached.[9] For example, there were millions of posts on collective action events, such as protests and riots, which are highly sensitive subjects. Posts can even predict actual organized protests in the following days.

Although the Chinese state keeps close tabs on the internet, the common assumption that social media is completely censored is incorrect. For one thing, it's not easy to block posts and trolls, which are widely forwarded instantaneously. Despite government surveillance, millions of bloggers post in the middle of the night, and before the government can filter out the innumerable threads of the topic a national commotion may already be under way. Even if some are completely deleted, the footprint left on the memories of netizens cannot be erased (however, this may change as artificial intelligence and machine learning are increasingly deployed). More important, top leaders are aware of the value of letting people express their opinions. Tuning in to this information also allows the government to respond swiftly to negative public opinion before it gives rise to social unrest. So long as postings do not touch the third rail—subversive views of the party itself or attacks on very senior party officials—a wide range of politically and socially sensitive issues are tolerated.

It is also useful to have social media whistleblowers helping the government monitor the party's cadres. According to the same *Journal of Economic Perspectives* study, 11 million of the 13.2 billion blog posts were government related, and of that 11 million, more than half involved corruption cases. Amateur civilian paparazzi of the Chinese variant are interested not only in chasing celebrities; they use their telephoto lenses to catch corrupt officials. When a senior official from Beijing paid a visit to a local official, a hawkeyed photographer noticed a band of lighter skin around the local official's wrist. A little digging into local archives uncovered images of that same official's wrist gleaming with a variety of luxury watches; posting the images online led to an official investigation and charges of corruption. Amateur and freelance investigators snap and post photos of officials sneaking out of a luxury mansion at night, or in other inappropriate situations.

Social media campaigns can also lead to change. In one high-profile case, a blogger shared a video about a woman who was abducted and forced into marriage, causing a national outrage that blamed government negligence for the episode and others like it. This quickly prompted the central government to launch a nationwide special campaign in 2022 to crack down on the trafficking of women and children. Another widely discussed campaign started when a student died from a heart attack after being defrauded of her tuition. It led the government not only to crack down on fraud but also paved the way for the enactment of one of the strictest data-privacy laws in the world. Although dissent on many sensitive issues is silenced on social media, the platform embodies a complex interaction between government and people, one that constrains the ability of the government to act without oversight and plays a broad role in the dissemination of information and propaganda, surveillance, and the aggregation of public opinion.

This emphasis on quality and safety is part of a new set of governing principles from the state's playbook. It marks a significant shift from an era when GDP creation was the holy grail and much was countenanced in its pursuit, including outright corruption. For a long time the state's attitude toward officials at both high levels and low was one eye open, one eye closed, so long as targets were met. But today the approach is both eyes wide open with a third eye in the back of one's head, as a broader set of social indicators—one that is inherently much harder to measure than GDP growth—has come to dominate the all-important process of performance evaluation.

In addition to addressing pollution and corruption, the state's new agenda includes one of the most glaring problems of the day: income disparity, which invariably comes along with rapid growth. Markets do not resolve this on their own; instead, they can exacerbate it. Rising inequality has become a critically important issue around the world, leading to polarized societies, rising populism, and widespread discontent with government.

Once again, the onus falls on local governments to tackle it; they have been given targets for the number of people who need to be lifted out of poverty each year in their jurisdictions, and their success or failure will be based on these metrics. President Xi put on the table a list of specific measures to bring prosperity to the most vulnerable. These include relocating people from rural areas prone to natural disasters or hardship to cities and towns; providing incentives and resources for people to start small businesses; improving rural infrastructure, and providing public goods in these areas, such as healthcare and public services; and education and vocational training for the young. Qualifying households are even provided contact information for those officials responsible for poverty elimination in their region. As a result of this program, the number of very poor rural residents declined from nearly 100 million in late 2012 to 16.6 million by the end of 2018. By the end of 2020, the target of eliminating extreme poverty altogether was achieved when the last cohort of 40 million people in rural areas were lifted out of abject destitution. The next milestone for the government, as we will discuss further in chapter 10, is to attain to the ambitious goal of common prosperity promised by Deng Xiaoping at the very outset of reform and opening up.

To opt for slower but higher-quality and more sustainable growth is the right approach. In fact, it is the only feasible strategy for an economy that has exhausted itself of low-hanging fruit and quick wins. But incentive mechanisms for local governments are put to the test. In the past, their performance was easily measurable under a single set of quantifiable targets related to GDP growth. But a multifaceted, broader objective that spans employment, environment, pandemic controls, to growth itself can sometimes lead to confusion and mismanagement of the local economy. Local officials can veer too much in one direction to avoid punishment at all costs rather than balance a wide range of objectives that ensure an improvement in the overall well-being of for their citizens.

China's unique system of government intertwined with the economy and power sharing at the local level creates both outsize opportunities and notable obstacles. And despite the limits China imposes on free market forces, and the absence of a free press, independent judicial system, and the individual right to vote, we see that there are other mechanisms in place to respond to the needs of its citizens and to address the threats posed by income inequality.

Different systems lead to different trade-offs. As economist Pranab Bardhan points out, centralized regimes can be good when it comes to making a long-term commitment but less effective when it comes to accountability or flexibility. Political pluralism has its benefits in terms of representing diverse populations, but it is often achieved at the cost of weak collective action. Democratic deliberations contribute to social legitimacy, but competition between political parties in a democracy can also lead to a race to the bottom. Rather than serving broad-based inter-ests as originally intended, democracies can be distorted through the power of money and the process of lobbying. People of different persua-sions prize certain values over others. Some may emphasize freedom, where others are more interested in prosperity, stability, or security.

Borrowing from a distinction made by Markus K. Brunnermeier in his analysis of post-COVID societies,[10] China's political economy system is robust, but is it resilient? Resilient societies are supple: they can absorb shocks and get back on their feet quickly. Robust societies are sturdy: with their many layers of buffers they are resistant to shock waves. But a robust system can be knocked off course by an extreme event, taking a long time to recover or potentially never fully recovering at all. As we have seen throughout this chapter, China's structure, with its centralized powers, financial muscle, and administrative capacity for policy imple-mentation, has made it robust. It also possesses qualities of resilience; it is an agile state quick to trigger the decision-making process with a readiness to change tack in real time. But overall, robustness still outbal-ances resilience in China: its growth model is reliable but not flexible. To keep it going, credit needs to be pumped constantly into the economy, and property prices and stock prices need to be propped up. To maintain stability, huge costs must be incurred—whether it is to save the economy from plunging into deep financial crisis or to maintain a strict zero-COVID policy.

Resisting downward pressure on the economy at all costs or main-taining stability at all times does not help build resilience. Like a body living in a sterile environment, it eventually loses all immunity. To be able to withstand turbulence one has to experience it and draw lessons from it. Brunnermeier's metaphor of a reed that "bends often but does not break" is apropos: an economy, or a system, is most sustainable when it can be more like a reed than an oak. That would be a worthy goal for China's new playbook.

SIX

THE FINANCIAL SYSTEM

T he financial system is the heart of any economy. Similar to pumping blood and oxygen to the body in a living organism, the financial system supplies money to the marketplace where goods and services are produced, bought, and sold—sometimes referred to as the real economy. As we saw in chapter 3, consumers earn money by working; they spend much of what they earn and save the rest. Unless those savings are hidden under the mattress, they flow into a financial system where banks, insurance companies, and stock exchanges facilitate the movement of those monies to wherever they're needed. This is where firms go for funds when they want to build capacity, constructing bigger facilities or hiring more workers to produce more goods or services. The state is an actor here too, regulating financial institutions to curb risk and predatory practices; the state also raises funds itself, by issuing government bonds, for instance.

When storms hit the financial system in the form of a stock market crash or a big company going under, the system rocks a bit, but so long as that rough weather stays contained within the system, it's manageable; when a storm breaches the levees of the financial system, however, it wreaks havoc on the larger real economy. Throughout history, such systemic financial crises have posed a profound threat to developing and advanced economies alike, including the debt crisis that disrupted Latin American economies in both the 1980s and 1990s, the Nordic and Japanese banking crises in the 1990s, the Asian financial meltdown in 1997, and of course, the US financial crisis of 2007–2009. This last example led to GDP contraction and job losses whose effects lingered for well over a decade and spilled over into other countries to an unprecedented degree.

One would expect the Chinese economy to have suffered a similar seismic event during its long market transition after 1978, but in fact the number of systemic financial crises in China is exactly zero. As we will see, there have been frequent steep plunges in the stock market, and nonperforming loans in some major state banks reached 20 percent in some years, but none of these events has led to a financial meltdown causing a serious contraction of the wider economy. At least not yet.

This oddity is just one of a number of financial puzzles in China. Another is the fact that despite the nation's preternatural economic growth, its stock market has been one of the worst performing in the world. As one study shows, between 2000 and 2018, China's economy quadrupled in size, yet a Chinese citizen who invested $1.00 in a diversified portfolio of domestic Chinese stocks in 2000 still would have had just that $1.00 eighteen years later, after adjusting for inflation. By contrast, in the US that same investment would have been worth $2.00, and $3.00 in Brazil or India. Incidentally, investing in Chinese stocks listed in international exchanges would have returned $3.50.[1] A Chinese citizen with access only to the domestic financial system would have fared better by stashing the cash in a savings account, upending the conventional wisdom that stocks generate the best returns over the long term.

China's stock market is no anomaly; it's just one reflection of the country's inefficient, topsy-turvy financial system. Another is the housing market, where residents of Beijing and Shanghai scramble to pay prices at Boston and San Francisco levels, even though their annual per capita income is less than a fifth of that of American households in those cities.[2] Shadow banking—unregulated or under-regulated banking activity—can be a risky affair, as we know from the US financial crisis in 2008. China's opaque shadow banking system expanded at a phenomenal rate until 2017, when the government finally applied the brakes. Yet, despite all this, China has still managed to avoid a massive financial implosion.

So why should you and I care about the many strange quirks in the Chinese financial system? Considering how intertwined all our fortunes have become in the increasingly global network of commerce and finance, we have little choice but to care. Just because financial shocks can be contained within China doesn't mean they won't cause shock waves elsewhere. In 2015, a stock market plunge in China wiped out US$2 trillion of global stock market value.[3] That same year a sharp depreciation of China's currency set off another global rout that eliminated US$5 trillion of global equity value.[4] In the second half of 2021, the regulatory body struck a heavy blow to the technology and education companies, wiping out more than US$1 trillion of value among these public companies, many of which are listed on the American stock exchanges and owned by a wide range of global investors. That amounts to a significant wealth loss for investors.

And the effect of these economic tremors can be surprisingly widespread. In 2021 the failure of a large property developer in China, Evergrande Group, to meet its loan obligations sent copper prices plunging and dragged down other property developers, who had to default on their obligations owed to foreign investors. For many of the financial institutions that own Chinese assets, a series of major domestic defaults linked to these assets can put them at substantial risk, and through a domino effect, spread to many other players in the system.

On the positive side, we might want to understand China's chaotic and clamorous financial system because its inadequacies open the door to opportunity. American and European insurance companies, investment banks, and asset management companies can readily offer Chinese consumers a vast array of financial products and services. And China's private fintech industry is wildly successful precisely because it fills many of the gaping holes in China's jealously guarded formal financial system.

Whether your interest is based on understanding the financial risks you may face, capitalizing on alluring opportunity, or simple intellectual curiosity, the baffling dichotomy between China's erratic financial system and its economy's rosy exceptionalism is well worth a closer look.

Understanding the Basics

Whether measured by breadth or depth, China's financial system is underdeveloped. For one thing, it's overly dependent on banks. Bank credit is the main source of financing in China and stood at around 165 percent of GDP in 2019; in the US, by comparison, bank credit accounts for only 52 percent of GDP.[5] In advanced economies, capital markets such as stock and bond markets play a much more important role in financing growth and innovation, allowing start-ups and mature companies to draw from large pools of capital by issuing stocks or bonds. In the US, the stock market size (measured by the value of outstanding shares) was around 150 percent of GDP in 2019, and its bond market size was around 205 percent of GDP. In China the stock market is a mere 60 percent of GDP; its bond market size grew from 35 percent in 2008 to about 113 percent by the end of 2020, but it lags in size, depth, and maturity compared with the US bond market.[6] An important measure of credit, sometimes referred to as "total social financing," gauges the aggregate amount of funds provided by the financial system to the real economy. By the end of 2021, more than 60 percent of total credit was accounted for by bank loans, while the stock market and corporate bond market contributed to a meager 3 percent and 10 percent of total credit, respectively.[7]

Heavy reliance on banks is a common feature of financial systems in developing countries. One can readily imagine why it is a sign of primitivism: bank loans cannot adequately provide smaller, riskier companies with stable and reliable financing, or transparently provide information to market participants on the state of the economy or on important prices such as interest rates. Neither can banks satisfy Chinese households with a diversified enough pool of income or offer them a sufficient stake in the country's growth. The equity-based American financial system, in contrast to the debt-based Chinese financial system, allows for broader sharing of risk and financial upside across all participants. But few developing countries have deep and well-functioning capital markets.

China's domestic financial landscape has a notable shortage of such typical financial players as investment funds, insurance companies, ratings agencies, and international investment banks. Assets managed by investment funds, for instance, make up only 12 percent of GDP in China, compared to more than 100 percent in the US.[8] Also missing is an active derivatives market, trading in futures contracts, or options. This significant room for development offers a host of opportunities to foreign players as the country opens up to the rest of the world and liberalizes its financial services. In the past, foreign investors have accounted for less than 5 percent of the investment in the domestic stock market. That number could potentially mushroom to 20 percent, which is good news for China's financial system, but will result in even more global exposure to China's economic fluctuations.

None of these numbers reflects a powerful variable unique to China's economy: active government involvement in the system. The government not only controls the financial and policy levers that determine interest rates and affect stock and property prices, but also wields power over where central bank money goes—to what sectors and to which firms within those sectors. Unfortunately, the policies dictated by the central government are often mercurial. Not long ago, for instance, shortly after having encouraged homeowners to sell in order to avoid a sharp upturn in housing prices, the government prohibited Chinese households from selling homes in order to avoid a big *drop* in housing prices. Not long thereafter, the government started to clamp down on housing investment, which caused nationwide panic in 2022. Chinese citizens justifiably complained about not being able to sell on the way up or buy on the way down. In addition, the financial market often reacts so sharply to these sudden changes in government policy that authorities are left unsure about whether to continue, slow down, or even roll back these policies.

Government intervention affects every segment of China's financial system. This urge to control stems from a strong sense of paternalism that has deep cultural and historical roots. As we will see in greater detail, it looms large in making sense of China's various financial puzzles—from roller-coaster stock exchanges and frothy property markets to the unbridled manipulations of shadow banking. But consumers and private companies were also driven to misbehave: private households speculated, firms exploited legal loopholes, and local governments behaved like venture capitalists. The last decade saw an explosion of financial activities outside the formal banking system, from shadow banking to peer-to-peer lending platforms. It was in part a way to circumvent formal rules and regulations, in part financial innovation, and in part a solution to existing deficiencies. As we will see, all of this contributes to a turbulent yet exciting financial system.

The Financial System as a Tool

A good financial system galvanizes the larger economy by connecting household savings with businesses in need of financing, pooling and diversifying risk, providing a market for price and value discovery, and becoming a springboard for technological progress and innovation. America's financial system, despite its problems and occasional failings, has largely served these ends. I believe it's fair to say that the US economy continues to thrive thanks to a well-functioning financial system, whereas in China the economy has boomed *despite* the nation's financial system.

Historically, the Chinese financial system was an instrument of the state, pure and simple. The stock market was opened to help ailing SOEs, as was the bond market. The government put a cap on deposit rates so that firms could borrow cheaply and mass industrialization could materialize quickly, but at the expense of households that earned negligible or even negative real returns on their savings, thanks to decades of low deposit rates and a dearth of investment options. State-owned banks lavished preferential loans on state-owned enterprises, and state-directed lending in infrastructure, technology, and industry worked to advance government-planned objectives. Directing the financial system to serve state purposes may achieve wonders when it comes to meeting strategic goals and managing emergencies, but it also spawns a series of stubborn problems.

A bit of history reveals how all this began. Until the late 1970s the nation's financial system was nonexistent in the modern sense. Beyond the Bank of China, which focused on foreign exchange and overseas business, there was strictly speaking only one bank, the People's Bank of China (PBC), which served a dual function as both central bank and commercial bank. It controlled 93 percent of the country's financial assets and handled most of its financial transactions. Only in 1978 did China give birth to a banking system by creating commercial banks from spin-offs of the PBC, the four largest being the Industrial and Commercial Bank of China, Agricultural Bank of China, the Bank of China, and China Construction Bank. As their names suggest, they were each given a specific sector to service. Today, along with the Bank of Communications, they are known collectively as the Big Five and control about 40 percent of China's total banking deposits.

Apart from providing loans to build the nation, these banks were assigned another task from the very outset: to support ailing state-owned enterprises that the government was reluctant to liquidate. As we've seen, SOEs enjoy soft budget constraints, and their finances are cushioned by government support. But this indulgence breeds risk. Protected by explicit and implicit government guarantees, banks have had few qualms about extending loans in excessive amounts, either to make an anticipated windfall or because they were under government pressure to lend. In the 1990s and early 2000s, the result was massive capital losses, and as a growing number of state enterprises got into trouble, nonperforming bank loans reached a stratospheric high of 20 percent in the early 2000s, rendering the banks that had made those loans technically bankrupt. (Even during the height of the US financial crisis in 2009, this share of bad loans was no more than 5 percent.) A crisis was averted only when the government swiftly recapitalized the banks, improved their balance sheets, and listed them on domestic or international stock markets. This last action reflected a significant government pivot toward stock and bond markets that it had previously held at arm's length.

When the stock market reopened in 1990, most of the companies listed on the two exchanges in Shanghai and Shenzhen were state-owned enterprises. Originally, the purpose of Deng Xiaoping's experiment was not to help private firms raise funds, or to offer investors risk-management opportunities, or to create price discovery; its aim was to raise money for ailing SOEs and to subject them to market discipline. Share prices, after all, reflected managerial capabilities and firm performance. The same held true for the bond markets, which were set up for bonds to be issued primarily by the local governments and SOEs.[9] In 2000, 70 percent of listed companies were still SOEs, although as private firms became more active, that number fell to 30 percent by 2018.[10]

Best-Performing Economy, Worst-Performing Stock Market

Although China's economy has enjoyed miraculous growth over the past few decades, easily eclipsing the likes of Brazil, India, Japan, and the US, its equity performance during China's fastest growth spurt (2000–2014) has lagged them all by a country mile, even Japan's sluggish Nikkei. In a typical economy, the stock market does well when the economy does well; in other words, the correlation between stock market returns and economic growth is high. When you take the average five-year stock market return of most major economies and connect it with GDP growth rates, you get the expected result: a high and positive correlation of about 50 percent for Germany and the UK, 30 percent for the US, and even above 40 percent for emerging economies like Brazil and Thailand. In China, however, that number is zero—that is, there is *no* correlation between GDP growth rates and stock market returns.[11] This puts China in the same bucket as Iran. This disconnect between economic growth and the stock market returns means that individuals and households cannot consistently enjoy the fruits of the economy's fast growth through its capital markets, and that a given company's stock performance is not always linked to its fundamental value.

Fortunately, we now have some data to help explain China's underperforming stock market. This includes financial and accounting information from close to four thousand companies on the A share market, which is where the majority of mainland Chinese companies are listed—and where most shares are bought and sold by domestic investors. China's two exchanges are the Shanghai Stock Exchange and the Shenzhen Stock Exchange. The B shares market is made up of shares issued by Chinese companies listed in these two exchanges that are sold and held by offshore foreign investors (it accounts for less than 1 percent of the A share market cap). There are also another one thousand or so Chinese companies listed in overseas markets such as the Hong Kong Stock Exchange or the New York Stock Exchange, but the investor base in these international stock exchanges is global rather than domestic.

One telling piece of evidence is that listed and unlisted Chinese companies that are otherwise similar have very different performance levels. In the data, we see that return on assets, return on equity, and net income growth of the listed companies are all inferior by a significant margin compared to their unlisted counterparts. They also lag behind Chinese companies listed overseas. Interestingly, when we omit domestically listed firms, returns for the remaining companies *do* become more highly correlated with economic growth—about 40 percent. It is the domestic Chinese companies that skew the numbers, which leads to the following question: Why does being listed on China's domestic stock exchanges equate with unusually poor performance?

It turns out that there are two factors. The first is the selection process for being listed itself. The other relates to what happens to companies once they become listed. Let's begin by exploring the first factor, the process for getting listed, which differs in China from typical market economies. Rather than being registration based, where firms disclose their financials and then register for an initial public offering (IPO), in China the process is approval based. Any company wishing to be listed on the A share market (with the exception of the Star Market—the Chinese-style Nasdaq launched in 2019) needs to receive the blessing of the state regulatory authority, the China Securities Regulatory Commission (CSRC), which is the equivalent of the SEC in the US. This process is lengthy and arduous, and its outcome far from certain. To qualify for approval a company must meet stringent criteria, including showing a profit in each of the three years leading up to the IPO, and it must meet significant thresholds for both net income and assets. Only when those criteria are met does the CSRC evaluate the company and approve or reject its application. Companies often wait for years to find out whether they have been approved. Even if they are already successful, they may still have no clue as to when the IPO can take place.

This listing process creates lots of room for interference by manipulating the rules and seeking special privileges. Companies that enjoy cozy relations with the government can move the process into the fast lane. Unfortunately, this also means that exciting, innovative firms can be shunted aside in favor of companies with stronger political connections. As a result, the Chinese stock market has missed out on listing many dynamic companies on its exchanges. Put off by the slow, uncertain process, firms like Alibaba, Tencent, JD.com, Baidu, Youku, and Pinduoduo have all chosen to list abroad instead. Also, many successful high-tech companies don't show any profits for years—think of Uber and Amazon, which would never have met the Chinese profitability requirement. JD.com, China's second-largest online retailer after Alibaba, would not have made the cut for domestic listing because two years before its IPO in 2014, it registered a small loss. So it chose to list on the Nasdaq instead, where its market capitalization (the market value of its publicly traded outstanding shares) shot up to US$115 billion. The hugely successful social media app Weibo, which posted losses of US$38 million in 2013, is another case in point, as are such famous internet companies as Sina, Sohu, NetEase, and Youku (the Chinese version of YouTube), all of which have chosen to list abroad.

Some observers characterize the difference between the US and

Chinese equity markets this way: the Chinese market looks to the past, whereas its US counterpart looks to the future. In China, you have to be profitable in order to step into the arena; in America, investors judge you by your potential. The Chinese A share market embodies much of the old growth model—it's heavy on the industrial sector and light on services. Even as its economy has surged ahead by embracing technology and innovation, China's domestic stock market has remained firmly rooted in the past. Central SOEs (state-owned companies controlled by the central authority) are at the very bottom of China's stock market, performing even worse than the SOEs controlled by local governments.

For the reasons elaborated, between 2000 and 2018 the number of Chinese companies that chose to be listed overseas increased fourfold; in the middle of 2021, American stock markets host US$2.1 trillion worth of Chinese companies.[12] If the best and fastest-growing firms are not being listed domestically, it is little wonder that China's domestic stock markets consistently underperform. This trend, however, could easily change due to growing geopolitical tensions. Recently there has been a push by the US to delist Chinese companies in sensitive sectors from American exchanges. The Chinese government is also making it more difficult for companies with sensitive data to list on foreign stock exchanges, and it could always pass new regulations limiting their ability to be listed abroad altogether.

The selection problem extends beyond which companies are allowed to enter the stock market: it also includes those that leave it. Ordinarily, poor performance leads to being delisted from national stock exchanges. In the period between 2000 and 2018, 33 percent of companies in the US were delisted every year. In Brazil, this number was 13 percent. In China, however, the number delisted every year during that same period was around five stocks—less than 2.7 percent.[13] Many Chinese companies that would have been cut from other stock exchanges continue to linger on life support, dragging down overall domestic performance.

The listing process in China also incentivizes firms to make poor decisions during the period leading up to an IPO. In order to meet listing criteria, many pursue short-term profits as window dressing, but once they go public and these underlying weaknesses are exposed, the stock price takes a nosedive. All companies tend to cherry-pick the best time of year to go public, but domestically listed Chinese company returns drop far more than those in the US, India, Brazil, or Japan. In China, the return on assets roughly halves in the year after an IPO, whereas in the US it falls by less than 10 percent.

Another contributor to the underwhelming performance of China's domestic stocks is poor decision making after they go public. Chinese public companies top the global list when it comes to the amount they invest, but they also have the worst investment efficiency of any major economy. Often this relates to the Chinese zest for bending rules. Firms lend money to other firms closely related to the controlling shareholder (a move known as "tunneling"). They go on spending sprees, buying up companies unrelated to their core business. After going public, a Chinese motorbike company that was once a household name went on to buy pharma companies, while an equally well-known pharma company started acquiring golf clubs, hotels, and car companies; they both tanked. After becoming one of the largest companies in the world,[14] Evergrande, the real estate empire that became a debt bomb threatening China's financial stability in late 2021, expanded into areas in which it had no expertise, including electric cars, soccer clubs, bottled water, and pig farming.

A senior official once told me about investigating a company that sold softshell turtles, a popular Chinese delicacy believed to boost vigor and vitality. Management had decided to manipulate the stock price by conjuring up some bad news for the company, allowing them to buy shares as the price went down and enjoy a windfall when the stock price recovered. When local newspapers broke the story that the Yangtze River had flooded the company's softshell turtle farms, allowing huge numbers to escape, the company's stock price plummeted. Not long afterward, however, the company reported record numbers of turtles, to the consternation of investors who sold on the bad news. They insisted on a meeting with the chairman of the company, who came up with a remarkable explanation. When fish escape a hatchery, he said, they swim away and don't come back, but turtles are different; they have a strong instinct to return to their birthplace. And in this case, they miraculously brought a horde of new turtles with them!

Turtles and their habits aside, the Chinese stock market is a wild roller-coaster ride. The second-largest stock market in the world is the most volatile of all the major economies. So as a Chinese investor, not only do you earn much worse returns compared with an investor in the US, it is also much risker—the average volatility of these returns was twice that in the US market from 2000 to 2017. Chinese markets frequently run up to giddy heights followed by gut-lurching plunges. In 2008, China's stock market shrank a horrifying 70 percent only a few months after the Shanghai Stock Exchange (SSE) composite index reached a record high! In 2015, A shares on the SSE lost one third of their value within a single month, after climbing 150 percent in the months prior.

Clearly, China's stock market is no place for the faint of heart. This is especially true because in China, unlike the US, the stock market is dominated by retail investors, many of whom are noise traders, gamblers who rely on rumors and gossip to play the market rather than invest long term. In China, retail investors account for about 80 percent of the trading volume in the A share market, whereas on the New York Stock Exchange, it is institutional investors that account for 85 percent.[15]

The state's penchant for stepping into the domestic stock markets adds yet another element of uncertainty to an already capricious investment climate. Paternalism prompts the government to interfere on the basis of protecting retail investors, sometimes even calling on "Team

China"—a group of financial institutions—to rescue a tumbling stock market, or slapping on a range of measures (stamp duties, price limits, limits on SOE shares, etc.) to cool down a wild rally. But the end result is that the retail investors never learn from their mistakes and the government continues to feel a need to protect them. What's more, a long history of state intervention has become part of the calculation made by investors as they place their bets. Whether they guess right or wrong, the presence of the state as a major actor adds one more big element of uncertainty to the mix. In June 2015, the government attempted to curb unregulated margin credit, with the disastrous result of a monthlong stock market crash. This led the government to introduce a circuit breaker in January 2016, an automated process whereby a 5-percent move in the index that tracks the largest listed companies in Shanghai and Shenzhen would cause a fifteen-minute pause in trading; a 7-percent move would halt trading for the rest of the day.

The goal here was to stabilize the stock market during large swings and protect retail investors by setting a ceiling on selling, but investors quickly digested the new measure's implications—and acted accordingly. They rushed to sell before the mechanism could kick in, and consequently the market crashed the very first day the circuit breaker was introduced. Two days later, the Shanghai stock market shut down thirty minutes after the start of trading, making it the shortest trading day in its history. Ultimately it took all of four days for the government to indefinitely suspend this new, stability-enhancing mechanism. Not to mention that during this brief experiment the market lost more than US$1 trillion of value. In the US, the circuit mechanism was triggered only once, in 1997, until the COVID-19 pandemic required its use four times in one month, March 2020. What the Chinese government often failed to see is that for every action they take there is a medley of reactions they didn't expect, ultimately causing more perturbation or perverse behavior.

When it comes to the larger economy beyond the financial markets, the Chinese government has exercised control by using a gradualist approach, taking small steps at first, limited in scope, while carefully observing how the economy reacts. This strategy has largely been successful, and the government should be credited with having averted a number of disasters while China went through a profound transformation. But gradualism doesn't always work for financial markets,[16] where expectations are almost instantaneously reflected in market prices.

The stock market should be a place for price and value discovery, but in China it is often *People's Daily* discussion boards that determine its movement. More recently, however, stock market reforms have been moving things in the right direction, and as a result stock prices have become more likely to reflect a company's potential to generate future profits. But the road to a full-fledged market under professional and enforceable regulation and sound corporate governance is still under construction, much like those now-famous images of China's ghost towns.

The Great Housing Rush

Between 2003 and 2013, the average price of housing in major Chinese cities quadrupled. At US$550 per square foot, Beijing and Shanghai prices became comparable to those in Boston, with Shenzhen rapidly catching up to San Francisco. This is astounding given the wide disparity in income: Beijing, Shanghai, and Shenzhen's US$7,500 income level around that time was vastly lower than Boston's US$40,000 average income, or San Francisco's more than US$50,000.[17] Housing stock in the rest of China has participated in a similarly dramatic surge, growing at near double-digit rates every year, which makes the US real estate bubble during the early 2000s look modest by comparison. In many respects,

China looks like it's experiencing a classic housing bubble. As housing prices soar, signs of new construction are everywhere.

Real estate is considered part of the financial sector, but the importance of real estate to the wider Chinese economy is not to be underestimated. For one thing, the value of real estate affects all of the economy's major actors: consumers, firms, and the state. Property accounts for 60 percent of Chinese household assets, as opposed to 37 percent in Japan and 25 percent in the US.[18] Chinese companies rely on real estate as their most important form of collateral for financing. Real estate also acts as a lifeline for local governments, for whom a big chunk of fiscal revenue and debt financing depends on current and future land sales. By the broadest metric, property also accounts for almost 30 percent of the nation's GDP.[19] This is by far the highest among large economies (17 percent in the US, 15 percent in Korea, around 20 percent in the UK and France; even Spain during its peak housing years prior to 2008 did not exceed 30 percent).

While China has shown that it recovers easily from periodic nosebleeds in the stock market, many experts are holding their breath for fear of a housing sector collapse. Because so much of the larger economy relies on high property values, this leaves China perilously exposed. China's shadow banking sector also has been actively channeling funds to a broad range of entities using real estate as collateral. A meltdown in housing prices would trigger waves of default, not only in mortgage debt but also in corporate debt, local government debt, and shadow banking loans. The fear is that a housing crisis could lead to a *systemic* financial crisis, just like the 2008 US financial crisis.

As of 2022, the market value of housing in China is almost twice that of the US. This is reminiscent of Japan leading up to its housing bust in the late 1980s and early 1990s, when the market value of its real estate was more than twice that of the US, but less than a third three decades later.[20] All this means that understanding the forces behind the great housing boom—and its sustainability, or lack thereof—is crucially important. We begin by discussing the unusual factors that have come to shape the housing landscape in China over the last three decades in China. These include the state, the buying habits of a new generation (including the role of marriage and the "six-wallet phenomenon"), and the incentives of local government officials in China's political economy.

SOME MEASUREMENT ISSUES

Tracking trends in housing prices turns out not to be a straightforward task in China. Official statistics often rely on lists of month-to-month transactions, but there is an inherent problem with this method. Let's suppose that this month all the housing units sold were new builds on the south side of Beijing, and next month they were new builds on the city's east side. The units would be comparable in that all of them are new, but the east side of Beijing is significantly more expensive than the south side, so tracking these two sets of numbers from one month to the next would register a large rise in housing prices. The point here is that although they get lumped together in official statistics, a new apartment sold one month may be very different from a new apartment sold the next. Ideally, one would want to measure changes in price of truly comparable units. In addition to location and size, there are features like living amenities that are more difficult to measure. A common tool used in other countries is the Case-Shiller index, which tracks sales of the same housing units to derive price changes. But the problem in China, given its nascent property sector, is that there are still too few repeat sales.

For all these reasons we need to be wary of housing data from official Chinese sources, or even from unofficial channels like real estate agencies. To get around this, Chinese researchers have developed a more reliable housing index by looking at transactions within the same hous-ing complex.[21] A typical scenario in Chinese cities involves a developer building hundreds of apartment units in a number of high-rise build-ings all at once, gradually selling them off over a few years. Because these apartments share the same amenities, such as gyms, outdoor spaces, and concierge services, this makes it easier to control for quality differences. Researchers employ detailed mortgage data for 120 Chinese cities cover-ing the period between 2003 and 2013, and another data set up until 2017; together these two spans cover the period in China when housing prices grew the fastest. In addition to the actual price of the housing unit at the time it was sold, the data set provides a wealth of detailed informa-tion, including household income and the size of the loans. Micro-level data like this provided by a big Chinese bank gives us far more reliable statistics than official numbers provided by the state.

The first pattern that jumps out is that housing prices from micro-level data appreciated significantly more than was reported by official statistics, and were more volatile. Figure 6.1 plots the national average housing price index from 2003 to 2017 against a measure of household purchasing power in different regions.[22] Surprisingly, although across the nation the housing price on average appreciated 350 percent between 2003 and 2017, the rising trend did not deviate too much from income growth, a pattern that suggests that no major housing bubble was in the making.

But that picture looks different across cities. First-tier cities convey a very different picture from the rest. As Figure 6.2 shows, Beijing, Shang-hai, Guangdong, and Shenzhen display a remarkably large divergence between housing price growth and income growth, showing signs of a real bubble. But in second-tier cities, housing prices are rising in line with income growth, and in the third tier they're growing even more slowly than income, implying that in these cities price growth has fun-damental support.

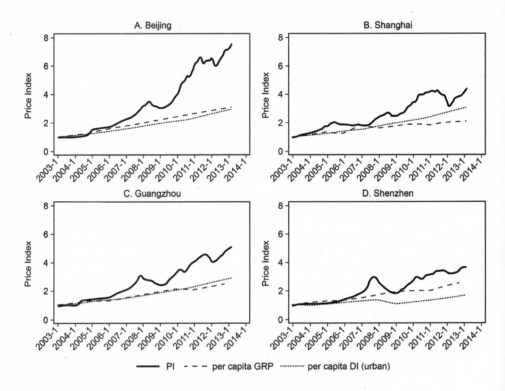

Figure 6.1: National Average Housing Price Index, 2003–2014

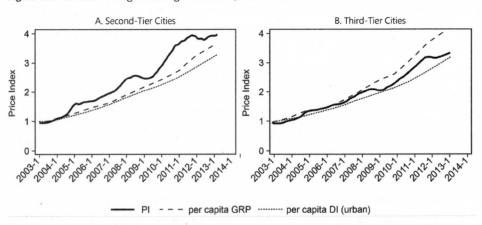

Figure 6.2: Divergence between Housing Price Growth and Income Growth in Second-Tier Cities and Third-Tier Cities, 2003–2014

Source: Hanming Fang, Quanlin Gu, Wei Xiong, and Li An Zhou, "Demystifying the Chinese Housing Boom," *NBER Macroeconomics Annual* 30, no. 1 (2016): 105–66; and National Bureau of Statistics.

Concerns about frothiness in the big-city housing market should come with a caveat. Unlike current income, which is fixed, housing prices reflect a value that includes expectations about the future. If we believe Beijing or Shanghai is on its way to becoming one of the world's most cosmopolitan cities over the next twenty years, for instance, then that expectation also will be reflected in the price: it's more expensive *today*. Therefore, a high housing price–to–income ratio doesn't necessarily indicate a bubble. It could also reflect people's rosy expectations of the future. How realistic are those expectations, and how susceptible are they to change? To answer these questions, we need to fill in some historical context.

A BRIEF HISTORY OF A HOUSING MARKET

Until some twenty years ago, the housing market in China was virtually nonexistent, which is yet another indication of the phenomenal pace of change there. Civil servants, employees of SOEs, and others working in the formal sector were allocated housing by their government employers. In 1997, the central government privatized the housing market, seeing housing demand as a way to stimulate economic growth in the aftermath of that year's East Asian financial crisis. China's housing market was born, and in just two decades it became the largest housing market in the world.

In China, all land is owned by the state except rural land, which is owned collectively by local villagers. The state can sell the right to use its land by way of leases of varying durations: thirty years for industrial land, forty years for commercial land, and seventy years for residential. Industrial land was traditionally sold at a discount and used solely for production purposes; commercial and residential land prices were determined by the market. Although most land is the exclusive property of the state, it is controlled by local governments that traditionally financed their activities by collecting taxes and using this income to pay for local economic development, local institutions, and various regional social programs.

However, in 1994 two changes in the legal system—Tax Sharing Reform and the Budget Law—brought about a seismic shift in this arrangement. Prior to 1994, taxes were largely under the control of local governments. That year, almost 80 percent of all tax revenue was collected and spent by the local governments. From that point forward, however, local governments were no longer allowed to keep the majority of these tax revenues, but had to hand them over to the central government. In the years that followed, the share of tax revenue collected and spent by local governments fell to below 50 percent. To make matters even more challenging, the 1994 Budget Law forbade local governments to borrow or run budget deficits, yet they still had to spend the same amount to maintain local operations and programs and to deliver growth. Stripped of their ability to keep most of the taxes they levied, and forbidden to borrow in order to finance their expenditures, how were local governments supposed to fill the gap between revenue and spending? The central government gave them one lifeline: the right to lease land that had formerly been the central government's exclusive province.

When local governments lease land, they are in effect selling a stake in the future growth of their region. This land becomes most valuable when it's developed and populated by a mix of residential and commercial tenants, which requires building infrastructure: roads, highways, bridges, schools, parks, and hospitals. This creates a powerful incentive to deliver these public systems and services. In a fascinating turn of events, since 1994, local governments have become equity owners in search of venture capital financing for various stages of commercial and residential development.

In the past, local governments wooed industrial firms to build manufacturing plants and factories in their jurisdictions. But after 2008 the industrialization frenzy gave way to an urbanization craze, as the old model of promoting growth based on manufacturing and exports was replaced by real estate development motivated by local officials who now relied on leasing for revenue. Local governments could sell pieces of their equity to property developers, who would then invest and make the holdings of both parties more valuable. This mechanism worked almost seamlessly—at least in the beginning.

Incentives were perfectly aligned. Local governments were enthusiastic about new construction, which brought with it capital investments and GDP growth. High profit margins due to the low cost of construction allowed real estate developers to amass vast fortunes. Prices for everything but industrial land (whose prices were deliberately kept low to support industrial companies) grew rapidly: for commercial land, the national average grew sevenfold between 2004 and 2014, followed by residential land prices, which grew fivefold.[23] In Beijing, land prices soared eighteenfold, and even in second-tier cities like Wuhan, land prices rose fifteenfold.[24]

Sales of land-use rights quickly became the primary source of revenue for local governments—as much as 30–40 percent of the total. Taxes on real estate development and apartment sales also contributed, but mostly it was the rapid growth of land sales revenue that allowed local governments to raise funding to finance local projects. Because local governments controlled the supply of land, they could bring it on the market at a pace that prevented a glut that might drive prices down. And they used tools like restricting or subsidizing home purchases to tighten or loosen controls on new development. By tightly controlling the supply of land, they caused land prices to soar, the government coffers were filled, and housing prices went through the roof.

Property developers in China enjoyed a good ride for an extended period of time. With the support of local governments, they engaged in

a frenzy of expansion through low-cost financing. They presold properties to home purchasers before they were built, and with virtually free
financing started to hoard new pockets of land and construction materials even before there were any projects to speak of. They became the
most indebted public property companies in the world.[25] Unscrupulous
behavior was not uncommon: the property giant Evergrande—before its
downfall in 2021—got so big and leveraged that it could use easy money
to expand into other areas entirely unrelated to real estate. Businesses in
other sectors, on the other hand, were so enthralled by the risky but
profitable real estate sector that many got distracted from focusing on
their core operations.

Over time, the overheated real estate market became a larger social
issue. As we've seen, young people these days may not be having more
children because space is too limited and too expensive. High housing
prices also make affordability an issue for lower- and middle-income
households, raising concerns about inequality. Thus, with firm determi-
nation, the government started to tighten the market in 2020, with the
high-pitched moral suasion that "property is to be lived in, not to be
speculated on." New restrictions led to a severe downturn in the property market, where sales declined by as much as 30 percent in 2021. A
wave of defaults ensued, and in less than a year, the majority of the top
one hundred property developers came under severe financial duress,
many on the brink of collapse. For all of its tough stance on an overheated property market, the government is unlikely to leave the powder
keg to explode unattended. But the great housing boom of the last two
decades has likely come to an end.

HOUSING FOR A NEW GENERATION

Even with the havoc that was repeatedly wreaked in the housing market—
three up-and-down cycles in the last decade—housing prices have not

seen a major correction. Even though property sales have declined significantly between 2021 and 2022, so far there has been no calamitous bursting of a great bubble as seen in the US, where prices dropped 36 percent from peak to trough, or in Japan, Spain, and many other countries. To understand why there is a basic support level for housing prices, we need to turn to the demand side of the story.

Difficult as it is to imagine, it takes an average of forty years of income to buy a house in many places in China, whereas in other parts of the world it usually takes just ten. So why don't people in China just choose to rent apartments, given the low cost relative to buying? (The housing price–to–rental ratio is 70 in Beijing or Shenzhen, compared to less than 20 in New York or San Francisco.) Let's imagine you're in your late twenties, facing some big life decisions. You earn a decent salary, save as much as 30 percent of it, and currently you're renting the space you live in. You could choose to continue to rent, put your savings in the bank, and earn an annual deposit rate of about 2 percent; given an average inflation rate of about 2 percent, your real return would be about zero. You could also elect to put those savings in the stock market and earn a low rate of return coupled with a high degree of risk, as we've seen. According to a household survey, only the top-10-percent-income-bracket households in China earned positive returns on their financial investments in the 2010–2018 period.[26] A third alternative would be to buy a place to live and earn a real rate of return of about 20 percent per year as your equity in the property grows in value. The substantial down payment would require three to four years of savings, but the good news is that your parents are likely to contribute, if they possibly can. This way you could take out a thirty-year mortgage at a 6 percent interest rate.

Given these options, your most likely choice would be to go ahead with the purchase of a property. This would be even more true if you're a bachelor looking to elevate your profile in the competitive market for a spouse. Owning a car and a home would certainly boost your appeal relative to that of a tenant with a slow-growing savings account. According to a *Shanghai Daily* survey of Chinese mothers with young daughters conducted in March 2010, 80 percent objected to their daughters marrying a non-homeowner. For all these reasons, it seems that everyone in China wants to own a house. The home ownership rate there is the highest in the world—more than 90 percent for the 276 million urban households, compared with 65 percent in the US or 42 percent in Switzerland.

An important factor when it comes to affordability is what the Chinese call the "six-wallet phenomenon." Many current homebuyers were born under the one-child policy that took effect in the early 1980s. So when the time comes for that only-child couple to purchase a home, there is not just one wallet available, but perhaps as many as six to chip in for that big down payment (the couple as well as the parents and in-laws) and to help out further if needed. It's not just the parents of the buyer, but also the spouse's parents who will want to contribute. And if grandparents join in, there could be as many as ten wallets opening up to contribute to a home purchase. Since the one-child policy has been rescinded, the next generation of home purchasers may not enjoy as much family support, and the six-wallet phenomenon may become a thing of the past.

A friend explained to me that it was almost impossible to buy a new apartment in Shanghai given the stringent scoring system instated by the government to curb the housing craze: purchasers need a high score just to be eligible to enter a lottery to buy a new property. To acquire an apartment in a coveted district in Shanghai, my friend would need to adopt an elaborate strategy to circumvent the rules, beginning with having her father buy the apartment for her. Then her father, who is more than sixty years old, would need to divorce her mother, marry someone who had accumulated a high score based on a number of metrics, including social security contributions, previous purchases of housing, etc., and then enter the lottery with his new combined high score—and win! (In a few years he would be free to get a divorce and then remarry his first wife.) A new market has emerged of people with high scores who are willing to marry and divorce in return for a fee—not so uncommon a practice in Shanghai. Even in this oddball dynamic, we can see the workings of a high-octane blend of social pressures and market forces that drove China's housing prices higher and higher, even saving it from a nosedive as real estate ran into serious trouble in 2021.

WHAT ABOUT THOSE GHOST TOWNS?

Not long ago, China was well known for its ghost towns—not the old, abandoned mining towns you might find in the western US, but newly constructed offices and high-rises with no one to populate them, empty as lunar landscapes. These images from Ordos in Inner Mongolia and Zhengdong of Henan became imprinted on the world's collective consciousness. So why were there so many empty housing units in China— by some accounts enough empty properties to house two hundred million Chinese? This is the narrative of China's overcapacity—vivid descriptions of bridges built to nowhere and houses built for no one. It's true that in typical cities in China, the vacancy rate is high; in the biggest cities, it can reach as high as 20 percent in some years. By comparison, the average vacancy rate is about 3 percent in America, even during a housing boom like that of the early 2000s.

But there are also reasons why the ghost town image of China's overcapacity may be off the mark. For one thing, the most prominent ghost towns were all in the same region, Inner Mongolia; they are not representative of China as a whole. Perhaps more important, they need to be viewed not as an ongoing state of affairs, but as a snapshot of a particular moment in time. In China, developing a new region or neighborhood involves multiple stages.

The process typically begins with a local government outlining a master plan: how much land should be converted into commercial and residential communities, how much infrastructure will be needed to support them, and so on. Then local officials engage property developers in a joint venture, and once the finances are settled, construction begins. This first stage in the process can take anywhere from one to five years. Some people will start to acquire housing units as soon as they go up in this early phase, but generally occupancy rates will be very low.

The second phase, during which most of the construction is completed, can take up to six to ten years from the launch of the project. This is the time when local governments move employees, agencies, and bureaus into the new area, priming demand for its commercial products and services. Occupancy gradually rises, but it takes another ten years before the district has become a dynamic new place to live and work. Only then do commercial businesses in the district become profitable, and a secondary housing market gets activated.

Given this long gestation period, it should be no surprise that districts once dubbed ghost cities are now thriving new urban centers. Pudong in Shanghai was one of the earliest ghost districts, but is now one of the most thriving parts of the city. Zhengdong once had a 10 percent occupancy rate, but today that rate is above 70 percent in a city that hosts hundreds of financial institutions and many more companies and services. Changzhou and Lanzhou were two other ghost towns, their new neighborhoods visible only as a few solitary lights in a sea of darkness, but both now are bustling cities. Many such nearly empty towns have since urbanized, built supportive infrastructure, jump-started their local economies, and roared to life.[27]

Of course, there are always exceptions. Some remote towns have remained empty for a variety of idiosyncratic reasons. In general, however, it might be helpful to know that in China, property development by local governments has been described by the homily "Poor kids wear oversized clothes." Growing into loose-fitting garments makes as much sense for urban development policy as it does for children. Time takes care of the rest.

Yet time alone may not always be sufficient to resolve the growing bubble in China's housing market. Data for the period between 2000 and 2015 reveals that other types of investments have suffered due to the property boom, a phenomenon directly linked to the use of land as collateral for borrowing. It turns out that even companies unrelated to housing construction set aside between 20 percent and 40 percent of their budgets to acquire land—not just industrial property, but also commercial and residential land not slated for production. Some companies use this land as collateral to acquire more land, which is then used to fuel even more borrowing.

All of this creates a dangerous too-big-to-fail mindset in the property market. Because local governments depend on real estate, companies and households believe it's impossible that the central government would allow the price of housing to drop. This expectation just fuels more speculative behavior, redirecting ever more resources to the housing sector, distorting its prices from the fundamentals of simple supply and demand.

By all accounts, a great housing bubble has already been created in many cities in China. Yes, there are social and financial reasons that justify those soaring prices, as we have explored. But future trends do not present a rosy picture. China's aging population and the younger generation's reluctance to have more children portend a decline in housing demand. There are also fewer and fewer people getting married: in 2021, only 7.6 million new marriages were registered, a 30 percent drop from only a few years ago. The younger generation, born under the one-child policy, may be delaying marriage or choosing not to marry at all. The pace of urbanization and income growth are also slowing, even with 200 million more people yet to move from rural to urban areas over the next decade or so. On the supply side, the state has sent a strong signal to keep a tighter rein on the market, dampening the insatiable appetite of both developers and home buyers.

The government has a wide range of administrative controls and tools at its disposal, such as restricting new builds and home purchases, or adjusting mortgage requirements and interest rates to control prices on the way up and the way down. This perhaps makes China relatively immune to a classic housing crisis witnessed in other market-based economies. But sometimes, the remedial actions and methods applied are so drastic and heavy-handed that they threaten macroeconomic and financial stability.

The addictive steroid of the housing market poses an ongoing dilemma for China. The government would like to wean the economy off it, but the state finds it hard to do so in ways that will neither stunt growth nor trigger a crisis. Each time the market crunches, the government softens its grip and chooses to buoy it up again. These repeated cycles of cooling and reheating the market are akin to tackling the symptoms without going after the root cause. And over time, the quick fix of inflating property values as a way to stimulate the economy becomes less and less potent. The mayor economy, heavily dependent on real estate, will need to change course.

The Dark Doppelgänger

Some of the gravest perils to China's financial system can be found in the aptly named shadow banking sector. The word "shadow" carries with it a hint of mystery and potential danger, and when "shadow" and "banking" come together that sense of threat gets magnified. Shadow banking, after all, was the source of the Great Recession of 2008 in the US, where banks peddled low-grade mortgage bonds with byzantine layers of hidden risk to unknowing buyers. Only a few years later, China's shadow banking had expanded far beyond its American sibling. Since 2009 it has grown at the ferocious pace of 20 percent annually, causing disquiet and sometimes outright alarm in the financial world.

As its name suggests, shadow banking refers to bank-like activities—various forms of lending and transferring funds—that take place outside the formal banking system. Unlike commercial banks, shadow banks are not heavily scrutinized, nor are they subject to liquidity and capital requirements. In China, shadow banking is ubiquitous, and the players range from pawnshops to mobile payment companies, from peer-to-peer lending platforms to savings and loan associations. Even commercial banks and local governments play an active role in shadow banking.

It makes perfect sense that shadow systems should find an ideal host in China, whose enterprising people are constantly trying to navigate a multitude of rules, constraints, and regulations. The desire for freedom in the pursuit of profit runs high among the Chinese people, as we've seen in the markets for stocks and housing. Today you can peel away a few layers of any formal institution or official sector and find its shadow counterpart—in education, foreign exchange, employment, and banking.

Shadow banking took firm root when conventional banks decided to skirt government regulations by moving much of their lending activity "off balance sheet." Local governments eager to showcase their zeal turned to this alternative system for funds in order to splurge on high-profile building projects and infrastructure. Households impatient for higher returns joined in the rush for easy loans. In this seeming Garden of Eden, lots of forbidden fruit was ostentatiously consumed. Back channels opened up for investment in sectors that previously had been off-limits, like real estate and mining. "Financial experts" bilked naive individual investors of their savings by promising exorbitant returns, and peer-to-peer lending platforms provided fertile ground for Ponzi schemes. People with good intentions were stirred into the same pot with the greedy and unscrupulous, as shadow banking embraced both the good and the bad.

Surprisingly, shadow banking was especially important for the state. The first hint that this might be the case came when the central government chose not to clamp down on shadow banking in its unruly infancy. Aware that a state-controlled financial system could no longer adequately serve the needs of an increasingly complex economy, the government treated shadow banking as a pseudo-experiment, a testing ground for the next big round of reforms directed at financial liberalization. To the degree that shadow banking mimicked a more free and open financial system, its lessons could serve to teach and forewarn. If successful, financial liberalization could help transform China from a country whose economy was based on cheap labor to one driven by technology and flush with capital, bolstering its international status.

In the past, big commercial state banks sat comfortably on mountains of profit owing to the large gap between the deposit rate and lending rate. All banks needed to do was collect as many deposits as possible and keep on lending—primarily to state enterprises, considered much safer than other clients. But as government regulation loosened to allow small and medium-size banks onto the scene, including a few private banks, competition for deposits became fiercer. In addition, government regulators began enforcing capital and liquidity requirements more stringently, which meant the banks had to scale back their lending. After 2007, a strict loan-to-deposit ratio of 75 percent was imposed, which meant that for every dollar of deposits a bank received, only seventy-five cents could be lent out. At this point, banks had to come up with ways to poach more deposits, lend more, or both.[28]

Shadow banking became the ideal medium. In 2005, Chinese banks started to sell their customers new savings instruments called wealth management products (WMPs). These were like term deposits, with an average maturity of a few months, but they were not subject to a capped interest rate. More important, banks no longer needed to guarantee the principal, allowing them to move WMPs off their balance sheets. In the years following 2009, the total amount of WMPs outstanding took off as funds from corporate and retail depositors came pouring in. From less than 2.6 percent of GDP in 2008, these wealth management products grew to 40 percent of GDP in 2016. In 2013 alone, RMB 3.1 trillion worth of WMPs were sold, and by the end of 2017 unguaranteed WMPs stood at RMB 22.2 trillion (or US$3.36 trillion).[29] Banks funneled the proceeds of these WMPs into outside trust companies, which subsequently invested the funds in the bond market, in credit instruments, or directly into specific companies or projects.

Once again, the crucial difference here is that unlike banks, trust companies were not subject to regulatory oversight. Free from loan restrictions or capital requirements, they effectively became off–balance sheet vehicles for banks by making loans on their behalf. Thanks to this financial sleight of hand, areas that had been off-limits to investment were now wide open, and trust companies controlled by banks or central SOEs took full advantage by pumping money into real estate, mining companies, and local government financing platforms—essentially, to high-risk borrowers. Between 2010 and 2015, trust company assets surged from 6 percent to 24 percent of GDP.

Commercial banks were not the only ones trying to find a way around rules and regulations. Enterprises of all kinds saw in shadow banking an opportunity to make big profits by lending money. Ordinarily, companies outside the financial sector were prohibited from doing so, but through shadow banking, anyone with privileged access to official financing, including large SOEs and public companies, could borrow money cheaply and lend it at high interest rates to those less privileged, making an immediate gain. These so-called entrusted loans are essentially firm-to-firm loans. Along with wealth management products and trust loans, they have become a major component of shadow banking.[30]

LOCAL GOVERNMENTS GO ALL IN

One of the biggest players in shadow banking turned out to be local governments, drawn by a pressing concern. In response to a financial downturn in the US, China's central government decided to roll out a massive fiscal stimulus program, bigger than anything ever seen up to that time. The decision was made in September 2008 in Shanxi, where President Hu Jintao, his policy advisers, and several Politburo members had been considering how best to manage the devastating aftershock that would inevitably follow the US financial crisis.[31] Their conclusion was that they needed to undertake a lot of fiscal spending. If they did not roll out the largest stimulus package imaginable, China might suffer a lost decade like Japan.

Two months later, in November 2008, Premier Wen Jiabao announced a fiscal stimulus package of RMB 4 trillion intended to boost the economy until 2010. It was going to be a fiscal splurge, with RMB 1.5 trillion directed to railways, roads, airports, water conservancy, and urban power grids; RMB 1 trillion to post-disaster reconstruction of Wenchuan Province after its devastating earthquake in May 2008; RMB 1.14 trillion to low-income housing, rural livelihoods, and local amenities; and another RMB 0.36 trillion directed to environmental protection and education.[32] Internationally, China earned praise for the speed and scale of its response.

But the big question was, who was going to enact the plan? Who was going to provide the money itself, and who was going to implement the projects themselves once that money became available? The central government was unprepared to take on the budget deficits needed to finance such massive spending, and it couldn't rely on funding from abroad. By 2009, the central government had placed the onus of steering China clear of the disastrous fallout from the Great Recession of 2008 directly on the shoulders of municipal governments. But there was one seemingly insurmountable problem: local governments were not allowed to run deficits, as decreed by the 1994 Budget Law! If they couldn't borrow, how could they spend? This time they could not turn to land leasing for an answer, for it would be neither sufficient nor swift enough.

By 2010, the full amount of China's RMB 4 trillion stimulus package had been disbursed—and on schedule. But only RMB 1 trillion had been financed by the central government. Where did the other RMB 3 trillion come from? Local governments had turned to an entity called a local government financing vehicle (LGFV) to borrow on their behalf. These LGFVs were nominally independent corporations, but in reality, they were owned by local governments. They could turn to commercial banks or shadow banks to borrow funds, and their debt would be considered corporate debt rather than local government debt. Local governments injected land assets into these companies, giving them land-use rights and the ability to build bridges and highways. With these resources as collateral, they could borrow prodigiously. The beauty of this scheme was that none of the debt, which was essentially the obligation of local governments, would show up on their balance sheet. So technically there was no violation of central government regulations.

The first of these LGFVs was the Shanghai Municipal Investment Corporation, founded in 1992 and authorized by the central government to issue a bond financing construction in the less-developed eastern part of Shanghai, the Pudong area. The Shanghai Pudong Construction bond issued that same year had a face value of RMB 500 million each year for ten years. In the following years, although the local governments used these vehicles to finance some borrowing, the special purpose vehicles were heavily restricted—limited to building roads and investments in urban development. But propelled by the exigencies of the 2009 stimulus package, local government financing vehicles proliferated. In 2009, there were only 3,800 LGVFs, but by 2013 the number had nearly doubled to 7,170, and thirty of China's thirty-six provinces and municipalities had LGVFs set up at the municipal level. The total debt borne by these vehicles rose from RMB 6 trillion in 2009 to an estimated RMB 45 trillion six years later.[33] In recent years, LGVFs have funded megaprojects like the US$2.4 billion Shanghai Tower, the second-tallest building in the world.

The central bank endorsed the practice at first. It accepted the local governments' circumvention of the 1994 Budget Law, since off–balance sheet borrowing was the only available alternative. The charade worked: on one end the Ministry of Finance encouraged local governments to use LGVFs to borrow, and on the other the central banking regulator (at the time it was the China Banking Regulatory Committee) encouraged state banks to lend generously to them. Of the RMB 4.7 trillion in new bank loans extended in 2009, half went to LGFVs. Whereas in normal years new bank loans constituted 15 percent of GDP, in 2009 that number had shot up to 27.5 percent. The consequence was a much-enlivened GDP, primed by swelling local government debt.[34]

It was in this context that shadow banking became increasingly important as a source of funding for local governments. In addition to bank loans, LGFVs began to issue urban construction and investment bonds known as chengtou bonds. These were considered corporate bonds, but everyone understood that they were implicitly guaranteed by the local government. The primary funds channeled to these bonds were coming from the shadow banking sector, which became an instant steroid as the ease and rapidity of raising funds through this new channel galvanized local governments. As the rate of chengtou bond growth picked up speed, money from shadow banking came pouring in. The number of new bonds issued climbed from 79 in 2008 to 1,704 by 2014, an astonishing growth rate of 85 percent each year. Every municipal government was now using their LGFVs to issue chengtou bonds.[35]

The shift from relying heavily on conventional bank loans to shadow banking picked up even more momentum after 2012. By the end of 2014, RMB 4.95 trillion was outstanding in chengtou bonds, which had become the primary staple for local governments. The share of bank loans in local government financing had dropped from 80 percent just six years earlier to less than 20 percent.[36] The trigger was that local governments had been pushed into a new corner. Alarmed by spiraling debt, the central bank decided to roll back the easy credit environment in 2010. But by this point, local governments were stuck. The huge bank loans they had taken on in 2009 would be due in three to five years, but these monies had been plowed into infrastructure projects that would take a decade to complete—and two decades before they generated material returns. There was enormous rollover pressure: local governments needed to pay back a significant amount of these bank loans. At this point local governments gave up any lingering restraint and fully embraced the new playing field of shadow banking. The baton had now been passed from the formal banking sector to its doppelgänger.

To summarize, with the new sources of funding provided by shadow banking, local governments were able to successfully implement the central government's ambitious response to the threat posed by the Great Recession of 2008. Moreover, they could funnel these funds wherever they wanted to, including property, local industry, and their favorite firms. Over the six years following the US's Great Recession of 2008, the size of the Chinese economy doubled from US$4.5 trillion to US$9 trillion by 2014. However, total Chinese debt rose to more than 230 percent of GDP. A significant portion of this was channeled through shadow banking.

BANKING IN CHINA VERSUS IN THE US

The backdrop of shadow banking in the US and China is actually not dissimilar: in both countries, banks wanted to circumvent regulations and chose to create off–balance sheet vehicles as a way of doing so. In both cases banks succeeded in raising short-term financing for lucrative but risky investments. In the US, this money went into exotic, hard-to-understand financial products; in China, it went into overheated sectors such as property. The difference, however, can be found in the structure of shadow banking in the two countries, as well as in the interrelationship of its various players.

A large part of US shadow banking revolves around complex forms of securitization—carving up tranches of loans and then repackaging them into a wide variety of securities catering to every taste for risk, maturity, and liquidity. The prime example of this is mortgage-backed securities. In China, things are much simpler: banks collect money from retail and corporate investors by offering high-return WMPs and trust products. There is no long, complex, opaque chain of intermediation that characterizes American shadow banking; instead of seven intermediary steps there are just one or two, and mostly plain vanilla loans.

Nor are there a great number of different financial entities tangled up in China's investing web. In the US this is far more common. Heading into 2008, Goldman Sachs was linked to hedge funds by a swap agreement that was used to offset obligations through another swap agreement with Bear Stearns, which had another swap agreement with a private equity firm. In the meantime, money market funds bought Lehman Brothers' debt, and when insurance companies like AIG sold several hundred billion dollars' worth of credit default swaps, a lot of those buyers also owned Lehman bonds. This intricate web of interconnections means that when one domino tipped over, the rest went with it.

The lack of financial complexity in China may seem to offer one compelling reason why a full-blown financial crisis is unlikely to occur, but it may not be reason enough. Bad lending lies at the core of most financial crises, and things can quickly turn sour in the subpar lending that underpins some of China's multitrillion-dollar market in WMPs and trust products. Evergrande, the fallen property giant, counted 40 percent of its financing from trust companies before it became financially embattled.[37] When it formally defaulted on its debt, it triggered a cascade of losses for trust companies, which used retail investors to fund the property group's projects. Anxin Trust, which lent money to a property company that then used those funds to buy SeaWorld and the luxury travel company Abercrombie & Kent, went into default when the property group failed to make payments on its loans.

When companies fail, investors get hurt, especially retail investors with little knowledge of finance. But even people with financial experience can mistakenly believe that shadow banking's investment products are safe, assuming they are guaranteed by the large state or commercial entities that sell these products. A relative of mine, a manager in a state bank, was a veteran of the financial system. The trust products she decided to buy had themselves invested in various real estate projects, and those loans were backed by valuable collateral, including land and housing developments. At first she was delighted by her investment—after all, it was generating annual returns of 10 percent, and it was backed by both valuable land and strong local government support. If ever the project ran into trouble, that property could be sold to repay creditors. However, when the government decided to cool off the overheating property market, the value of the collateral dropped sharply, and the projects themselves fell on hard times. Five years later, my relative was still waiting to recover the principal on her investment.

The potential for disaster in shadow banking is as vast as the sector itself. WMPs alone amounted to about 35 percent of China's GDP at its peak—four times the value of Citigroup, Bank of America, Wells Fargo, and JPMorgan combined as a share of US GDP.[38] The weakness in the system is the potential for a run on WMPs and trust products in China should investors suddenly lose their appetite for risk. Panic is contagious and could lead to waves of default. These risks associated with the dramatic rise of shadow banking in China are very real, but to cast this sector in only a negative light would do it an injustice. Shadow banking has enjoyed such spectacular growth because it served as a remedy, however flawed, for the glaring deficiencies of the traditional financial sector. Principally, it filled a void in the Chinese economy when it came to a pervasive credit shortage. Small and medium-sized private companies without access to formal channels for borrowing have found relatively cheap and available capital in shadow banking, improving the impact of allocations that would otherwise have gone largely—if not completely— to state-owned enterprises. Households found higher returns on their savings than they had been getting, albeit with much greater hidden risk. Shadow banking also accelerated the development of the corporate bond market, which before 2013 was small and primarily used by commercial banks; today, China's corporate bond market is the third largest in the world.

In the end, shadow banking is another theater for the maelstrom of China's financial sector. In all of the markets we have seen—stocks, housing, and banking—the regulatory framework is incomplete, prompting actors to take advantage of various loopholes. Sometimes, its anomalies are also a consequence of the central government's mercurial policies, or of cases when too much state intervention in one part of the financial system shifts the issue elsewhere. At times it can look like the government is playing a giant game of Whac-a-Mole, one more indication that the financial system—a significant part of the Chinese economy—is still very much a work in progress.

China's Financial System: Risks and Trajectory

Each of the past three decades has ushered in its specific cause for concern. In the 1990s, it was large nonperforming loans supplied by state banks; in the first decade of the twenty-first century, it was the looming property bubble that would bring the banking system down along with it when it burst; next came the relentless expansion of shadow banking with its plentiful easy credit, leading to mountains of debt. In 2001, Gordon Chang's *The Coming Collapse of China* predicted, "The end of the modern Chinese state is near. The People's Republic has five years, perhaps ten, before it falls." *The Economist* ran several articles under the banner "The Great Fall of China," one in 2004 and one in 2015. However, none of these dark predictions has come to pass. So how has China managed to avoid a full-blown crisis?

In his book *Stress Test: Reflections on Financial Crises,* former Treasury secretary Tim Geithner, one of the key firefighters of the US 2008 emergency, said that every financial crisis is a crisis of confidence. When people lose faith that the money they have put in banks or bonds or stock markets is safe, or if investors believe that the government will not bail out important financial institutions, they will flee as fast as possible. When the US lent a helping hand to Bear Stearns, the market calmed; when it refused to bail out Lehman Brothers, the bottom fell out. But in China, politics won't get in the way of saving a financial system from collapse.

The state not only regulates the banks, but it is also their majority owner, and banks, in turn, own the debt of local governments. This means that it is unlikely that a major bank will be allowed to fail in the way Lehman was. No ideological battles within different branches of the government will prevent emergency rescues from taking place. Yes, this creates both moral hazard and a sense that investors will be protected from serious losses, but the government can respond by stripping CEOs of troubled institutions of their power, and even indicting and convicting them. This could provide sufficient warning and reassurance to successfully navigate these dangers in the future.

China's state capacity also extends far beyond backstopping any particular bank or brokerage firm, given its exceptional ability to mobilize resources wherever they may be needed. During the US financial crisis, a severe credit crunch froze up the system. Banks were hoarding cash, ordinary borrowers who wanted to finance a new car or a college education were unable to do so, and financial intermediaries stopped lending. At this point, if the US government had injected liquidity into the system, the spasm could have been averted. But Congress was not interested in further bailouts. In China, the government would simply *order* the banks to make more money available.

The most alarming aspect of the Chinese financial system is pervasive debt. We have seen how the need to carry out China's central government mandate for a massive stimulus in the wake of the 2008 Great Recession led local governments to rack up debt. As a result, the overall debt-to-GDP ratio in China reached a record high of 275 percent in 2022, making it one of the highest in the world. But debt crises occur when borrower and lender cannot agree to a mutually acceptable resolution, and when lenders do not act in a coordinated way. In China, where most of the debt is owned directly or indirectly by local governments or state-owned companies, state control of both borrowing and lending makes default resolution much simpler. If necessary, the central government can just step in and resolve things.[39] But sometimes, rescue plans come a little bit too late and too little, such as during the property market crisis in 2022. This can spook investors and cause larger-than-expected remedial costs.

Debt is only one side of the equation. To examine creditworthiness, the asset side also matters. Local governments are heavily indebted, but many also have substantial amounts of assets. By one credible estimate, local government assets totaled roughly RMB 126 trillion at the end of 2017, far exceeding liabilities of RMB 29 trillion (it has since grown to an estimated RMB 61.3 trillion).[40] Their annual revenue was significantly impaired by a deflating property market and an economic slump in 2022, to the point that some were so financially strained that they had to hold off salary payments to civil servants. Nevertheless, there is a consolidated national balance sheet with a wealthy central government, meaning that in times of emergency, funds can move from one coffer to another. Chinese households, on the other hand, are even better positioned. Although their debt levels are rising, particularly mortgage loans, their ability to service these interest payments is extremely high thanks to their vast amount of saving. It is several times higher than that of Americans, Japanese, or Spanish residents leading up to the bursting of their housing bubbles.[41]

Evaluations of China's debt levels are based on the same standards applied to Western economies, but there is a fundamental difference between the two situations: the gap between the economy's growth rate and the interest rate. This is a crucial variable in determining debt sustainability. When interest rates are lower than growth rates, then interest on the debt is low, and debt-to-GDP ratios will fall over time. When interest rates are higher than growth rates, then debt-to-GDP ratios will rise, and debt sustainability becomes an issue (interest rates are currently rising in the US). Emerging markets like China normally enjoy significantly higher growth rates than advanced economies, and growth rates are likely to remain higher than the interest rate. Therefore, one cannot apply the same standards to evaluate debt. This is not to say that China won't suffer the consequences of excessive and risky lending over time. But even if bad lending and state support for zombie companies continues, this is more likely to lead to gradual corrosion of the economy rather than to a series of acute outbreaks.

China's extraordinary amount of national saving is more than enough to cover its domestic investment needs. This means that the economy does not need to rely on foreign capital, and as a result, China is unlikely to be at the mercy of outside speculative money, or to suffer the reverse international capital flows that most emerging market economies have had to endure. Strict capital controls, which limit how much money can flow in and out of the country, keep savings bottled up inside China. In other countries, such as Japan, residents have simply divested their assets domestically and moved them abroad after the housing market collapsed, catalyzing a much larger asset price correction. In China, as long as these controls remain effective in preventing sudden capital flight, Chinese savings can provide the nation with financial ballast. This is not necessarily optimal for Chinese residents, or for economic efficiency in the long run, but it does prevent an amplification of financial shocks.

Die-hard prognosticators of doom are still predicting the collapse of the Chinese financial system, and it does no harm to take these countdowns to a meltdown as a warning to prepare for the unexpected. Anything is possible, and China's financial stability does depend on an important condition: that distress in one realm of the financial system is kept isolated and not allowed to infect the system as a whole. If several big banks run into financial difficulty, or if a few WMPs and trust products default, then the state's ability to stave off these threats is high. But in the event of a perfect storm—if in addition to a property price plunge the stock market were to drop precipitously, the big banks were to fail, and a wide swath of defaults were to happen simultaneously—the government's ability to save the day would be called into question. Expectations could quickly reverse, confidence could erode, and a financial tsunami could inundate banks, local governments, companies, households, and firms. Given the way the Chinese government has handled all the challenges of the last forty years, such a scenario is not likely in the near future.

In recent years, the government has also ramped up its efforts to deleverage the financial system and the economy as a whole. In 2020–2021, its refusal to bail out China's largest property companies when they went insolvent shows that it has the power and willingness to stave off significant financial peril even when its actions are unpopular. These efforts have been largely successful, and the country is more financially sound than it was a few years ago. But the economy slowed down considerably at some point, as companies found it hard to borrow and banks did not want to lend, and the near-death experience of property developers spooked the market. Stability may ultimately be achieved, but businesses also suffered in the process of ever-changing regulatory rules and financing conditions; costs for bailing out and stimulating the economy mount with every delay and hesitation, each time exacerbating moral hazard. In the financial system in particular as in the broader economy in general, China scores high on stability but low on efficiency.

The financial system in China is faced with a perennial dilemma: because it is not yet mature, the state feels the need to constantly intervene and preserve its stability. But the more it intervenes, the more distortions are created, and the slower it is to mature. Market mechanisms clearly need to weigh in more than the state in the future. One remedy for China's financial weaknesses would be to introduce competition from private domestic players and foreign players who can challenge the status quo with its cumbersome state entities. Just as private firms made SOEs more productive by challenging their comfortable existence, a greater number of foreign participants—the likes of JPMorgan, Fidelity, and BlackRock—may help sweep aside the web of perverse incentives and distorted behavior endemic to China's domestic financial realm. Over the long term, opening up and letting go—something the state has only on occasion been prepared to do—may be the best approach to averting the dark fate so many have imagined for China's financial system.

SEVEN

THE TECHNOLOGY RACE

Since the first stone tool was created nearly two million years ago, technology has transformed human experience. We have harnessed the power of science to feed ourselves, extend our life expectancy, and expand our cognitive capacity. Today, gaining a global competitive edge as a nation has less to do with the clash of armies and more to do with the mastery of cutting-edge technology and cybersecurity. Most trials of strength between nations will be resolved by who prevails in setting international technology standards, who gains more market share in high-tech industries, and who can develop the best algorithms to process the vast amounts of data that shape our daily lives. Technology dictates geopolitical winners and losers.

Technology also plays a key role in every economy: when infusions of capital and labor eventually run their course as drivers of economic growth, boosting productivity becomes the best way forward. (As economist Paul Krugman puts it, "Productivity isn't everything, but in the long run it is almost everything.") In chapter 2 we saw China lift itself up from poverty, but in order for China to join the world's wealthiest countries, constant progress is essential.

The last time China led the world technologically was in the fourteenth-century Song dynasty, when it invented the compass, paper, gunpowder, and printing. Today, first-time visitors to China can see a shopper pick up a live crab and scan it with a mobile phone to identify its source and nutritional value. On Singles Day they can join the online shopping craze on Alibaba with fully automated customer service managing 540,000 orders *per second*. During a spike in COVID-19 cases, they can see robots delivering food to apartments and disinfecting public spaces.[1] On the street, they can run into a panhandler holding up a QR code for mobile payments on a sign that reads I'M HUNGRY.

This is the China that built the world's fastest supercomputer and the world's first solar-powered expressway, and conducted the world's first 5G-enabled remote surgery. This is the China that launched the world's first aerial passenger drone, the EHang 184, which can transport a person in the air for twenty-three minutes with a range of thirty-five kilometers. This is the China that is moving ahead of the US in internet- and perception-based AI, as well as in 5G, digital payment, quantum communication, and speech technology, where Chinese firms are beating American firms in every language, including English. This is the China whose new smart cities feature autonomous vehicles that communicate with traffic lights and parking lots as they move past smart poles that measure wind direction and gauge levels of CO_2, transmit data in real time, and charge electric vehicles. For the first time in history, a developing country with only a quarter of the living standard of leading industrialized nations is a master of leading-edge technology. This seems to have flown in the face of Western predictions. In 1999, *Time* magazine's special issue "Beyond 2000" asserted: "China cannot grow into an industrial giant in the 21st century. Its population is too large and its gross domestic product too small." People did not believe that it would have enough money to buy advanced technology products—let alone the resources to invent them.[2]

Despite all the highly visible signs of technological prowess, experts are still divided as to how ready China is to assume the mantle of global innovator in chief. Some observers point out that this is also the China that still relies on an education system that emphasizes test taking and rote learning, on weak intellectual property laws and enforcement, and on the heavy hand of the state for planning, all of which work to limit imagination and creativity. They contend that Chinese technology still falls short of the technological frontier by being critically dependent on America or Europe for core competencies, including the creation of cutting-edge semiconductors.

As we seek to reconcile these contradictory views of China, it is helpful to distinguish between two different types of innovations: fundamental breakthroughs and creative adaptations. The first category takes us "from zero to one." This technology is revolutionary, giving rise to general-purpose technologies like computers and artificial intelligence that permeate the economy and inspire streams of new spin-off technology. The second category takes us "from one to N." These innovations are incremental: evolutionary rather than revolutionary, they feature continuous improvements rather than discontinuous leaps into existence. While China is achieving remarkable mastery of "one to N" technologies, particularly when it comes to internet applications and business model design, it is not yet poised to consistently make "zero to one" trailblazing innovations. In order for this to happen, there will need to be profound changes to China's civil society, its markets, and the role of the state.

From One to N: China's Sweet Spot

So, what *is* innovation? It's commonly understood as the development of something new—a first-of-its-kind device, method, or process. By this definition, the invention of the iPhone would count as an innovation, but not the Samsung Galaxy, even though with its one third of the global market share, Samsung is bigger than Apple. However, when it comes to capturing the impact that technical progress can have on society and the economy, this definition is too narrow. Any significant improvement of an existing product, process, or service should count as an innovation. In his book *The Economics of Technological Change*, economist Edwin Mansfield tells us that innovation can take many forms, including new ways of producing existing products, designs that add important new characteristics. By this definition an LG mobile phone screen that can be rolled up like a newspaper, or running shoes that can track your heartbeat, count as innovations. Facebook does too, even though it was not the first social networking platform, because its improvements on the original idea have transformed the way the internet is used.

In addition to product innovation, we also have *process* innovation—the discovery of cheaper, cleaner, and more efficient ways to produce something. Putting a new idea or scientific discovery into practice is yet another important kind of innovation. Many important contributions were not first-time inventions. James Watt did not invent the steam engine, but his machine was a significant improvement on Thomas Savery's invention patented a century earlier. At Kitty Hawk the Wright brothers came up with the precursor to the modern airplane, but a much earlier flying machine was conceived in 1799 by Sir George Cayley. As American economic historian Abbott Payson Usher puts it, invention proceeds from "the constructive assimilation of pre-existing elements into new syntheses," and according to sociologist S. Colum Gilfillan's more succinct definition, an invention is a "new combination of prior art."[3]

Chinese innovation tends to be based on new applications of existing technology. Machine learning—the core technique behind artificial intelligence—may not have been invented in China, but Chinese applications of AI are world class, including self-driving cars, autonomous drones, facial recognition, and robotics. For urbanites coping with limited living spaces, Chinese companies have come up with paper-thin treadmills capable of being folded in two and conveniently tucked away in a closet. For parents eager to start early education for their young children, robots have been designed to both entertain and teach. For police officers coping with high levels of city air pollution, Chinese manufacturers offer air-purifying nasal devices to wear as they perform their duties.

The Chinese are particularly good at making existing technology both better and cheaper. Huawei's top-end handset is half the cost of an iPhone, while Xiaomi's equally sleek smartphone costs even less. Xiaomi was ranked number one as a global smartphone brand in 2021. The Chinese manufacturing process itself is swift, agile, and lean, making it possible to produce high-quality goods at a fraction of the cost typically incurred in other countries, even before factoring in the cost of labor. Using modular manufacturing technologies, for example, Chinese companies can build a sixty-story hotel in less than three weeks.

Perhaps above all else, China has been creative in developing business models. Everyone is familiar with video streaming platforms, but China's iQiyi allows viewers to purchase products and clothing from the very shows they are watching. Right in the moment! Pinduoduo encourages members shopping online to form teams to get group discounts and play games with friends and family to win prizes. This novel shopping experience has allowed the company to become the fastest-growing company in history—from an upstart novelty in 2015 to a US$30 billion company at the time of its IPO three years later. Meituan has combined the services of Groupon (group buying), Grubhub or Deliveroo (food delivery), Tripadvisor (travel), and Yelp (recommendations) all on one platform. These Chinese companies, and countless others like them, are finding new ways to monetize their services, attract customers, and encourage them to buy, which is a good thing for a country with the world's highest saving rate and a global trade imbalance on the export side.

What we're seeing here is that when it comes to innovation, Chinese companies are remarkably clever at taking existing technologies and applying them in new ways, expanding them from one to N. Although some may dismiss these adaptations and new implementations of existing technologies as mere tinkering, they are significant so long as they contribute to growth by increasing productivity and generating income, which is certainly the case in China. Electricity was a zero to one technology, for example, but its countless spin-offs, including those that allow us to light, heat, and air-condition our homes, have allowed us to be far more comfortable and more productive. Cheap smartphones loaded with features may not change the world like the discovery of electricity, but if these gadgets enable Chinese farmers in rural areas to get real-time feedback on pricing and demand for their produce, they can lead to huge gains in people's welfare. Under this broader definition of innovation, China can be counted as a highly innovative nation.

BEYOND COPYING AND PROTECTIONISM

Perhaps because these are not splashier, fundamental breakthroughs, the West tends to discount China's high-tech achievements by ascribing them to copying or to protectionism. While these practices did give China's economy traction early on, they are no longer the primary drivers of Chinese innovation, for the simple reason that such cruder types of opportunities have already been fully exhausted. Instead, China is replete with first-of-their-kind companies, like Mobike for bike sharing; and Ant, the payment–cum–financial technology company that spun off from Alibaba, is easily the most innovative such company in the world.[4] Even though TikTok is not the first short-video sharing app, its AI-powered technology is the best of its kind in video feeds.

For decades, it was common practice for Chinese people to copy what they liked, a practice that emanated from within society rather than from government. Replication has long been considered simply pragmatic, and widely accepted as a way of doing business and catching up. The first generation of Chinese internet companies in the early 2000s consisted of carbon copies of Western models: Xiaonei, a Chinese social networking site, was a pixel-to-pixel imitator of Facebook; the Chinese version of Yahoo! was Sohoo (later Sohu, where "So" refers to "search"); and China's variant version of YouTube was called Youku. Nor was the highest form of flattery limited to technology. The founder of Xiaomi (touted as the "Apple of China") loves to wear black turtlenecks that unabashedly evoke Steve Jobs. The fast-food company KFC has multiple Chinese copycats with the same red-and-white logos, but branded slightly differently as MFC, KFD, or KFG. The Chinese car company Chery has a logo eerily similar to that of Nissan's Infiniti.

Not only was copying not considered disreputable, it was sometimes even a way of boasting. I once met a local mayor who had encouraged building bridges across the small rivers flowing through his town, all of which were unabashed copies, including diminutive versions of London Bridge and the Golden Gate Bridge. The clubhouse of a golf course outside Beijing replicates a famous château in France. And a wealthy businessman once told me proudly that his residence was a precisely scaled model of the White House. But as the world snickered at such imitations, Chinese companies were catching up to global industry leaders, and in recent years started to surpass them. This same pragmatic attitude informed the Chinese state's lax approach to enforcing intellectual property protections.

It's also important to bear in mind that all economic success stories include a stage that involved copying and mimicking the technologies and products of industry leaders. Imitation is a basic aspect of nature and of economic life. No one would argue, however, that stealing British designs for looms and mills made America an economic superpower, or that copying turned Japanese companies such as Nintendo, Hitachi, and Sony into household names worldwide. No economy copies its way to the top. And today we see the imitation phenomenon starting to run in a new cycle; now it is Chinese companies that are being copied, this time by their Malaysian, Indian, and Philippine competitors.

Some technologies also prove difficult to copy. In an attempt to accelerate its absorption of advanced technologies from the West, China implemented a long-standing quid pro quo strategy of "trading markets for technology." When outside firms wanted to operate in China and take advantage of its lower costs and vast market, they were required to form joint ventures with Chinese companies, which often entailed sharing proprietary technology. In recent disputes over trade, the West has referred to this policy as "forced technology transfer." The reality is a bit more nuanced: many multinational enterprises accept the arrangement, figuring out that they can invent new technologies fast enough to remain ahead of their domestic competitors and still earn lucrative profits in China's vast market. And although China benefited enormously from what it learned in this way, there was also a major flaw in this strategy: frequently China did not succeed in gaining access to the core technology it sought because foreign companies shared only the technology necessary for those products—or parts of products—manufactured locally in China; they withheld the master blueprint, or critical information needed for fully independent production of a competitive product.[5]

In the book *China as an Innovation Nation*, Professor Kaidong Feng describes how this policy of requiring foreign companies to share technology fell far short of its intended purpose. The automotive industry provides perhaps the best example. Chinese teams in the hundreds of joint ventures formed with foreign car companies did not even develop the capability to make high-quality engines on their own. Instead, it was purely domestic players like Chery and Geely that succeeded in cornering substantial market share. Today, trading markets for technology has fallen from favor as a policy. Instead, spurred by geopolitical tensions and trade wars, China has shifted from importing technology to a strategy based on self-reliance. Tesla, for instance, which is producing a record number of vehicles from its Gigafactory Shanghai, has full control of its technology and IP.

There is nothing inherently wrong with technology transfers, so long as all parties involved are aware of the trade-offs and sign a mutually beneficial deal. As China becomes the leader in many novel areas of technology, the pendulum of technology transfers has begun to swing the other way. This is particularly true for green innovation. As author Scott Malcomson observed in an article in *Foreign Affairs,* Ford and Toyota invested in Chinese EV companies so that their technologies could be brought to the American, Japanese, and European markets.[6] Tesla has opted to use the cobalt-free battery produced by the innovative Chinese company CATL. These investments could be restricted by China, but that would be unhelpful for everyone. If all nations choose to develop their technologies in isolation for geopolitical reasons, technological advancement will slow down for all. The German government is encouraging its automakers to raise their own game in producing electric vehicle batteries, but even that effort builds off ten years of collaboration with innovative Chinese companies.

In addition to copying, protectionism is also popularly cited as a reason for China's technological success. Again, there is some truth to this claim. Information-related foreign tech companies such as Google, Facebook, and Twitter were heavily restricted in China and were either ultimately blocked or pushed to leave. Had Google been able to freely operate in China, Baidu (China's homegrown search engine) would have had little chance of building the 70 percent market share it does today. Similarly, if Twitter and Facebook had been allowed to compete in China, they would have had a good shot at taking over domestic services like WeChat or Sina Weibo, which have flourished, albeit under the watchful eye of government censors.

Although protectionism did give some Chinese technology companies a chance to take root, it was not the ultimate cause of China's tech-sector successes. For one thing, most domestic tech companies were not protected from foreign competitors. Amazon did not pull out of China in 2018 because its domestic competitors were given unfair advantages. It lost out to competitors like JD.com, which was well aware that Chinese people love discounts but distrust memberships like Amazon Prime. They also like to have fun shopping and found Amazon's interface dull compared with JD.com's busy, festive design. Alibaba successfully took on eBay by making radical changes to its business model: it made listing free, charging only those sellers who opted for higher visibility, and it slashed fees levied on suppliers. Uber's fierce trial of strength with Didi in China ended with Didi acquiring Uber's local operations because Didi understood Chinese drivers and customers much better. In most cases, like these, the Chinese companies simply outcompeted their foreign rivals.

It's difficult to convey just how ferocious competition is in China. The rivalry between Chinese technology companies today is reminiscent of the Warring States period between 475 BC and 221 BC. Modern tactics—price wars, undercutting competitors by uninstalling their software, sending each other to prison, and blocking each other's payments systems—are every bit as ruthless, just without the bloodshed.[7] On the more positive side, competition in China pushes companies to relentlessly upgrade their products, find new ways of monetization, and aggressively cut costs. The expression "nine-nine-six" captures the work ethic in China: 9:00 a.m. to 9:00 p.m., six days a week. A more updated version, "double-oh-seven," refers to being available 24/7, with no personal life.

THE BENEFITS OF SCALE AND BIG DATA

The past several decades have seen a paradigm shift in the corporate world. In 2008 the companies with the largest market capitalization were the likes of Chevron and Walmart. Microsoft was the only representative from the technology sector. Ten years later, tech companies including Alphabet, Amazon, Tencent, and Alibaba occupy seven out of the ten top slots. And there's a reason most of these companies are either American or Chinese. Both countries possess the advantage of scale—large markets and access to massive amounts of data.

In the latter part of the twentieth century, China leveraged economies of scale—the cost advantages that come from producing in large amounts—to build a manufacturing powerhouse with vast networks of supportive infrastructure and the logistics needed to achieve high efficiency. But in the age of information, scale takes on an altogether new significance. Because tech companies are based on data, they become capable of harnessing what economists refer to as "increasing returns to scale," which means that if you double the inputs, you more than double the output. Artificial intelligence, for instance, can create a virtuous loop where the more data that flows into one's algorithms the more efficient these algorithms become—and the better the final product will be, whether it's a search engine, a real-time translation, or an autonomous vehicle.

Once again, Chinese companies enjoy a clear competitive advantage with their giant domestic market. Toutiao has perfected its news feed technology, which matches people with news they might like, thanks to a huge customer base. The founder of Ctrip, the largest online travel company in China (Trip.com in the US), tells me that its size allows it to learn rapidly from its vast number of customers. And of course, the same holds true for Alibaba, with its eight hundred million users on various platforms, and five hundred million consumers borrowing money from its Alipay service. Information harvested from the more than a billion users of Tencent's services, which include social networks, music, e-commerce, internet services, payment systems, smartphones, and multiplayer online games, helps make the company's products more useful and more fun.

Scale is not everything, which explains why India does not have nearly as many tech giants as China. Other crucial factors include human capital, physical and digital infrastructure, and long-term financial capital. But still, scale matters, and in ways that are far more pronounced than they were in a predigital economy. Tech companies mark a distinct break from the traditional industrial companies. There, when a factory made an additional shoe, its production and sale incurred an additional cost. However, the additional cost of delivering a digital product over the internet—an extra subscription to Spotify or Netflix or Zoom—is next to nothing. Tech companies become more profitable by acquiring as many customers as possible, which makes it easy to see why having 1.4 billion consumers connected by the internet and accessible via smartphones is a tremendous advantage for Chinese companies.

This is why many tech industries are substantially more concentrated than manufacturers: Google has captured 90 percent of the global market in online searches, while Uber and Lyft together control almost 100 percent of the US ride-sharing market. This characteristic of the new economy has important implications for society as a whole, affecting everything from social inequality to the equilibrium interest rate—the interest rate at which the supply of saving matches investment demand.

In a digital economy, data is the new input that informs production. Medical data contributes to better diagnoses, consumer data improves

Amazon recommendations, and traffic data produces navigation apps like Waze. Biotechnology, city planning, transportation logistics, and supply chains: all these use data as a key input. "Data is the new oil" contains a lot of truth, although the analogy is not totally accurate.[8] Oil cannot be reused; that gallon of gasoline you consumed to drive to the store is gone forever. Data, on the other hand, can be shared by individuals, researchers, companies, and governments for as long as it's useful. This means that owning data is not as important as having *access* to it.

In principle, small countries may not be at such a significant disadvantage compared with large economies so long as they can tap into a global pool of data. In reality, however, data is a highly politicized commodity that raises national security and privacy concerns for policy makers and citizens alike. When data in customer-focused applications carries a lot of information that is specific to a particular culture, then large countries such as China and the US enjoy a significant advantage.

China generates not just troves of data, but troves of *useful* data. More than a billion Chinese use mobile phones to make payments. On a given day, Chinese digital payments exceed US digital payments for a given *year*. China's obsession with digital services means that many aspects of daily life are transformed into digital data. Online food delivery is ten times more prevalent than it is in the US, and shared bike rides are more than three hundred times more common. Prior to the 2020 pandemic, one quarter of retail transactions took place online in China, compared with about 10 percent in the US, and payments for coffee, a bus ticket, or a parking fine reveal a lot about a shopper's personal profile. With this kind of information, companies can sell you things more effectively and improve their services. Also, as we'll see, they can revolutionize banking.

Data collection and data-driven governance raise issues of surveillance and privacy, about which people tend to feel very differently in China. China has one of the most advanced facial recognition systems in the world. In Shanghai, individuals in public spaces purportedly can be identified within seconds. I once crossed the street close to my home and minutes later got a text saying that I had been fined for jaywalking. People in China are also monitored for irregular or bad behavior: so-and-so dumped the trash outside the bin, or someone posted illegal advertising in a building hallway, and so on. Such technology proved to be highly effective during the COVID-19 pandemic, when phone apps kept track of people's whereabouts and whom they had contacted. Without multiple green passes on my digital health code app and location app, it would have been impossible for me to travel to another city in China, or even enter a restaurant or a shop.

In the West, this lack of privacy and pervasive surveillance would be considered invasive (at best), but in China, many citizens value safety over privacy. Many profess that they don't mind sharing their data if it means that there will be less crime, better social behavior, and fewer public health risks. As mentioned earlier, according to the World Values Survey, 93 percent of Chinese people value security over freedom, whereas 72 percent of Americans value freedom over security. In China, a large number of people have even signed up for the (so far) opt-in social credit system, which gives you bonus points for being a good citizen (by paying bills on time, volunteering to help the poor, and committing a "heroic" act, for example), and deducts points for poor behavior, which includes anything from committing a traffic offense or participating in illegal protests to not visiting aging parents regularly. Higher scores can earn you cheaper public transport fares, a short security line in subways, or tax breaks. This may all seem mystifying to the Western eye, but many ordinary Chinese citizens find the scheme attractive with its numerous practical benefits.

However, it is a myth that neither the Chinese government nor the Chinese people care about privacy. Room for differences of opinion is slowly emerging. When citizens in the city of Hangzhou denounced its health code app for collecting too much personal information, local officials had to cancel the project. Civilian pressure is also prompting the government to ramp up data protection laws and strengthen consumer privacy. It took the shortest amount of time in the history of Chinese legislation for the government to come up with one of the most stringent data protection laws in the world. A much stricter approval system for governments at various levels to collect data from private platforms is also now in place.

The West denounces the export of Chinese surveillance technologies around the world, but this overlooks the fact that there has been high *demand* from other countries to purchase from China—rather than from the US or Japan—due to high quality at a low price. More than eighty countries have adopted Chinese surveillance and public security platforms since 2008, including liberal democracies as well as repressive regimes. American have been supplying them too—to over thirty countries in 2019. A study by the Brookings Institution in 2020 found that countries with high crime rates are more likely to adopt these technologies, rather than those that are less democratic and free.[9] They are also used to power smart city platforms and smart policing. Crime reduction has been very successful in these countries. For instance, thousands of Indian children who disappear can now be recovered in days; drug criminals are more easily captured in Latin America; in the UK, ubiquitous CCTV cameras have led to improvements in public security.

TECHNOLOGICAL LEAPFROGGING

As we saw with industrialization, it turns out that starting out from behind conveys some surprising benefits. For one thing, a backward economy can adopt the latest technologies directly from advanced economies, thereby skipping all those long, slow, costly intermediary steps. Some developing countries have elected not to build broadband infrastructure, for example, putting their focus on mobile networks instead. Others are circumventing traditional consumer banks by going straight to mobile banking. And developing countries can also make the shift toward the technologies of renewable energy without having to build—and later discard—power plants based on fossil fuel. It is almost always easier to start from a clean slate than it is to demolish an existing structure in order to make way for the new.

When New York International Airport, today known as John F. Kennedy International Airport, was built in 1948, it was the most advanced airport of its time. Today it still functions, so it's still in use, but its infrastructure is far from state-of-the-art. By contrast, in 1948, when JFK was under construction, Beijing was still relying on a converted military airport for domestic air travel, but today its Daxing airport has facial recognition security access, heating and cooling systems based on geothermal heat pumps, and radio frequency identification for baggage tracking. Tearing down JFK to build a smart airport like Daxing makes less sense given the heavy investment already made in the past. The obstacle of legacy is less about the ability to create new technologies than it is about escaping from old ones.

Because mature economies have extensive experience with old technologies, this often makes new ones seem less worthwhile—especially those that appear to offer only incremental benefits in the beginning. There is an argument to be made that sometimes the biggest barrier to creating something truly great is having something already good enough. Several decades ago, the US doubled down on its credit card payment network and became the most advanced player in the payment space. Being so invested in that system led the US to spend the last decade upgrading its bank-based magnetic strip cards into chips.[10] American consumers kept getting new credit cards in the mail from banks and credit card companies as the chips improved, and retailers kept upgrading their chip readers at the point of purchase, all at great expense. China, on the other hand, was free to ride the wave of a revolution in financial technology and create a totally new ecosystem of digital payments. As a result, Chinese consumers scan a QR code with their phones to pay instantly for purchases. And with a few clicks, Chinese consumers can pay, borrow, invest, or even purchase insurance products tailored to their specific needs. Having once been the front-runner, the US now lags far behind in digital payment technologies.

A further burden of legacy is that it creates powerful incumbents with deep-seated interests in maintaining the status quo. Kodak was the first company to develop the digital camera, but it intentionally held back for fear of losing its lucrative business selling rolls of film. Eventually that decision would prove fatal to an iconic company whose future and that of the camera seemed inextricably entwined. Toyota and Ford are well positioned to lead in electric vehicle technologies, but instead it is outsiders like Tesla that are charting new directions; for them the only way to become market leaders is to embrace disruptive technologies. This is the same kind of leapfrogging that has allowed China to take a lead recently in many new fields in technology, including renewable energy, of which it is now a leader.

Backwardness provides another advantage by occasionally spurring radical innovation as a solution to previously unresolved problems, which leads to technological leapfrogging. E-commerce sprung up in China because residents living outside large cities had few traditional retail options. In this arid landscape, companies like Alibaba found an opportunity to bloom and flourish, and now Chinese e-commerce companies are the most innovative in the world. The same holds true for China's financial technology companies, which sprung to life in response to China's inchoate financial industry, which, as we have seen, failed to serve Chinese households and firms. Innovative fintechs also provide the most dramatic benefit to those who live in remote areas, far from the nearest bank branch or even ATM—the customers who first turned to e-commerce. A variety of studies have shown that Ant's big data technology promotes inclusive financing. Ant's MYbank, for instance, services thirty-five million of the country's one hundred million small and medium-size companies. What's more, borrowers' digital footprints serve as a new type of collateral and this additional information can lower default rates.[11]

Legend has it that Jack Ma, Alibaba's cofounder, once bought *yang rou pao mo* (lamb broth) from a street vendor in Xian (the city famous for its ancient terra-cotta soldiers) and took the opportunity to inquire about the seller's experience using Ant's microlending business. The street vendor, not having recognized Ma, described how he was able to get RMB 80,000 (more than US$10,000) in loans that year, allowing him to successfully expand his business. Having no collateral or credit history, the vendor would never have been able to qualify for a loan from a traditional bank, but within a short period of time Alipay gave him one, and a few seconds after it was approved the money was credited directly to his Alipay account.

The first time I tried the app Huabei, it offered me an instant $150 line of credit that I could spend on a new phone or cosmetics, or add a temporary boost to my spending power on Singles Day. The majority of Huabei's five hundred million borrowers are millennials who don't want to miss out on that fabulous sale online because they're waiting for their next paycheck. Another product, called Jiebei (just borrow), gives you access to amounts from $150 to $8,000, typically for a period of twelve months. And those are just consumer products. Tens of millions of small businesses and individual vendors like the lamb broth seller are also taking out loans from MYbank.

During COVID-19, China's fintech allowed financial support to be targeted precisely and delivered conveniently and rapidly through mobile payments—getting insurance products to frontline health workers or small-value coupons to those who needed them.[12] The central bank also provided RMB 590 billion of interest-free loans to MYbank, and encouraged them to use their reach and expertise in lending to assist a group of small businesses to which the central bank had little access. All in all, RMB 8 trillion of loans were extended to over 10 million entities over a three-year time frame.[13]

But along with innovation come new risks, some of which are undetectable at first. Leapfrogging can happen so quickly that policy makers and regulators have difficulty keeping up. Are Ant and Square (now Block) technology companies or financial institutions? If they offer banking services, should they not be regulated like banks?

The situation reminds me of the hedge funds and investment banks in 2008 that eagerly created and sold risky new financial instruments, leading to the great financial meltdown. The perils posed by today's new breed of financial institutions are still unknown, as technology continues to outstrip regulation. Policy makers want to ensure that they're not stifling innovation with cumbersome rules, but China's government is also unwilling to give its billionaire tech entrepreneurs unbridled power. This is why the government has been clamping down, particularly on companies with huge, consumer-facing internet platforms, even ahead of the US, which is trying to legislate limits for giants like Meta Platforms—parent company of Facebook, Instagram, and WhatsApp—and Alphabet, Google's parent company.

CHINA VERSUS THE US: WHO HAS THE EDGE IN ONE TO N TECHNOLOGY?

Of the twenty-five most valuable internet companies in 2020, eleven were American and nine Chinese. Of every ten venture capital dollars invested in AI in 2018, five went to Chinese start-ups and four to American ones.[14] On many fronts, from e-commerce to ride-sharing, it is Chinese and American companies that are competing toe-to-toe. Interestingly, few in the same league have emerged from Europe and elsewhere; the internet technology sphere is split between the two largest economies in the world, partly as a result of the benefits of scale. So a natural question is whether people around the world will be using Instagram or TikTok, riding with Didi or Uber, shopping with Amazon or Alibaba. The die may already have been cast in China and the US, but other parts of the global marketplace are up for grabs. As we try to predict the outcome of competition between the major tech players, some interesting patterns emerge.

In 2017, the Chinese ride-sharing company Didi made its first foray into the Mexican market, where Uber had already taken a dominant position, controlling almost 87 percent of the market. In addition to the handicap of being a newcomer, Didi had some glaring disadvantages compared with Uber. Mexico shares a border with the US, English is more widely spoken in Mexico than Chinese, and Mexicans know much more about American culture than they do about Chinese culture. Yet only a few years later, Didi surpassed Uber as the biggest player, with 56 percent of the market in 2022.[15] While it makes sense that Didi would be the dominant player in the Chinese market and Uber would hold sway in the US, it's significant that in countries like Mexico and elsewhere in Latin America, where the two companies compete head-to-head outside their home markets, Didi is winning the battle.

A closer look at this example points to two very different approaches to new markets. Uber took the model that had proved so successful in the US and tried to replicate it in other countries. Didi's strategy focused on adapting their model to accommodate demographic conditions, cultural norms, and other national characteristics. In Brazil, for instance, where many drivers live from hand to mouth, Didi paid them on a daily rather than monthly basis, which Brazilian drivers vastly preferred. Most didn't have a bank account, so Didi created a one-click bank account application button inside its app for drivers, which also allowed Didi to apply for an account on the drivers' behalf, guaranteeing quick approval and allowing new drivers to receive a bank card within just a few days.

During COVID-19, Didi provided free disinfectant and face shields. Because most Latin American transactions were cash based and exchanging money was particularly dangerous during the pandemic, Didi added a digital wallet to its app. Didi also invested heavily in training centers for its drivers, facial recognition technology to make rides safer, and relationships with local banks to make payment easier. The ride-sharing business model did not originate with the Chinese company, but Didi adapted it in ways that made it more attractive to local markets. By creating what has become the most popular ride-sharing app in Latin America, Didi has now firmly established itself in the US's backyard, despite originating halfway around the world in a completely different culture.

This story speaks volumes about tactics that can tip the balance in competition between US and Chinese tech giants in markets beyond their borders. It is not simply a matter of who has better technology or who commands more cultural appeal. In order to detect some general patterns that can inform us about the future, we need to better understand the structural forces that shape these companies and the markets they compete in. Different tech sectors exhibit distinctive market profiles. Internet search engines are dominated by one player in the world, Google. When it comes to 5G telecom equipment, there are just four global players—Huawei, Ericsson, Nokia, and Samsung. This degree of dominance makes sense given the enormous cost of developing your own alternative. Instead, many countries grant established global giants access to their market, to the benefit of their residents. In other words, it's less than optimal for the Malaysian government to try to build its own search engine, aviation sector, or semiconductor foundries from scratch if that's not necessary.

But the situation is different in the ride-sharing sector, for instance. Unlike search engines, ride-sharing has significant *local* players. For instance, in Southeast Asia, Grab is very popular. In Russia, Uber was forced to merge with its local competitor, Yandex. Ola, an Indian company, wrestles for primacy with Uber in that country. When we turn to e-commerce, the pattern of competition looks similar to ride-sharing, with even more significant local players vying with the global giants, in this case Amazon and Alibaba. In Indonesia, for instance, Shopee and Tokopedia together capture the majority of the market share. In India, the domestic Flipkart is ahead of Amazon in e-commerce, but many other local players are splitting the rest of the market. Even in China, Alibaba now has less than 60 percent of the market, as domestic rivals JD.com and Pinduoduo aggressively stake their claims. By contrast, when we look at online service bookings and recommendations, we see no global giant to reckon with; local services like Yelp in the US or Dianping in China dominate the market.

One important factor that makes market competition look very different in each of these sectors is whether a sector has a global or local externality—that is, whether its technological spillover is more universal or more local. Google's search engine is a prime example of technology with universal benefits. Whatever Google does in India, for example, including the information it collects, is good for the company worldwide; its algorithm is incredibly deft at sorting through an enormous amount of worldwide content to deliver accurate results for each query, regardless of where it's being posed or the language of the user. Amazon also has significant global externalities because its extensive network of global suppliers and sellers means that consumers all around the world can benefit from its wide variety of offerings to buy goods that local e-commerce vendors cannot offer. They also enjoy better matching thanks to Amazon's recommended products, and lower prices due to Amazon's superior global supply chains.

In sectors like these with significant global spillover, whoever has the better technology or product is most likely to dominate the entire global market. This is why the likes of Google, Huawei, and Bitcoin have been clear winners in their respective domains. By contrast, sectors with significant local externalities, such as online delivery and to a certain extent ride-sharing, can accommodate a wide variety of local competitors. Where local taste, niche marketing, or variety is more important, this gives a range of different players an advantage, not just one. Economists categorize products or services in terms of their substitutability. Google and Bing are highly interchangeable in terms of what service they offer. However, Facebook, WhatsApp, TikTok, or Twitter are not the same, even though they all fall under the category of social media, which is why multiple giants, be they American or Chinese, can emerge to grab global markets in this sphere.

This analysis oversimplifies the situation because there are other factors involved, such as entry barriers to competition, the extent of network effects in each sector, and the degree of customer trust required, all of which shape market competition. But having sorted these companies along several important dimensions, we can now look more closely at the state of competition between the two major players in technology, the US and China. Both enjoy the benefit of large domestic markets, but differences in culture, strategy, entrepreneurial approaches, and the role of their government will play a role in shaping the future. Chinese companies may be more successful at producing more anonymous technologies—the kinds that have universal reach without the need for cultural appeal, at least for now. For instance, if Chinese robots, drones, and blockchain technologies become best, they can succeed in capturing significant global market share; the Chinese company DJI controls 76 percent of the drone market in the US, despite the obstacles posed by the US-China trade war. And in areas of artificial intelligence, team China would have an advantage if the next era were all about AI implementation. If it has more to do with breakthrough leaps in algorithms and hardware, the advantage lies with team US.

But there is a reason why WeChat, despite being a truly fantastic app and a massive success in China, has enjoyed less international appeal. Social media has an important cultural dimension, and WeChat is designed mostly to suit Chinese customs, tastes, and demands. However, if the new generation of Chinese entrepreneurs can produce goods that appeal to millennials around the world in the same way that K-pop and TikTok have, then Chinese companies may become serious competitors in this sphere. Until this happens, however, American companies enjoy a significant advantage thanks to the more universal reach of the English language and American pop culture.

Perhaps because Chinese companies have significant experience in dealing with regulatory uncertainty, and also because they have seen how foreign companies have failed in China as a result of their inability to adapt to local circumstances, China may be better at adapting to markets in developing countries where local institutions are incomplete and rules and regulations are not well defined. The fierce domestic competition from which these Chinese companies emerged may also make them more willing to do the grunt work necessary to gain even a slight competitive edge. (The colloquial term for this is "eat bitter.") American companies may be more likely to take their proven model and try to replicate it in as many markets as possible, since often they have the advantage of being the first mover. Chinese companies may be more likely to invest more resources and time in each market, choosing depth over breadth. Their competitive advantage may lie in their ingenuity to win over market share previously held by their competitor. This could explain why Uber is in many more countries than Didi, but Didi has higher average revenues in each market.

Lastly, when it comes to international competition in technology, the role of the state looms large once again. Governments around the world are contemplating reining in big tech, even breaking it up, in the name of antitrust, consumer welfare, and data security. These concerns may be justified. Strong increasing returns to scale means that technology companies are not bound by the natural limits to growth faced by traditional industrial companies. To prevent tech firms from getting too big and using their data in ways that are detrimental to consumers, killing off competition, and suppressing innovation, governments may feel it incumbent upon them to step in and regulate. But the argument becomes more complex when it's applied to international competition. To keep tech companies globally competitive in foreign markets, the governments may be more willing to tolerate these problems and allow firms to stay big or grow even bigger.

Government concerns about consumer protection can lead to very different policies on international competition. In Europe, consumer protections trump efficiency and profits. In China, efficiency and economic success have typically outweighed considerations of consumer welfare, allowing the rapid rise of behemoths and national champions. The US lies somewhere in between. But in the new era in China, as economic equality and consumer welfare rise up the ranks of national priorities, the government is starting to seriously limit the once pampered companies by invoking antitrust laws and new regulations. It also doesn't want a firm to get large enough to challenge the power of the state—an important factor driving the onslaught of regulations and clampdowns that began in 2020.

From Zero to One

China's glitzy, futuristic landscapes of AI-powered smart cities and autonomous vehicles may make European cities look dowdy and middle-aged, but these images belie the reality that China is not yet a pioneer of cutting-edge technologies and pathbreaking inventions. It is one thing to be a fast follower, or an equal peer, and quite another to be a creator. Preeminence in cutting-edge technology, such as software, new materials, or next-generation communications, is important not only because its commercial applications can garner international market share and set international technology standards, shaping norms and the institutions that adopt them. Deep knowledge and know-how also give rise to general-purpose technologies, or GPTs, like electricity, computers, the internet, and artificial intelligence, whose benefits can spill over into the larger economy, creating jobs and inspiring new spin-offs. It gives pioneers a first-mover advantage in securing a lead and shaping markets for years to come. Creating zero to one technology is critical to a country's competitive edge and national security, where advanced technology leads to advanced military capability. When it comes to creating these fundamental breakthroughs, China is rapidly catching up and in some areas even leading the pack, but the gap with the West for the most part is still sizable.

China can manufacture generic drugs, but not branded pharmaceuticals. It is proficient in designing semiconductors, but it doesn't have foundries that manufacture integrated circuits. Chinese medical companies are successful service providers, but they still rely on imports for the latest medical equipment. It is the world's manufacturer and deployer of green energy technologies, but not their inventor. Meanwhile, American start-ups are working on nanobots that can roam around inside our organs, patching up stomachs and performing heart surgeries, like a science fiction novel sprung to life. Even in artificial intelligence, where Chinese companies are highly advanced, their comparative advantage lies in data rather than in the algorithms used for calculation, data processing, and automated reasoning.

Semiconductors, considered the core of future technologies, provide the vital materials and circuitry necessary to produce microchips required to operate everything from a smartphone to an advanced satellite weapons system. But China still cannot make its own highest-grade chips; for years it has been importing critical semiconductor parts. It was not until late 2019 that China's most modern foundry, SMIC, began to create chips from the fourteen-nanometer technology node. (This refers to the physical size of the transistor; the smaller the transistor, the more transistors you can fit in a small space; the faster they switch, the less energy they require, and the cooler they run.) This still put China at least two generations behind the global leaders, Taiwan, South Korea, and the United States. TSMC in Taiwan has been producing seven-nanometer nodes since 2018, is producing three-nanometer nodes in 2022, and will soon have two-nanometer nodes.

Despite investing astronomical sums in research and development over the last few years, China is still dependent on other countries for equipment, materials, or core intellectual property. China imports the advanced equipment required to produce semiconductors, including the extreme ultraviolet scanner—dubbed the most complicated machine on the planet[16]—from Dutch company ASML. Self-reliance here is not easily or swiftly attained. High-end semiconductor production requires skills and advanced processes based on decades of cumulative learning and refinement; that ultraviolet machine, for example, was developed after seventeen years of research at a cost of $9 billion. Huawei's precarious situation after it was banned through US sanctions from producing its chips with its partner TSMC illustrates the fragility behind China's seeming technological strength.

Huawei has since responded by gearing up its chip production capabilities, launching new product lines and services, and rolling out 5G infrastructure unlike anything its closest competitors have seen. It has managed to keep expanding its number of international partners and has seen rising profitability over the years. Despite US sanctions, China's largest chipmaker SMIC started to ship out seven-nanometer chips in

2022, neck and neck with companies like Intel.[17] The race for techno-logical supremacy is often spurred by external pressure—moments like the embargo on semiconductors to Chinese companies. The sense of urgency was intensified by President Joe Biden's sweeping controls in 2022, announced a few days before the convening of the Twentieth Party Congress, which reelected President Xi to a third term. The new set of controls not only added more Chinese companies to the sanction list and banned international companies that use US technology from selling chips and equipment to the Chinese, it also prohibited US personnel from working for Chinese semiconductor companies.

When the Soviet Union launched Sputnik, the first satellite, it galvanized the US to regain its lead role in space exploration. China, awakened with a jolt, has made technological self-sufficiency a national priority in its fourteenth Five-Year Plan (2021–2025) and a spotlight in the party's Twentieth Party Congress, which introduced for the first time a category called *ke jiao xing guo*, which means bolstering the nation through science, technology, and education. The Chinese government is invoking a *juguo* approach, or an "integrated whole-nation scheme," concentrating all sorts of national resources in an attempt to achieve breakthroughs in key technologies, or as the Chinese call it, "throat choking" technologies. This campaign is now in full swing, with an intensity not seen since Chairman Mao launched the Two Bombs and One Satellite program, which succeeded in developing the atomic and hydrogen bombs in record time, and to the musical accompaniment of "The East Is Red," lifting a Chinese satellite into orbit just a few years after the Soviet Sputnik. (Interestingly, that happened under a trade embargo imposed by the West.) This achievement was remarkable, considering that China barely had a modern industrial base and scarce resources at the time.

When a strategic objective has been given a *juguo* designation, cost considerations are set aside. Waste will be tolerated. The essence of the *juguo* system is that the whole nation mobilizes to achieve a strategic goal; it casts the net wide for a big catch, as China did in the quest for Olympic medals to boost national pride and prestige. President Xi Jinping himself has taken over the job of overseeing China's technology advancement, previously under the supervision of a government minister. Mobilizations of this kind are primarily triggered in wartime, but China sees being at the forefront of developing key technologies as a matter of survival.

WILL THE *JUGUO* APPROACH WORK?

We all tend to think of tech superstars like Steve Jobs and Elon Musk as solo trailblazers, but even in the US, government has played a crucial behind-the-scenes role in major technological advances like the internet, personal computers, GPS, touch screens, and microprocessors.[18] The government underwrites important programs like DARPA, the US's Defense Advanced Research Projects Agency, which uses some of its annual budget in the billions of dollars to recruit top talent from university computer science departments around the country. Taking inspiration from the Manhattan Project and the Apollo program, China is building a fully integrated incubation chain linking key national labs, universities, and high-tech industrial parks. In addition, the state aims to create a hundred new tech centers and a hundred more high-tech industrial parks around the country. It has already attracted thousands of researchers and scientists from abroad to reside in China. And as Chinese scientists and academics face growing scrutiny in the US, some find the prospect of returning to China—where research and development in the sciences and technology are generously funded by both the government and private companies—increasingly attractive.

As part of its effort to make China more desirable for basic scientific research, the state has been focusing on strengthening its intellectual property protections. Disputes with other nations over IP set China in the right direction, but the lack of proper safeguards was also posing a major obstacle for domestic companies striving to develop core technology. Enforcement of intellectual property has historically been weak in China, where appropriation of someone else's ideas was never considered a big problem, but now the government has set in place a system of substantial penalties, implemented by IP protection centers around the country, and is working on changing the culture around ideas, beginning in primary school. China has also been building a comprehensive legal framework that promises to be the fastest in the world to investigate and handle IP violations.

As is the case with any grand state objective in China, the central government develops the strategic plan—in this case a *juguo* approach to achieving breakthroughs in key technologies—and local government is called on to deliver. Officials I have met with speak ambitiously of building "unicorn islands," agglomerations of billion-dollar tech companies that they will help nurture. In 2020, I visited a Suzhou high-tech park where companies in biomedicine, semiconductors, and information technology enjoy cheap land, tax breaks, and reduced social security costs. The local government official in charge there explained to me how this "one-stop shop" helps companies find financing and create a high-quality life for employees on a spectacular, Google-like campus. It helps promote research and development collaboration, attracts talent from nearby universities, and takes advantage of national initiatives to recruit overseas talent. All this support allows companies to focus on developing breakthrough technologies without external distractions.

Who could afford to create the new infrastructure for computing, the Internet of Things, and 5G that will allow autonomous vehicles, robots, drones, and facial recognition to function smoothly in society? Only the state, or a company like Google or Amazon, which has the patience and resources needed for risky, imaginative enterprises that may have a significant impact downstream but promise no short-term return on investment. Certainly the ability to provide massive funding, a large pool of internationally trained scientists and engineers, and the will to give its mission a wartime sense of urgency adds wings to China's quest to become the global leader in technology. In 2019, China launched a US$1.4 trillion stimulus plan to invest in new technology infrastructure over six years. Instead of building more bridges and highways as it did post–financial crisis in 2009, China is rolling out wireless networks, installing sensors, and building platforms for an industrial Internet of Things to rejuvenate the post-pandemic economy and make headway in the global technology race. The semiconductor industry benefits from a "Big Fund," which is channeling more than a trillion RMB of private and public investment. Quantum communications, equally, has a "megaproject."[19]

Although these funds are often wasteful and inefficient, the *juguo* approach works particularly well in areas where state funding is paramount, or where costs are of less concern, like space programs, quantum communications, and cybersecurity. Despite the popular wisdom that large state pushes are ineffective, China's have a decent track record. Of the thirty-five or so critical technologies where China is striving for self-reliance, twenty or so have allegedly seen breakthroughs: those in essential algorithms, software, and high-end manufacturing, although less so in semiconductors or biomedicine. Where cost competitiveness and mass production are important, such as advanced chips for end users, the *juguo* approach works less well.

In other novel high-tech sectors where everyone is starting from a relatively equal footing, like renewable energy, electric vehicles, and the green tech supply chain, China is already charging ahead of the US and its other global competitors. However, even if China can take a commanding lead across a wide swath of high-tech areas, this is still not the same as being the consistent *instigator* of technological breakthroughs. Who will be the first to give machines cognitive abilities comparable to or better than our own? Develop a cure for cancer? Create medical therapies that can repair all of our various body parts? Zero to one technology emerges from cumulative learning based on repeated trial and error, countless successes and failures. All of this takes time. It cannot be appropriated, copied, or imported from abroad.

Behind breakthroughs in critical technologies are three key factors: markets, money, and talent. China has arguably the first two of the three. But its weak point is talent, which has led to a dearth of basic research. Although there are a plethora of programmers and engineers, and the greatest number of STEM students graduating in the world, many of them do not go on to pursue a science and technology career. As an example, in semiconductors, less than 15 percent of graduating students majoring in the field actually choose to work for the industry. There will be an estimated gap of three hundred thousand skilled workers in the chip industry by 2025.[20]

Ultimately, quantum leaps emerge from basic research—a deep, broad knowledge base acquired without a specific commercial purpose or aim. It expands through collaboration between universities, national labs, and industry to produce and share knowledge in an environment that fosters learning, curiosity, and exploration. Despite its recent efforts to catch up, China has fallen way behind in this regard, partly because its universities and research centers have historically placed an outsize emphasis on quantity—focusing on the number of academic publications and patents, for example, rather than their quality. Although China leads the world in the number of patents produced, the average quality of these patents is not first rate.[21] Scholars are pressured to publish a large number of papers to get promoted, or to show results to the government cadres, but this doesn't win Nobel Prizes. Close supervision of researchers can also produce a stifling effect on creativity.

AN IMPATIENT NATION

The biggest barrier China faces in becoming the world's leader in zero to one technology is located in its society as a whole. We must not forget that China today is still a $10,000-a-year income nation, and it behaves, thinks, and acts accordingly—with the impatience of a young country, a teenager whose desires and ambitions exceed present capacity. China's youthful national psyche has inspired a nationwide sprint: start-ups become billion-dollar companies within just a few years, high-speed train stations are built in a matter of months, academics are pushed to publish frequently in prestigious journals, and the Chinese government trades access to its markets for foreign technology that fills specific gaps. These are all signs of a nation eager for instant results, quick fixes, and overnight wins.

There is a saying in China that captures its state of mind: *duan, ping, kuai,* or "short, flat, fast." This was originally used to describe a winning strategy in volleyball, but now it serves as a popular prescription for investors: make short-term investments, keep them simple, and look for rapid returns. It also reflects a more general attitude in society at large. It has even been used cynically to describe the marriage marketplace: a brief courtship before tying the knot, limited emotional investment, and a fast track to divorce. An energetic, hardworking, fiercely competitive, and intently focused young nation may produce remarkable short-term gains, but the creation of transformative zero to one technology requires patience—from creators, investors, and institutions alike. It requires learned people—students, researchers, professors, and other scholars—to dedicate themselves to the pursuit of knowledge for its own sake. In other words, creative breakthroughs require patient capital, patient people, and a patient nation.

Fundamental innovation places high demands on civic society. First, the general populace needs to prosper, or at least to be "rich enough."

Only then can it move beyond products that are "good enough"—that make incremental improvements on existing technology. China is not there, at least not yet. In a $10,000-income nation, *duan, ping, kuai* generates ready profits. Because money flows to wherever returns are highest, China's economy will need to exhaust those quick gains from low-hanging fruit before it dedicates its resources to knowledge-intensive sectors that promise the highest returns but also the risk of no returns at all.

The free flow of ideas and knowledge also requires openness, both within China and in its exchanges with the rest of the world. In this age of information, the ability to attract international talent and gain ready access to international technology is indispensable, as is the ability to develop trust. The mindset that encourages creativity by pushing boundaries, that has the audacity to relentlessly challenge established modalities, has hardly been China's strength so far. This is partly cultural: the Confucian virtue of deference to authority and seniority is still widely observed in contemporary Chinese society. It is also a practical accommodation to the reality of a strong state.

Another hindrance China faces is that in a country with now 1.4 billion people, the only feasible means of identifying talent is to rely on standardized testing, which emphasizes quick, tidy answers. Although this does highlight certain kinds of facility, it doesn't identify or reward the kind of deep analysis or out-of-the-box thinking that contribute to breakthrough innovation. So far, neat problem-solving and rote memorization have been more important to a Chinese student's future than creative thinking and imagination. In 2021, the government cracked down on the private tutoring industry, part of an effort to free children from the burdens of being overworked and from overemphasis on test-taking skills that will not prove useful to them or to the nation. In 2022, during the party congress, the leadership committed to improving the education system so as to foster better basic science and nurture talent.

Like the US, China also faces an ongoing dilemma when it comes to regulating tech companies, given their vast and growing power—exercised not just through their wealth (which exceeds that of many nation-states), but also through their pervasive social influence. How can governments establish necessary regulations without discouraging tech companies from innovating in ways that make them global leaders and drive markets? In China, those tech companies being targeted by new rules are largely consumer facing: social media providers, livestreaming services, e-commerce platforms, and delivery services. Both China and the US will continue to struggle to find ways to regulate a fast-moving sector without creating a chilling effect. But some might argue that by limiting the growth of these internet platform companies in China, more resources become available for the deep-tech companies advancing the national goal of breakthroughs where China still has a significant gap to close with the US.

Most important of all is the system of innovation—a construct that is both vertical and horizontal, interlinking many participants, both private and public. A well-functioning system creates the right kind of incentives: universities pursue the advancement of knowledge for its own sake, firms innovate and invest in emerging technologies, and the state plays a supporting role without imposing itself in ways that squelch innovation. Strong intellectual property protection provides additional incentives to come up with new inventions, and market forces contribute their process of "creative destruction" that renders the outdated obsolete while making room for the more technologically advanced.

This core feature of the market economy is an important one to keep in mind in the context of US-China technology competition. Competition can be constructive, as it forces companies to innovate when there is a close competitor in sight; this was the case with the US when Japan dominated semiconductors in the 1980s, or when France and Germany quickly converged on the US in terms of productivity and innovativeness in the 1960s. The response back then was not a series of protectionist pressures or threats to decouple, but geared-up innovation policy, like the research and development tax credit scheme of 1981 adopted by the Reagan administration.

Fast-forward forty years and technological rivalry is increasingly seen as a win-lose situation, evaluated through the narrow lens of national security. But innovation, in the end, permeates society and affects every aspect of our daily lives. Only by harnessing the constructive elements of "competitive cooperation" between two giants such as the US and China can we find vaccines, advance life sciences, and transition to clean and safe energy faster and better. The technological race between the US and China should be more like a race to win more Olympic gold medals—with proper rules and constraints—than like a downward spiral toward confrontation.[22]

Technology is also uniquely intertwined with trust: we choose to shop on e-commerce platforms that won't ship us counterfeit goods or take our money and run; we submit our data to companies, trusting them to handle it with caution; we use cloud services that we know are secure. Trust lies at the very heart of achieving a universal technological standard. Gaining this trust is a tall order, but here China's new generation is making its presence felt. Many founders and CEOs of China's unicorn tech companies are millennials. For many of these young people, making money is not the sole end in itself, but a by-product of providing high quality and value for consumers. Paradoxically, they are more successful as a result. Their influence is helping to create a more patient and measured society, and it is they—rather than the state—who will ultimately meet the nation's technological aspirations by turning whatever advantages the state provides into long-term benefits. They are China's hope of becoming a sustainable zero to one innovator with a global reach.

EIGHT

CHINA'S ROLE
IN GLOBAL TRADE

remember a pair of pink snow boots my father brought back for me in the 1980s when he returned from a business trip to Korea. They were snug, beautifully shaped, and made of full-grain leather. No one had seen anything like them back home, and as I paraded them around, they caused quite a stir in my kindergarten, and even in my father's ministry, where colleagues who went on the same trip got scolded by their wives for not having brought back something equally precious for their own kids. Well-made consumer products like those were simply not found anywhere in China at that time. But it did not take long, only about a decade or so, before the world-famous Silk Market in China became an international phenomenon—a multistory building filled with all kinds of garments, shoes, and textiles that attracted even the first ladies of Western countries when they came on state visits to China. As the story goes, when George H. W. Bush returned to Beijing in the late 1990s and shopped in the Silk Market, the vendor refused payment for his selections. What was so fascinating was that the country I knew when I was growing up, deprived of even the most basic consumer products, became the world's largest exporter of many of the same items less than two decades later. Those boots still remind me of how rapidly China ascended the trading ladder, and how its story is so different from that of many other developing countries.

In 1978, Deng Xiaoping forever changed the fate of the Chinese people when he announced that China was going to "reform and open up." We've seen reform play a crucial role in transforming a nascent Chinese economy and setting it on the path to prosperity, but opening up was every bit as important. With the support of the US after prolonged and difficult negotiations, China finally acceded to the World Trade Organization in 2001, the last step in flinging its trading doors wide open. As the world welcomed 1.3 billion Chinese consumers at that moment and their trillions of dollars of savings into the global economic system, few countries anticipated what would happen as a result of China's access to *their* domestic markets.

In less than ten years, China would become the largest exporter in the world, as Chinese manufacturers churned out a wide range of consumer goods, including clothes, sneakers, furniture, and toys, at prices more affordable than ever before. It would become the largest trading partner to more than 120 countries in 2020, taking over the role played by the US two decades prior. Now people in developing countries in Africa and Southeast Asia could stay connected, with smartphones made in China at a fraction of the cost of an iPhone. What's more, China positioned itself at the heart of the global supply chain by cheaply and skillfully assembling components from various sources into finished products like computers, which were then reexported to other countries. And the Chinese consumer went on a shopping spree, providing a welcome boost to sales of Italian handbags, German cars, Australian beef, American soybeans, and many other commodities around the globe.

Today, Chinese travelers abroad often discover something to buy and take home, only to be disappointed when a closer look reveals that it was made in China. It's not easy to find something that *isn't* made in China, or assembled in China, or built by the Chinese, or funded by Chinese capital. In remote parts of Africa, digital payments are made on platforms designed by Alibaba. Even the self-anchored suspension deck components of the eastern span replacement of the San Francisco–Oakland Bay Bridge were built by a company in Shanghai.

The impact of China's entry into the global trading system was simply unprecedented. The world had seen new markets open up prior to this, but those economies were mostly small—the likes of Korea, Mexico, or Belgium. Subsequently, these countries enjoyed stellar trade growth, but for them the impact *from* globalization was far bigger than their impact *on* globalization. China was different. The size and the speed with which it ramped up its already impressive production machine caught the world by surprise. After joining the WTO in 2001, China's share of global GDP more than doubled by 2020, rising from 7.8 percent to almost 19 percent. Low-wage work from around the world flowed to China, exports from China swamped global economies, and China's growing trade surplus confirmed the higher likelihood of purchasing from China than of selling to it. Before long, Chinese investors became owners of US cinema company AMC and prized brands such as Volvo, evoking memories of Japan in the 1980s.

As China gradually shifted its emphasis from cheap, low-end products to higher-quality goods that had been the exclusive province of wealthy countries, some saw the young trading nation as a blessing, others as a curse, still others as both. Trade frictions with the US came to a head when Donald Trump was elected in 2016 and the US levied new tariffs on the grounds of protecting American jobs. By 2018, the Trump administration had kicked off an all-out trade war with China, accompanied by a level of acrimony not seen since the normalization of diplomatic relations between the two countries. And populist leaders around the world took advantage of the opportunity to blame global trade for their economic troubles at home—including rising inequality, jobless-ness, and political polarization.

The Rise of Chinese Trade

China's swift ascent as a global trade power was not entirely the result of the internal conditions we explored in earlier chapters. Powerful forces in the background also set the stage. For the more than three decades between 1986 and 2008, the world was gripped by a phenomenon that became known as hyper-globalization. During this time, world trade doubled as a percentage of GDP. Cheaper international communication and internet access facilitated connections among people, suppliers, and buyers. The cost of goods fell precipitously. And the cost of transporting them also plunged, thanks to larger, faster, and more efficient ships and aircraft, along with improved logistics in container storage, delivery, and customs clearance.

During this time, the world enthusiastically embraced a more open trading system. Governments rolled back or dismantled man-made trade barriers set up in an era haunted by the two world wars: the world average tariff rate was cut by half from 14 percent.[1] This period saw the rise of the European Union; the signing of the North American Free Trade Agreement (NAFTA) between the US, Canada, and Mexico in 1994; and the creation of the Mercosur trade bloc in Latin America. In Asia, the ASEAN Free Trade Area of 1992 and its later expansions created a trade bloc of ten East Asian nations. The World Trade Organization, established in 1995, slashed average tariff rates to single digits, lowered most-favored-nation tariffs, and granted access to new members.

China came into this receptive environment with a virtually inexhaustible supply of extremely low-cost labor (in 1990, its labor cost was only 1.29 percent of that of the US)[2] as well as a large consumer base. As hundreds of millions of its workers shifted from agriculture to industry, China was unwittingly preparing to become the world's largest factory.[3] It could export labor-intensive goods that didn't require sophisticated production, while countries like the US could focus on producing capital- or skill-intensive goods. Everyone stood to benefit.

Toward a New Paradigm for Global Trade

Today "made in China" is largely a misnomer; it's more accurate to say of most products that they are "made in the world."[4] Countries and regions in the global trading system are deeply intertwined. US goods rely on Chinese parts and Korean components assembled by Taiwanese intermediates, and Chinese parts are made up of Japanese and German components. The new paradigm of trade, accelerated by the information revolution, features the cross-border movement of parts and components like chips, microprocessors, and chemicals. These intermediate goods—goods that are used in the production of larger, more complex products—account for an astonishing two thirds of global trade.[5] An iPhone may be designed in California, but its various components converge from South Korea, the Netherlands, and Taiwan before being assembled in mainland China by Foxconn, a Taiwanese company.

This geographic splintering of production gave rise to what is known as the global value chain. Each phase of production adds value, from initial design and development to assembling the necessary materials, including complicated parts or modules, all the way to the assembly line that churns out the final product for shipping to its eventual destination, where it will be marketed and sold to customers. Each stage can take place in any country, wherever production is most efficient and has the lowest cost. Complex products take shape gradually, often crisscrossing national borders many times before finally being ready for sale or export in finished form.

To make a Mini Cooper, for example, China ships tires to Britain while sending engine parts to Japan for assembly and shipping to Britain. The engine parts, the assembled engine, and the tires are all considered intermediate goods that contribute to the final product. A Boeing airliner has twelve thousand active suppliers from all around the world; the back-and-forth trade in these components is greater than the trade in the airplanes themselves, which is why these intermediate trades dominate the global marketplace. Even the components of a chip can travel twenty-five thousand miles from the US, Korea, and Taiwan to Germany before they are combined into a finished product.[6]

If we map out of a global network of trade, we will see that almost all countries are interlinked. With the exception of Greenland and a few sub-Saharan countries, *every* nation is part of the global supply chain. China, Germany, and the US are the central nodes for most of this global trade flow in goods. Regional trade creates regional hubs: China's strongest trading partners are its neighbors—Japan, Korea, and Vietnam. For the US, Mexico and Canada are its primary trading partners, and for Germany these partners are Italy and France.

When countries work together in this way, each occupies a particular position on the value chain. For a long time, China was mostly doing assembly, receiving intermediate goods like electronic chips and components from countries like Japan, Korea, and the US, and then putting them together and shipping out the final products. For China the benefit of making an iPhone, for example, was very low. In 2009, for instance, out of the $100 retail price, only $1.30 went to the Chinese. In 2018, that number was $10.40.[7] Over time, China has steadily moved to the center of the global supply chain, displacing nations previously holding that position. In 2000, China played a more modest role in the global value chain for textiles, but by 2017, China had become the largest node of the entire chain.[8] In the information and communication technology (ICT) sector, China displaced Japan to take a central place in the supply chain.

Despite the game of musical chairs, having China in the global trade system was an opportunity for everyone, particularly in the new paradigm of trade: China's low production costs and high degree of efficiency lowered the price of intermediate goods, which created a ripple effect throughout the network, boosting profits. Firms could hire more workers and pass on lower prices to consumers. However, a new peril also emerged from this increasingly interconnected world, and from China's prominent position in particular. Trade disruptions in China now had serious knock-on effects for all its trading partners—and ultimately for their consumers.

When factories in China first shut down in response to the global pandemic in 2020, the impact was felt broadly across the entire production network. Korea, which had sourced lots of inputs in China, could no longer supply the components it was producing for countries such as Germany or the US. And when the US could not import these parts from Korea, this disrupted production in other countries, including China—which was sourcing inputs from the US (high-tech products in particular). Supply shocks became demand shocks as the postponement of purchases struck China a further blow. According to the Institute for Supply Management (ISM), about three quarters of American firms were affected by the supply chain disruption emanating from China.

Another event that underscored just how interlinked global trade has become was the trade war between the US and China. On the surface, imposing tariffs on Chinese goods coming into the US may look like a form of punishment for China, but given the elaborate network of interconnections we've seen, American firms and consumers were not spared the negative effects. President Trump's stated intention was to have the Chinese pay for the tariffs, but in reality that cost was borne by American consumers; prices of US intermediate and final goods rose by some 10 percent to 30 percent,[9] which was roughly the size of the tariffs.

American firms were hit hard because they sourced so many intermediate products in China. Higher tariffs on these inputs meant that American firms faced higher production costs, which then squeezed their profits and forced them to lay off workers or raise prices or both. After equipment maker Caterpillar had to pay higher duties on Chinese intermediate goods that increased its production costs by more than $100 million, it had to raise prices on the machinery it produced—a cost hike that eventually hit the pockets of American consumers. And the effect on prices didn't end there. Firms in the same industry jumped on the bandwagon and hiked prices even if they were unaffected by Chinese tariffs. A study by economists at the University of Chicago found that a 20 percent tariff on washing machines resulted in a 12 percent increase in the cost for US consumers. That might be expected, but it ended up driving up the price of dryers to the same extent, because the products are often bought in pairs.

China as a Global Trade Partner: Weighing Opportunity against Threat

These days we hear more about trade friction, disputes, and job losses than we do about the benefits of interdependence, which tends to give populists an amplified voice and nudges countries down the slippery slope of greater protectionism. So, when it comes to trading with China, has it proved to be an opportunity or a menace? Given the high-profile trade clashes between the US and China, this is a good place for us to focus.

Chinese imports appear to have wrought havoc on a certain segment of the population in the US. Between 2000 and 2010, six million manufacturing jobs disappeared in the United States.[10] In some cities that make furniture, like Hickory, North Carolina, the unemployment rate jumped to 50 percent over the national average of 9.6 percent.[11] In the Southeast, overall manufacturing employment dropped 38 percent in the decade following 2000. These events took place during a time of intense penetration of Chinese imports into the US, and economists estimate that roughly two to three million manufacturing jobs lost in the early 2000s were directly attributed to imports from China.[12]

But the full picture appears in more shades of gray. It turns out that two important developments in the background also contributed to the disappearance of US jobs. The first was a boom in technology, especially information technology and the adoption of robotics.[13] Right around the time China joined the WTO, American firms were aggressively acquiring more advanced production equipment. Between 2000 and 2003, the percentage of American manufacturing firms purchasing computers and using electronic networks shot up from 20 percent to 60 percent.[14] This wholesale adoption of technology inevitably affects labor: computerization, supply chain management, and automation rendered skilled workers more productive while making other workers redundant.

The second important trend was that American manufacturing had already been in decline *decades* before China came into the picture. Manufacturing employment in the US peaked in 1979 and started to decline with the use of labor-saving technologies and outsourcing to countries like Mexico and Japan. What's more, researchers found that manufacturing employment declined substantially in the early 2000s even in areas where there were virtually no Chinese imports—or trade, for that matter.[15] But the reason the China shock hurt so much was not just the number of jobs lost, but the fact that it hit the most vulnerable sectors—like toys, footwear, and apparel—which were already on the decline.[16] Affected workers had lower levels of education, and the geographical areas hardest hit had higher unemployment rates before the arrival of Chinese goods. Chinese imports made these preexisting vulnerabilities painfully apparent. And as one industry, like automobiles or apparel, got hit, employment in surrounding areas was likely to suffer too. Locating producers of specialized inputs nearby makes production more efficient, but the downside is that entire regions can get hollowed out by external shocks.

A big part of the problem in the US is that manufacturing, which was previously open to low-skilled workers, has become increasingly skill oriented over time. The skill mismatch in the country explains much of the decline in labor demand in manufacturing. As Anne Case and Angus Deaton observe in their thoughtful book *Deaths of Despair and the Future of Capitalism*, globalization and China are often held up as villains because they replaced uneducated domestic workers with cheaper foreign labor. But the US's long-term stagnation of wages is unique compared with other rich countries that equally faced globalization and technological change. As the authors suggest, "There is something going on in America that is different . . . and particularly toxic for the working class," which they ascribe to oppressive monopolies and American institutions that have consistently weakened unions and empowered employers, allowing them to profit at the expense of ordinary workers.[17]

As difficult as the surge of inexpensive Chinese imports was for certain sectors in the US, Chinese imports created many jobs as well. When Chinese businesses build factories in the US, they create employment. According to the US-China Business Council, Chinese multinationals employ 197,000 American workers, and US exports to China support another 1.2 million American jobs.[18] Where job losses from trading with China tend to be concentrated in a small subset of manufacturing sectors, job creation is spread throughout the US economy, including many modern service sectors. This is also true in Europe, where Chinese companies like Huawei and Lenovo have established a substantial presence and employ tens of thousands of employees, while Alibaba's e-commerce is ranked among the top in Eastern Europe and is now expanding into other parts of Europe. Jobs can also be created there through substantial Chinese investments in European infrastructure.

Studies find that, on balance, at least as many US jobs have been created through its exports to the world as have been lost due to imports. Another study finds that when considering the entire supply chain with upstream and downstream channels, trading with China created more jobs on net.[19] Others show that manufacturing jobs that were displaced were more than offset by more productive jobs in marketing and management, data processing, or finance.[20] Apple is the paragon of this model: shift physical production of the products outside the US but grow the design, marketing, and retailing part of the business at home. It raises American profitability, productivity, and value-added. Of course, this is good news for the more educated workers and bad news for the less educated. The problem, however, is not trade itself, but rather the erosion of jobs and community destruction that have brought into sharper focus the unequal distribution of trade gains and the failure of governments to remediate and compensate those who have lost out. China's arrival made that point even more painfully clear.

These facts tend to be ignored amid the sometimes heated political rhetoric. When jobs are lost to competitors overseas, it's more palatable politically to frame global competition as "us against them" than it is to admit that government could be doing more and better. Viewed from an economist's perspective, without the distraction of politics, there are roughly seventy thousand steel workers in the US, but close to ten million workers in the auto industry, and hundreds of millions of American consumers. Slapping tariffs on products from the steel sector could arguably save a few thousand jobs, but many more would be lost in downstream sectors like the automobile industry, which uses steel as an input. Nor does this consider the cost to companies hit by retaliatory tariffs, and to consumers in terms of higher prices. Ultimately, protectionist efforts to resuscitate sectors threatened with extinction may create political cover or render favors for special interest groups,[21] but they distract policy makers from more productive solutions, like supporting emerging technologies that contribute to high-paying jobs and a vibrant future.

It is interesting to note that Chinese imports affected Western European countries less.[22] The reason is that these countries were already exposed to low-cost competition from countries such as Greece and Turkey. China's arrival went on to displace jobs in those countries, especially in industries such as textiles and apparel, rather than those in France, Germany, and Scandinavia. Germany in particular also benefited substantially from integration with Eastern European countries early on, and its surging exports to both China and Eastern Europe offset manufacturing jobs that were lost. Moreover, European governments did a much better job in retraining their workers and finding them new jobs. Germany, France, and Denmark devoted 0.20, 0.37, and 0.60 percent of GDP, respectively, in 2015 to public spending for worker training, while that number was 0.03 percent in the US.[23] Sweden has an efficient network of job security councils, jointly run by industries and unions, that retrain laid-off workers and help them find new jobs. Germany's national unemployment agency transformed itself into a job-matching entity that gives not only career advice but also vouchers to cover retraining costs. For these reasons, Chinese imports caused less of a disruption in their labor markets.

The negative impact of Chinese imports on low-wage workers in America is indelible, and irreversible for many. But the story of trade wrecking the economy is seriously distorted without carefully examining the benefits of trading with China. As Case and Deaton observe, it has also brought about a "great upheaval" in America. Firms are more productive and more profitable thanks to less expensive intermediate imports. And by offshoring to China, American multinationals reduced costs and located themselves close to a huge market with growing disposable income. More efficient supply chains that included China in a central role led to gains for the large number of countries involved. When it comes to the customers for these products, Chinese imports have provided American consumers with more affordable furniture, clothes, toys, and gadgets at increasingly higher quality.[24] And with remarkable variety. Goodbaby, for example, offers a massive selection of strollers, car seats, bassinets, and playpens—four times as many different options as its closest competitor—all at mass-market prices. Haier has made its wine storage refrigerators a mainstream category sold through America's Sam's Club at less than half the original price.

Less-well-to-do consumers benefit most. They spend a higher share of their income on traded goods than rich households (which spend proportionately more on services), and many of these goods come from China. This has significant implications. Although trade can widen wage gaps between the skilled and unskilled, it can also reduce *real* income inequality between these groups. If a household's income remains unchanged but the price of the goods it consumes fall by 20 percent, it is effectively 20 percent richer; real income disparity shrinks. An important study estimates that if trade were to be shut off, the bottom 10 percent income bracket would lose 63 percent of real income on average, in comparison to only 28 percent for the top 10 percent income group.[25]

There are also positive effects from competition, which can be unforgiving but also generative: European or American companies faced with an existential threat from Chinese rivals were forced to innovate and raise their game. Consider a manufacturer of athletic footwear in America or Europe that enjoyed a profitable position in a mature market. The sudden influx of sneakers made in China could potentially be catastrophic for this company, were it to compete solely on the basis of cost. Only by focusing more clearly on its clients and catering to their specific needs—by customizing and adding unique features like ergonomic benefits, or ways to measure your pulse, for instance—could a company like this survive. Faced with competition from China, many such firms went into overdrive, investing in innovation, upgrading quality, developing new products, and seeking out new niche markets.

Ariens, a Wisconsin snow remover and lawn mower company founded in 1933, had never faced competition as stiff as Chinese imports in the 1990s and early 2000s. It responded with a huge investment in research and development and training its workers, giving birth to a revolutionary new mower that went on to dominate the market.[26] When Marlin Steel Wire Products, a Baltimore producer of wire baskets for bagel shops, was pushed by Chinese competition to the brink of insolvency, the company started investing in automation.[27] After spending millions on modern equipment, not only did it survive, it prospered, and now exports to both China and Mexico.

In a seminal study, three economists showed that the threat posed by Chinese imports spurred innovation in Europe, accounting for 14 percent of Europe's technology upgrades between 2000 and 2007.[28] Increases in patenting, IT, and productivity in Europe can be attributed to pressure from Chinese imports. Although there is no conclusive evidence that Chinese competition did the same for US innovation, there is evidence that companies that invested more in research and development were substantially better shielded from low-cost Chinese competition.[29]

Trade's Thorny Issues

For all the benefits that can be enumerated, there's no doubt that the roses of globalization are accompanied by thorns. When those thorns prick, China, as the largest exporter in the world, becomes embroiled in disputes not just with the US but also with other advanced economies.

The most important of these focus on China's state subsidies, its restrictions on foreign investment, and its demands for technology transfers, subjects we've mentioned in earlier chapters. More broadly, these are emblematic of a whole gamut of disputes between developing countries and rich nations under the current global trading system. Leaving politics aside, there are real dilemmas in the global trading system to grapple with. One of the biggest challenges in the current system is that domestic agendas often get waylaid by obligations to the World Trade Organization.[30]

For one thing, what constitutes "fair trade" according to global trading agreements embodied in the WTO means different things to different people, depending on their perspectives and interests—and the views held by advanced economies and developing countries are often diametrically opposed. Many developing countries feel that WTO rules or conditions imposed on lending by international organizations like the World Bank and the IMF are too stringent and hamstring these economies in their bid for development. Developing countries have good reasons to nurture and protect infant industries through subsidies, since exposing them too early to international competition would nip them in the bud. *Selective* opening up, such as using capital controls and liberalizing their exports before their import sector, was always how nations succeeded in globalization. Great Britain and the US were no exceptions: both engaged in nationalistic policies such as subsidies, supporting state-owned enterprises, and government direction on banking credits, at the same time they reduced tariffs.[31] The same strategy allowed Japan and Korea to nurture global giants such as Toyota and Samsung, whereas Latin American and African nations that followed the rich nations' advice of flinging open their doors were never able to develop the same capabilities.

What's more, as developing countries see it, the advanced countries that established the rules of global trade game stacked the cards in their favor, protecting their own weaker or interest-laden sectors like agriculture and textiles, for example, while requiring developing countries to lower barriers in their weaker sectors, like advanced manufacturing. Developed countries make the rules, such as what constitutes subsidies, and then play around these rules. Korean economist Ha-Joon Chang makes this point forcefully in his book *Bad Samaritans*. He cites the example of Japan and the US, which were so keen to pry open Korea's financial sector and industry that they made that access a precondition for financial support from the IMF during the East Asian crisis in 1997.

On the other side of the debate, advanced economies argue that countries like China have taken advantage of the WTO system by using their status as developing countries to subsidize state companies and violate intellectual property rights. (WTO rules give developing countries more leeway to pursue their domestic strategies and tolerate a certain amount of infringement on intellectual property.) When it first joined the WTO, China undisputedly qualified as a developing country with roughly a thousand dollars of per capita GDP. But there is growing external pressure for China to change its status. A nation hovering around ten thousand dollars of per capita GDP twenty years later still qualifies it as a developing county, but Beijing and Shanghai also enjoy income levels almost on par with rich nations like Korea. China's mature industries and technology in some areas rank among the best in the world, as we saw in the previous chapter. But the situation is complex, as the country still has also over six hundred million people with US$140 monthly income.

In 2001, when the World Trade Organization finally gave China an admission ticket, China had a small footprint in the global economy. Agreements negotiated then made sense at the time, but China transformed itself at a pace that far exceeded anyone's imagination. When exceptions carved out for developing countries were applied to China, few could have predicted the impact on the rest of the world. When

China provided subsidies to its steelmakers and solar panel manufacturers, for example, this resulted in a significant tumble in global prices and massive oversupply. Even if lower prices for clean tech may have been good news for the environment, the friction they caused in the trading system has largely overshadowed that benefit.

WTO rules prohibit state subsidies for exports that distort foreign markets. The problem is that all nations provide state subsidies, sometimes huge ones, for sectors like energy, agriculture, and manufacturing. Advanced economies are no exception. And where the marketplace does not provide sufficient incentive to invest in sectors essential to mitigating the effects of the climate crisis, for example, then it makes sense for the government to step in. Furthermore, it is often difficult to discern whether this support is aimed at exports and adversely affects fair competition. In the US, companies like GM, GE, Ford, and Boeing all receive subsidies. Arguments that this doesn't distort international markets seem implausible, but establishing that the US has violated WTO rules requires proof that other countries were hurt in the process—a difficult evidentiary threshold to meet. This is why disputes over subsidies are so difficult to resolve. And it's not just subsidies that spark contention. The WTO's reach extends to domestic tax systems, food safety rules, environmental regulations, and industrial promotion policies, all of which can be challenged by the organization's trading partners.

There is a growing general consensus that the design of the WTO system is flawed. It has many loopholes, and enforcement is spotty. Bringing a large number of very different economies under one roof with a system of fair rules is inherently challenging, and there is work to be done in getting it right. The rules need to be updated with regard to data flow, e-commerce, environmental protections, and labor rights; they also need to focus more on the flow of goods, and less on trade in services, which disproportionately benefits the US. In order for the WTO to stay relevant, it will have to get both the US and China on board. But in the last few years, the two countries have mostly wrestled with trade disputes bilaterally.

For China's part, there are a number of things it can do to ensure continued engagement with the global trading system. It could acknowledge its higher level of development relative to other developing economies in many areas. Subsidies to state-owned entities also could be phased out for China's own good. State support may succeed in bolstering a few strategic industries, but it also keeps unproductive state enterprises afloat for too long, diverting resources from productive firms and wasting money. This change would also create a more level playing field for foreign companies competing in the same areas, thereby improving China's image. Direct state subsidies in China outside of strategic SOEs are becoming fewer and farther between, but pressuring China to abandon its state capital model for the sake of trade negotiations is unrealistic and unlikely to lead anywhere.

Still, in many ways outside pressure on China to change some of its practices may be a gift in disguise. China's new foreign investment law prohibits forced technology transfers (one of the core areas of dispute), and stipulates punishments for government officials involved in the process. Years back, China scrapped thousands of laws and created new ones to meet conditions for WTO membership, making domestic companies more efficient and disciplined. China also modified its practices when it lost a WTO ruling and recorded a better track record than the US. Since 2001, there have been forty-seven WTO complaints lodged against China, but more than twice that number against the US in the same period. And only two out of the forty-seven saw a second filing, indicating noncompliance, compared to fifteen ignored by the US.[32] This is what the Chinese refer to as *dao bi ji zhi*, a "lock-in" situation in which there is no escape route but to move forward, such as with reforms. In this way, opening China up further, making it more market oriented, and protecting innovation more forcefully are in China's long-term interest anyway at this stage. Bilateral skirmishes have accomplished little while inflicting losses on both sides. But the multilateral system has so far been the most effective and civil way to resolve trade disputes, pushing all trading partners—including China—to comply with its rules.

It's important to recognize that China's rise as a global trading power is based on the success of its own economy. It then rode the rising tide of hyper-globalization to become an important link in the global trade network. Higher waves are good for a skillful surfer, and China took full advantage of its productivity, low-cost labor, and streamlined infrastructure and logistics. These factors outweigh controversial subsidies and exchange rate imbalances, which, even if China fully addressed them, would not bring back American or European manufacturing jobs. Jobs in those vulnerable sectors would have been lost anyway, as we have seen, either to technology or to other low-cost countries.

Competition is rarely comfortable; what is good for Pepsi may not be good for Coke. But when one company creates a better product as a result of that competition, the consumer benefits, and eventually, if they survive, both companies do as well. Trade wars have proven to be a recipe for lost productivity and waste that, in the end, benefits no one. Ultimately, domestic problems and poorly devised domestic policies, not the success of foreign competitors, lie at the root of a country's loss of competitiveness. To create jobs in Europe or in the US, companies there will have to innovate and become more competitive, and governments will have to do their job of preparing their workers for transitions. That should always be the first line of defense, not protectionist policies. China, too, will have no one else to blame should it face declining industries, slowdowns in productivity, and financial crises that lead to a more divisive and unequal society. Unfortunately, "the ability to perceive adversaries as all bad and to perceive oneself as all good," as described by psychologist Charles Osgood, captures some of the current mood when it comes to global trade.

What's Next?

These days the future of globalization looks murky. Protectionism is on the rise, and against a backdrop of geopolitical tension and a global pandemic that disrupted supply chains for everything from microchips to N95 masks, talk of deglobalization and decoupling fills the air. Meanwhile, the US waged a "chip war" against China, adding to the disruption of an already fragile supply chain. For all the benefits globalization has brought, it has become a popular scapegoat for the problems the world is facing, and in this narrative, China features prominently. Yet despite these sentiments, experience tells us that globalization is, in the words of business writer Zachary Karabell, "easy to hate, convenient to target, but impossible to stop."[33] Beyond all the sound and fury, the data shows that no deglobalization is in sight. The pace of expansion has slowed down since the 2008 financial crisis, as the positive forces mentioned earlier in this chapter are running out of steam. But not only has global trade volume recovered after every setback, it quickly exceeded pre-crisis levels. This is true whether it was the financial crisis of 2008, when world trade volumes plunged more than twice as much as world GDP, or during the pandemic in 2020.

New forms and patterns of globalization are taking shape at the same time that some aspects are rupturing. Service trade enabled by technology has burgeoned. Digital trade is booming. Video streaming, online education, e-commerce, and telemedicine have all been boosted by greater internet connectivity and the remote participation technology so widely adopted during the pandemic. Companies around the world are selling their products on platforms like Amazon, Alibaba, and Facebook. Alibaba is making inroads into Europe, competing with Amazon. Shein, which sells Chinese-made fast fashion through TikTok and YouTube, has become a phenomenon with American millennials. Consumers are no longer just finding Chinese products in Walmart, Best Buy, Tesco, and Carrefour, but are purchasing them directly from Chinese and American internet platforms. Technology will continue to spur global trade to new levels, regardless of populist outcries.

For all that globalization itself will be a constant, the roles of its major players are very much in flux. As China's share of labor-intensive exports continues to fall and its share of research- and skill-intensive exports continues to rise, competing with China in the global trading system will take on new meaning. Rather than continuing to flood European and American shores with cheap clothes, toys, and furniture, China will be moving up the value chain to make more sophisticated products that directly compete with those made in Japan, Germany, and the US, from chemicals and electronics to batteries.[34] It also will be joining those countries in a new kind of manufacturing that deploys next-generation technology, such as artificial intelligence, robotics, and big data, making production more efficient and less costly while successfully improving its quality. For instance, in China artificial intelligence already powers production lines run by robots that operate 24/7, unattended and uninterrupted, replacing humans performing dangerous, high-intensity work. Haier, the company that exports refrigerators and washing machines to the US, has created "connected factories" so that customers with specific requirements can enter them into an interactive platform and come away with a tailor-made refrigerator or washing machine. Haier's delivery times have been cut in half, and operational costs reduced by 20 percent. Like that company, more and more Chinese manufacturers are adopting smart equipment and user-friendly interfaces.

This shift may sound alarming to advanced economies whose comparative advantage lies in highly trained workers and sophisticated technology. However, there is a fundamental difference between low-skill and high-skill industry. The former produces good that are highly substitutable; whoever makes that T-shirt cheaper will displace the competition. The high-tech sector, however, allows for more differentiation and variety, making it possible for more companies to find ways to coexist within the same sphere. Apple and Xiaomi phones are competitors, for example, but one features higher quality at a higher price, and the other offers good quality at a lower price. Chinese telecom equipment and cloud services are particularly popular in developing countries because they offer access to high-tech infrastructure at competitive prices, so developing countries may become the main destination for these high-tech Chinese products.

In the future, China will strive to be a bigger but more forward-looking Germany, with an unparalleled industrial capacity powered by disruptive technologies. In the fourteenth Five-Year Plan (2021–2025), upgrading manufacturing is a clear focal point. For China, it is not a version of the financialized and service-oriented US that will ensure its security and strength. Instead, the government explicitly states in the plan that the focus should be on building up the "real economy," investing in know-how and specialized skill so as to climb up the value chain and become an even more critical node in the global supply chain.

When the Japan shock hit the US economy for a decade beginning in 1975, it struck less swiftly and with less force than the China shock in the early 2000s. And low-skill US workers didn't bear the full brunt of new competition from Japan, which mostly affected high-ticket items like cars, electronics, and machinery; because these industries enjoyed above-average levels of income and education along with below-average rates of unemployment, they adapted quickly and were spurred to improve. Nor did it take too long before retrained workers were able to find new jobs. It didn't, however, prevent a wave of anti-Japanese sentiment in the US in the 1980s. This experience provides reasons to believe that China's move up the production value chain may not produce the same side effects on low-wage workers or cause massive dislocations such as the ones triggered by the earlier years, but at the same time, national angst is unlikely to subside.

Within China itself, things are changing. Labor costs are rising sharply and growth is slowing down, catalyzing a flight of low-end manufacturing to its Asian neighbors. A friend of mine recently reminded me that the type of inexpensive shirts he bought in America fifteen years ago that were made in China are now made in Vietnam. But it's not just T-shirts; the prolonged pandemic lockdowns and geopolitical tensions with the US have increasingly prompted companies like Apple and Google to shift some of their smartphone production to India and Vietnam.[35]

This may be an inevitable trend. But there are positive developments, too, that come with economic maturation and social evolution. Chinese companies are less interested in a race to the bottom—squeezing competitors out of the market by slashing prices and profits and working employees to the bone. Chinese firms are also subject to increasingly stringent environmental standards as the nation moves away from record levels of air pollution and toward a green, sustainable economy, leading to higher costs. And at the same time that young people in China are becoming more interested in leisure and less willing to put up with working long shifts on a factory production line, the government itself is discouraging the nine-nine-six work ethic so young people can have more children and help ease China's looming demographic challenges. Yes, there will always be highly motivated only-child trailblazers seeking to leave their mark on the country and the world, but other young people are choosing a life of carpe diem, or becoming part of the *tang ping* (lying flat) phenomenon, pursuing a minimalist approach to work and income. As all these domestic forces gather strength—and as countries like India,

Malaysia, Thailand, Indonesia, and Vietnam increasingly take on the mantle of low-cost manufacturing—they will support China's shift away from cheap labor and endless work and toward high-value production embodying more research, knowledge, and skill.

This also means that the time-honored complaint about Chinese trade—its large trade surplus against American deficits—is becoming less relevant to the debate. Trade surpluses resulted from Chinese working too much and consuming too little, and as we have seen from the trade wars, there is not much that tariffs, embargoes, or trade policies could do to change this trade imbalance. The changing behavior of people as they become more prosperous is far more likely to redress these imbalances over time. It also helps that where the focus of Chinese producers was once on how to sell more to foreigners, now it has been redirected to selling more to the Chinese.

THE RISE OF ECONOMIC NATIONALISM

Although globalism is a genie that refuses to go back into the lamp, geopolitical forces, trade policies, and ruptures in the supply chain ecosystem are pushing many countries toward economic nationalism. China's response has been to shift its priorities so that economic growth is accompanied by a new emphasis on its own domestic marketplace. This is reflected in the concept of "dual circulation" that constitutes a central component of China's fourteenth Five-Year Plan, of two engines simultaneously propelling its economy. One keeps China open to the world ("international circulation"), and the other develops self-reliance by developing its own market ("domestic circulation"), in ways that reinforce each other. To some observers, these policies signal an inward turn.

Indeed, the same Five-Year Plan and the most recent party congress place enormous emphasis on developing China's own high-tech sector, as we've seen. A full-on national effort is being directed to wean China off foreign-made, high-end microprocessors and other critical parts by developing its own. But there is no contradiction, in the minds of the Chinese, when it comes to continued openness and greater self-reliance. Quite the contrary. The data points to much greater opening up, which was reiterated in the Twentieth Party Congress. Sectors that were previously off-limits, such as financial services, are now open to companies with 100 percent foreign ownership. By joining a group of fifteen Asian countries that has formed the world's largest trading bloc, the Regional Comprehensive Economic Partnership (RCEP), in early 2022, China has committed to fully open at least 65 percent of its service sectors. At the same time, China is experimenting with creating free trade zones within the country, such as the Hainan Free Trade Port, where companies would be exempt from the usual customs controls and other government restrictions, giving them free access to overseas goods and funds. It is actively seeking new ties with trade partners and solidifying established connections in neighboring regions, where its near-term ambition of leadership lies.

China needs the world, and the world needs China—even if in some instances it is "cold politics but hot economics." Foreign direct investment in China continued to reach record highs even after the outbreak of trade wars with the US. A crucial factor is that foreign companies selling a lot to China will want to locate manufacturing facilities close to the "home market," so goods that are made there can be sold directly, avoiding extra shipping costs and customs. Tesla is a case in point. Its most advanced manufacturing plant is located in Shanghai, and the company is betting on its low cost, cutting-edge infrastructure, and logistics; above all, Tesla wants to sell directly to Chinese customers. For the same reason, very few Japanese companies in 2022 are planning to downsize or exit the Chinese market despite China's stringent COVID-19 restrictions, while many more plan to expand. Japanese automakers are convinced that China's lucrative market is worth the risk of overreliance on Chinese supplies, or even having their technology being transferred, to the point of cultivating domestic competitors.[36] Beyond selling to customers, many international companies speak of China as being the "fitness center" and "testing ground," where demanding Chinese consumers ruthlessly drive companies to offer better and more innovative products. Foreign clothing brands, some of which have suffered from backlashes resulting from provoking nationalist sentiments by broaching sensitive political issues, are willing to be more circumspect when engaging with the Chinese public. The Swedish clothing brand H&M returned to Alibaba's e-commerce platform a year after its stores were closed due to Chinese boycott.

Tim Cook, CEO of Apple, has described on numerous occasions how China has fashioned itself into a vital source for the company, with its unique mix of advanced manufacturing and craftsmanlike skill that meets the company's high threshold for quality and precision. Multinational trade of this type is massively important: about a *quarter* of global output is produced by multinationals like Apple, Nike, Toyota, and Unilever, with a large amount of that trade conducted through its affiliates in places like China. The US, for instance, has $5 trillion in sales that take place through foreign affiliates of multinational firms, compared to about $1 trillion worth of exports shipped out of the country itself.[37]

Thus, even in a post-pandemic world, global supply chains and global interdependency will still be as important as ever, and China's role still indispensable, albeit altered. Consumers around the world will still demand lower prices, and firms will still want to import parts from other countries if they are cheaper than those domestically produced. Global supply chains still provide more scope for diversification than if countries were to do it all on their own, as most shocks are local rather than global (pandemics being the exception rather than the rule). For all the sound and fury of the trade wars, their impact on the US-China trade deficit has been negligible. Instead, both imports and exports between the two countries *rose* in 2020. It is not so easy to shrug off China as a trading partner or replace the megasize manufacturing powerhouse, inconvenient as the truth may be. One fifth of South Korea's imports come from China, which is also Korea's top export market. China is Japan's largest trading partner. It is unlikely that small economies like that of Vietnam will be able to step in and take over a big chunk of Chinese production anytime soon, being the size of a second-tier city in China. And China's efficiencies go beyond scale to include infrastructure and logistics, thanks to the world's leading supply chain management system and to the ease of doing business relative to other developing countries. A number of global firms that explored moving their production to Vietnam had to battle with endemic corruption, only to find that overall costs were still lower in China.

China's connectedness with the world is likely to deepen, but the trend cannot be taken for granted. For all of its intentions of greater integration, China is juggling many priorities and struggling to balance domestic concerns against external pressures. Extended lockdowns and restricted travel, as well as the mounting tensions between the US and China, are driving foreign enterprises toward a wait-and-see mode. People-to-people ties are weakened without physical interaction, and some international companies are struggling to retain foreign staff. It won't be easy to rekindle the past excitement around the second-largest economy, but it may be equally difficult to pass off the opportunities presented by the world's largest middle-income group.

In the longer term, the world is caught in a dilemma with regard to China, ambivalent about this rising superpower that is in many ways different from any before. On the one hand, leaders in the West want to see China take up more global responsibilities, sharing the burden of maintaining international peace and security, as well as global economic and financial stability. On the other hand, they are not yet comfortable with China wielding influence on the global stage that is commensurate with its economic size and newfound power.

For China's part, it seeks a form of global leadership in which it plays an active role in shaping international norms and rules. To that end, China has become one of the largest contributors to the UN, the WHO, and the IMF, while helping fund the World Bank, the Asian Development Bank, and other multilateral cooperative mechanisms. It is unwilling to subordinate itself, but neither does it aspire to dominate. It strives to be self-sufficient only to avoid precarious dependence on others. It believes it has a right to prosperity for its people, and to a role in international affairs befitting its status as a major power. It has made strong official statements supporting a peaceful rise, while rejecting the notion idea that "great powers must be hegemonic" (*guo qiang bi ba*).[38] China's insistence on the coexistence of nations with different values, political systems, religious beliefs, and economic models departs from the US's advocacy of universal democracy. Reserving judgment on the absolute in favor of the practical, China believes that economic cooperation can transcend inherent national differences. Interestingly, for much of modern history it was European pluralism that was committed to an ideal of diversity, and it is the spirit of diverse opinions that permeates American universities today.

China's interactions with the rest of the world must also be seen as part of an evolution. For instance, its early economic ties with Africa were primarily driven by the desire to acquire natural resources. But over time China recognized the need to cultivate a more sustainable relationship, investing in a wide range of industries, helping African governments construct industrial parks that tap into China's own experience, and building hospitals, infrastructure, and schools for African communities.

China understands the need for cooperation when it comes to tackling threats to humanity. It would require a joint effort from the international community, and especially from China and the US. The challenge is whether the two economic superpowers can compartmentalize their differences from the areas in which they can collaborate, and not let one contaminate the other. Climate change, environmental degradation, global pandemics, terrorism, and cybersecurity cannot be successfully addressed without close cooperation between the world's largest powers. In important areas, China has turned words into deeds. It accounts for a third of the global investment in renewable energy. It invests over $50 billion of research and development into clean energy every year and is quickly becoming a global hub for energy innovation.

The country is also committed to achieving carbon neutrality by 2060. Chinese companies are deeply involved with their American, Japanese, and European counterparts in developing a variety of green innovations, including energy storage and electric vehicles. In spite of trade frictions and geopolitical disputes with major economies, China has met with much less distrust when it comes to leading the green revolution around the world. But as China and the US together account for 40 percent of global energy consumption and emissions, and 50 percent of global coal use, decoupling these two major powers would disrupt the green initiative when it is needed most.

Even when the rhetoric between sovereign states becomes heated and high-pitched, this cannot be permitted to stand in the way of those all-important shared interests. The finger-pointing that sometimes serves as diplomacy must give way to the real thing. Threats to information channels that link the young—the universities, the study-abroad programs, the collaborative projects, and the fluid movements of people—undermine stability and peace. Instead, we must nurture the ties that bind—global trade plays an important connecting role here—as well as keep seeking to understand each other as fellow global citizens.

With the possible exception of India, no country will ever emerge to match China's impact on the global economy. The world has transformed since China stepped onto that global stage, and in an age of information, other developing countries are unlikely to be able to produce and trade their way to middle-income status. The marginal cost of manufacturing is falling dramatically, especially for wealthy nations, as automation and 3D printing and other labor-displacing technologies come online. Yet as the trade chapter of China's dramatic impact on the world is drawing to an end, another is beginning. China's participation in global finance is still way behind the curve relative to advanced economies, but China is taking steps to close the gap and become an international financial power.

NINE

ON THE WORLD'S
FINANCIAL STAGE

f we were to fast-forward two hundred years and look back on global finance in the twenty-first century, we might see China stepping into a new role as the world's financial anchor, much the way Britain did in the nineteenth century and the US did in the twentieth. Those two countries shared important qualities. Both were the world's largest economies at the time, and both were responsible for making massive investments beyond their own shores. In the nineteenth century, Britain financed the creation of a far-flung colonial empire as well as infrastructure in various independent nations, including many in Latin America. The US accounted for more than 40 percent of the all the foreign investments made between 1975 and 1980,[1] taking on the mantle of the world's largest banker. And just as London and New York became preeminent centers of international finance, the pound sterling and the dollar became the reigning currencies of their times.

Globalization is not limited to the flow of goods across borders. It's also about the flow of capital. Chinese banks lend to African countries so they can build infrastructure; American companies finance new factories and assembly plants in China; and British citizens acquire Apple and Google stock on American stock exchanges. This global circulation of capital, which includes foreign direct investment, equities and bonds, and bank loans, rose 800 percent between 1990 and the financial crisis in 2008, concurrent with the period of hyper-globalization we saw in the world of trade. Just as liberalizing trade in China effectively brought more than a billion people into the global labor pool and consumer marketplace, China's more cautious financial opening up is still bringing trillions of dollars into the global economy. The Chinese are traditionally big savers, and whatever money is not being invested domestically gets sent abroad. These savings give it the financial muscle to fund gargantuan global infrastructure projects and drive global investments in renewable energy. China is also one of the largest holders of US Treasuries, making the two economies deeply enmeshed.

In the previous chapter we explored the impact of the trade shock when China became part of the World Trade Organization. Another such upheaval may be looming, this time in the world of international finance, where the dominance of the US no longer feels unassailable. While the US's share of the global economy is falling, its responsibilities as the world's liquidity provider and lender of last resort are mounting. As global appetite for dollars surges, a debt-burdened, inwardly focused US is straining to meet the world's demand for its assets and liquidity. History tells us this dynamic can be a harbinger of global financial instability—and an opportunity for a rising financial power to challenge a dominant power for its central role.

Today an ambitious China is taking steps to do just that. It's ramping up efforts to popularize its currency, the renminbi (*ren min bi* means "people's money"), by encouraging trade to be invoiced in the currency, and foreign investment banks, insurance companies, rating agencies, and other financial institutions to do business in China. The PBC, China's central bank, is also using renminbi to provide financial assistance to countries that have been left out of the rich countries' club in times of need,[2] providing emergency liquidity to Argentina during its recurrent economic and debt crisis,[3] and to Egypt in the face of its mounting debt in 2016.[4] Geographically and economically diverse countries like Austria, South Africa, and Japan are holding unprecedented amounts of renminbi as reserves in their central banks. In 2016, the IMF added the renminbi (with a 10.9 percent weighting) to the basket of five major currencies that make up the special drawing rights (SDR)—the international reserve asset.

But whether China is ready to take on the mantle of international economic leadership is still open to debate. China certainly has the hard power, given the size of its economy, its fire hose of global trade, and massive programs like the Belt and Road Initiative that increasingly connect it to the rest of the world. But does China have the soft power—the transparency, predictable policies and reliable mechanisms, and trust from the international system? And what would China in a position of leadership mean for the rest of the world?

There was a time in the 1920s and 1930s when the United Kingdom no longer had the capacity to stay the course as the world's financial anchor, and the US was not yet ready to lead. That period of transition, when economic leadership was passing from one power to another, was fraught with risks and volatility. Economist Ragnar Nurkse famously forewarned the world of instability in the international monetary system as the pound sterling and the dollar vied for supremacy and central banks around the world vacillated between holding these two reserve currencies. Successive devaluations of both in 1931 and 1933 ultimately led to the collapse of the gold standard.[5]

Are we bracing ourselves for another period of financial instability as a new currency vies for a position of global dominance? Already, tremors from China, whether in the form of inflation scares, clampdowns on the property sector, or corporate defaults, are rippling throughout global markets, in a context where China's level of financial integration lags far behind that of the US.[6] Now imagine a future when the Chinese economy is as internationally integrated as the US, and Chinese capital is flowing without restrictions, its exchange rate free to swing wildly up and down, its stocks and bonds occupying a major part of every global investor's portfolio. Under those circumstances, global financial markets will necessarily depend, moment to moment, on what is happening in China. This makes refining our understanding of China's financial and monetary system an urgent necessity.

Selective Openness

In 1978, Deng Xiaoping launched the opening-up program that led to the liberalization of trade, but there was no analogous drive to open up China's financial borders. They remained largely closed, until recently. The financial policies prescribed by the Washington Consensus for developing countries—full-scale capital account and exchange rate regime liberalization—didn't sit well with China, which instead chose to take more state control in a strategy that is sometimes referred to as the "Beijing Consensus." The Chinese government simply did not want the uncertainty of capital flowing in and out of China without regulation and exchange rates swinging wildly up and down. The state also held deep-seated suspicions about the desire of major powers to prise open China's financial sector, misgivings reinforced by the Asian financial crisis in 1997–1998, when speculators brought Malaysia, Indonesia, the Philippines, and even Singapore to their knees. Ten years later, when the US financial crisis ravaged its economy and spread throughout the world,

China became even less inclined toward the Western approach. Full-scale opening up of its financial system looked too dangerous.

As a result, China's financial integration with the rest of the world has been slow, especially when compared with trade integration, which has surged dramatically over the past twenty years. China's trade is 40 percent more integrated than that of the US, but its financial integration is less than a third of that of the US.[7] This reflects Chinese capital controls, which keep in check how much and what types of money can move in and out of the country.

Investors—Chinese or foreign—feel China's lack of financial openness directly. The ordinary Chinese family that wishes to invest its savings abroad faces restrictions. Currently, each adult in China is limited to exchanging the renminbi equivalent of US$50,000 into foreign currency every year, whether it is intended to pay for a child's education abroad or for tourism. Only those with offshore money can buy stocks on the New York Stock Exchange or the London Stock Exchange. Given these restrictions, the Chinese have few choices that can satisfy their appetite for foreign assets, based on their desire to find new places to park their savings outside of real estate and the roller-coaster Chinese stock market, or to diversify their wealth by holding a variety of assets in different currencies.

When it comes to letting the outside world in, limits are also in place, this time on foreigners who wish to invest in Chinese stocks and bonds. As of this writing, foreign investors own only 3–5 percent of China's A shares equity and bond market, and less than 2 percent of its banking assets. By comparison, foreign investors own 26 percent of America's stock market, 30 percent of its bond market, and 13 percent of its banking assets.[8] Only institutional investors granted specific quotas can invest in Chinese securities, which means that when retail investors around the world want to contribute to and share in the growth of Chinese companies, they are unable to do so. In this respect, China lags far behind other emerging economies like Korea, where 28 percent of its stock market is held by foreigners, or India, with 22 percent. Globally, Chinese stocks and bonds represent less than 1 percent of portfolio holdings.[9]

To get a bit more perspective on these numbers, let's consider a diversified portfolio of global stocks. If markets were completely open and frictionless, then a global portfolio would consist of stocks from each major economy, weighted to that economy's GDP. If America commands 24 percent of the world's GDP, China 16 percent, and Japan 6 percent, then in theory a global diversified portfolio would be allocated accordingly: 24 percent American equities, 16 percent Chinese equities, and 6 percent Japanese equities. But no global portfolio comes close to investing 16 percent of its assets in Chinese securities. The MSCI ACWI Index, a global stock index that asset managers use as a guide, recommends investing 58 percent in the US, 7 percent in Japan, and only 5 percent in China (a long way from 16 percent), due in large part to the difficulty of investing in China. This tracks back to the fact that China chose to selectively open up its financial markets, instead of pursuing a more open policy the way it did with trade.

Some of this caution is understandable. After all, the world has seen devastating consequences for countries that simply flung open their financial doors: when international capital rushed in, asset prices soared, only to collapse when foreign investors fled a bubble of their own making. The Mexican peso crisis of 1994, the collapse of financial markets in Thailand, Malaysia, Indonesia, and Korea during the 1997 East Asian crisis, the Russian crisis in 1998, and the Brazil crisis in 1999 all served as chilling cautionary tales. Many of these economies combined freedom of capital flow with the rigidity of a pegged exchange rate regime, a classic recipe for disaster.

So China chose a different path. It adopted capital controls and held fast to a stable exchange rate. It sought long-term capital in the form of foreign direct investment but discriminated against open flow into domestic stocks and bonds, limiting that access to certain foreign institutional investors with specific quotas. As a result of this excessive caution, China has avoided deluges of hot money, funds frequently transferred between financial institutions to maximize interest or capital gain. It has therefore been spared woes typical of developing countries: so far, no major exchange rate crisis, external debt, or banking crisis has wrought havoc on its economy. All in all, the system has steered clear of catastrophe.

That said, China's apparent stability masks the fragility inherent in any rigid system. For one thing, speculators tend to see tightly regulated systems as an invitation to make a killing. When the Chinese government launched a large fiscal stimulus in the wake of the 2008 financial crisis, it relaxed restrictions in order to tap overseas funds. Chinese corporations rushed to borrow at low interest rates abroad. And because China artificially kept its exchange rate stable, there were sure profits to be made through this "carry trade"—borrowing at low interest rates and lending at higher rates—knowing that the yuan wouldn't depreciate and erode these gains. From 2008 to 2014, China's corporate overseas borrowing totaled US$1.1 trillion. Capital flooded into China, but those rosy conditions were unsustainable. At some point, Chinese corporations and institutions would need to repay their foreign debt, and massive amounts of capital would flow back *out* of the country. And this is exactly what happened in 2015, when China experienced the greatest capital flight in history.[10] It lost US$500 billion in reserves,[11] and even government interventions could not prevent the renminbi from depreciating (a significant amount for a currency that has consistently been held to a stable value).[12] A total of $1 trillion fled China over the course of a single year.[13] The event rippled through the global financial system, causing a global rout.[14]

The moral of the story is that the very interventions intended to make the financial system stable—capital controls and rigid exchange rates—can trigger instability. Yes, it's laudable to want to steer an economy away from financial cliffs, but this is particularly problematic for a country that considers its power to control the economy sacrosanct, yet also has ambitions to become a great financial power in the larger world. Unfortunately, these two objectives are incompatible. To become a financial anchor, an economy must be open, which requires giving up control. In global capital markets, there's no room for machinations that take place behind closed doors. So long as the Chinese government continues to prize control and stability over flexibility and efficiency, especially in the financial sector, its aspiration of being a global financial anchor remains a remote dream.

The Allure of Being the World's Financial Anchor

It's easy to appreciate why a rising economic superpower would aspire to global financial leadership, given all the status attendant on the position. What's more, the position currently held by the US also comes with economic advantages and political leverage. Oil is priced in dollars, as are major commodities. More than half of international transactions are made in dollars, with banks and foreign corporations borrowing and lending in dollars. This is a major benefit for US exporters and importers, as well as borrowers and lenders, because it protects them from exchange rate fluctuations that could otherwise significantly alter the value of what they owe and what is owed to them. This dollar privilege is also self-reinforcing: because trade is invoiced in dollars, businesses are more willing to borrow in dollars.[15] Investors are also comfortable holding dollar-denominated assets because they are liquid and because historically the dollar has tended to maintain its value. This allows the US to finance its borrowing at lower interest rates, because investors are willing to forgo higher returns in exchange for a sense of security. And when a crisis comes, the world turns to the US in search of safe assets.

This power of the dollar translates into enormous political leverage. The US can grant its friends loans or privileged access to its currency, much the way the Federal Reserve arranged central bank swap agreements (agreements to allow foreign banks to borrow in dollars using their own currency as collateral) to provide liquidity to select countries in the wake of the 2008 financial crisis. At the same time, it can deprive its foes of access to international networks needed to clear payments. Any country paying or selling in dollars can be vulnerable to US political pressure, which is why US sanctions are so potent. This makes the dollar a mighty instrument of US statecraft.[16]

In 1988, when the US was determined to force Panama's leader out of power, Washington froze Panamanian assets in US banks and prohibited all payments or dollar transfers to Panama. This forced most local banks to close their doors, creating a severe liquidity shortage that significantly weakened Panamanian resistance to American pressure.[17] The US can prohibit companies from doing business with countries like Iran, because third parties generally pay in dollars transferred through the Belgium-based Society for Worldwide Interbank Financial Telecommunication (SWIFT) system.[18] In 2012, when Standard Chartered Bank was accused by the New York State Department of Financial Services of having hidden some US$250 billion in financial transactions with Iran, the bank had to pay over US$300 million in fines. In 2014, the French bank BNP Paribas was fined US$8.9 billion for violation of the sanctions against Iran and Cuba. During the Russo-Ukrainian war, major Russian banks were cut off from the dollar system, and a substantial amount of its central bank reserves—some 35 percent of Russia's GDP—were frozen. Money is no longer "neutral" in the face of geopolitics, and the fact that a country's access to its reserves can be contingent on its foreign policies has induced many countries to reduce their holdings of dollar assets. A number of countries, including China, are also seeking to establish alternative payment networks, namely CIPS, in order to move international payments outside the current dollar-dominated system.[19] CIPS processes only a tiny fraction of transactions compared to SWIFT, but its popularity is growing. The US's tight grip on cross-border transactions and weaponization of the dollar could boost the use of China's renminbi, or digital currencies, as many countries look to skirt the dollar. For instance, Indian companies importing coal from Russia since the outbreak of the Russo-Ukrainian war settled payments in RMB, even though the companies involved had nothing to do with China. Trade invoiced in RMB, along with the share of RMB reserves held by central banks around the world, also rose to unprecedented levels over this period. These developments could pose a challenge to US financial hegemony.[20]

China's Opportunity

When the UK's economic might was eclipsed by that of the US in the early part of the twentieth century, the UK no longer had the capacity to stabilize the international financial system. Its countercyclical capacity—the ability to lend to the world in bad times and borrow in good times—was no longer sufficient to cover global demand; it no longer had enough capital to provide liquidity at the requisite scale. Gradually that role was supplanted by the larger economy of the US. This made good sense after World War II, when the US accounted for more than half of the combined economic output of the great powers, and its roles included world's largest importer and primary source of global trade credit.

Even before that war ended, representatives from the forty-four nations that fought on the Allied side met at Bretton Woods, New Hampshire, in an effort to set up an international monetary system. The US insisted that it depend on the dollar and prevailed. However, in the 1960s, Belgian American economist Robert Triffin warned of major fault lines in the Bretton Woods system. As part of the agreement, the US had pledged to convert dollars to gold on request, but due to high global demand, the amount of dollars outside the US now exceeded the value of gold in the US Treasury. In what became known as the Triffin dilemma, Robert Triffin predicted that the system could not continue to maintain either liquidity or confidence. In 1971 he was proved right, and President Richard Nixon was forced to end the convertibility of the dollar into gold. This brought the Bretton Woods system to an end, and turned the dollar into what is known as a "fiat currency," which means that it derives its value solely from the faith placed in it. Now safety lies completely in the eye of the beholder.

The currency used for international reserves is expected to provide a stable store of value. Today the US's declining relative size in the world economy means that it will struggle to meet the responsibilities that come with its leadership role. While the US accounts for less than a quarter of the world's GDP, the demand for dollar reserves is huge, making up 60 percent of total global reserves. But there may well come a time in the not-so-distant future when dollar assets will no longer be perceived as safe. If the world loses confidence in the US's ability to repay the debt from its growing deficits, the dollar will plunge in value as those assets are abandoned. This is one important reason why there need to be additional big currency players besides the US.[21] During the Great Recession, banks around the world scrambled for liquidity.[22] The US Federal Reserve did set up the swap agreements mentioned earlier, but this emergency liquidity only benefited a dozen countries and excluded most developing economies.[23] The IMF offered loans, but with conditions that often made them unpalatable.[24] At this point the Chinese central bank stepped up to fill in the gap, signing swap agreements with a number of different countries to provide liquidity based on the renminbi. An alternative like this makes the international monetary system safer and more efficient.

Another complication for any nation with a dominant currency is balancing its own internal political and economic considerations against its global responsibilities. For instance, when the US pursues a domestic policy like quantitative easing—purchasing longer-term securities from the open market in order to increase monetary supply and encourage lending and investment—this has a knock-on effect for the rest of the world. Countries experience a lending boom and possibly inflation, even if these are not what their particular economies call for. There is also a temptation for the US to devalue in times of crisis, or inflate away some of the debt payments it owes the rest of the world, even though this runs counter to the obligations of a financial stabilizer. In 2017, President Trump tried to talk down the dollar in order to stimulate American exports,[25] but the move was met with criticism from around the world.

With privilege comes responsibility. This is the lesson of history. In the 1930s, when the US was suffering through the Great Depression, it closed itself off from other countries by ramping up protectionist measures like the Smoot-Hawley Tariff Act. This could have amplified the global impact of America's woes, but fortunately the UK came to the rescue. Britain, which was going through a milder depression, kept its markets open through the Ottawa agreements, extending countercyclical lending and providing a vital source of financial stability.[26] This kind of stabilizing influence is critical to an international system, but it is a lot to ask of any one country. The big question is whether China can rise to the occasion if necessary and complement the central role of the US. One obstacle is the global reach of China's currency, the renminbi.

Despite China being the world's second-largest economy and largest trading nation, its currency plays a limited role in international settlements in trade and finance; in fact, the renminbi is not even counted among the top five most traded currencies. A fully international currency must meet a number of criteria: it must be held as a reserve in central banks; it must be used to invoice trade around the world; and it must be the currency of denomination for corporate and government bonds and bank loans. The most prominent international currencies are also commonly chosen as anchors for countries that are pegging their exchange rates to a particular currency, or basket of currencies, to provide stability.[27]

TABLE 9.1 ROLES OF AN INTERNATIONAL CURRENCY

FUNCTION OF MONEY	GOVERNMENTS	PRIVATE ACTORS
Store of value	International reserves	Currency substitution (private dollarization)
Medium of exchange	Vehicle currency for foreign exchange intervention	Invoicing trade and financial transactions
Unit of account	Anchor for pegging local currency	Denominating trade and financial transactions
		Investment

Source: Chinn Menzie and Jeffrey Frankel, "Will the Euro Eventually Surpass the Dollar as Leading International Reserve Currency?" NBER Working Paper 11510, National Bureau of Economic Research, Cambridge, MA, August 2005; originally from Peter B. Kenen, "The Role of the Dollar as the International Currency," *Group of Thirty Occasional Papers* 13 (1983).

In all these respects, China's currency lags behind. The renminbi accounted for just 2.66 percent of total foreign reserves in 2021, compared with 59 percent for the dollar.[28] According to SWIFT, the renminbi accounts for 4 percent of global payments, significantly behind the dollar at 39 percent, the euro at 33 percent, and the pound sterling at 7 percent. Of all the international bonds issued, renminbi-denominated bonds only account for less than 1 percent of the total.[29] In foreign exchange markets the renminbi commands about 4.3 percent of total trade volume, compared with the US's 44.2 percent.[30]

A Long March

As a leading trading nation, China is well positioned to expand the use of its currency. By 2015, 25 percent of its trade was being settled in renminbi, up from almost nothing only few years prior.[31] And as private transactions are increasingly made in Chinese currency, central banks will hold more renminbi as reserves. There is also an added benefit of having the financial means to lend abroad and acquire overseas assets.

In the late nineteenth century, Great Britain was a major exporter of capital to the emerging markets of that time. Its current account surplus (an economics term measuring the flow of net lending abroad) rose as high as 10 percent of GDP right before World War I).[32] The British invested in railway construction, improving port facilities, developing urban infrastructure, and even creating a system of ranches and meat-packing facilities that supported the exportation of canned and chilled beef.[33] Britain's active role in real estate, securities markets, and banking activities accelerated the use of the pound sterling around the world, leading to a golden age for that currency between 1850 and 1914.

The US's current account surplus reached 7 percent of GDP in the period between the two world wars (compared with a current account deficit, or net borrowing, of 3.7 percent of GDP in late 2021), and the dollar rose to prominence as an international currency. Similarly, as Japan's net lending rose sharply during the 1970s and 1980s,[34] the Japanese yen gained significant momentum—accounting for more than 8 percent of the world's financial reserves in 1991.[35] China's current account surplus peaked at 9.1 percent of GDP in 2008 (amounting to US$450 billion of net outflows that year), and some of these funds went into accumulating massive amounts of US Treasuries. But over time, China started to lend to developing countries and emerging markets. As of 2018, the government of China holds more than US$5 trillion of the world's debt

(6 percent of world GDP),[36] making it the third-largest creditor in the world. China's trillion-dollar Belt and Road Initiative, made possible through China's colossal saving, can encourage countries to borrow in renminbi and to denominate business transactions in renminbi.

In a carefully calibrated strategy, the Chinese government is also trying to expand renminbi usage on other fronts: for instance, by inviting domestic and foreign firms to issue renminbi-denominated bonds, called dim sum bonds, which the likes of McDonald's and HSBC have taken up. Another action taken by the PBC bears a striking resemblance to a tack taken by the US Fed almost a century earlier. China has entered into swap agreements with forty countries around the world as of 2021, effectively providing liquidity (especially during emergencies) in renminbi to these countries. By one estimate, the use of a swap line leads to a 13–20 percentage-point increase in the probability of a country making or receiving renminbi payments.[37] As a consequence, cross-border usage of the renminbi has increased a phenomenal five thousand times since 2009. Along with its efforts to popularize its currency, China is also making its exchange rate more flexible, reducing its restrictions on capital movement, and easing quotas on foreign financial institutions doing business in China.

Despite these efforts, China's status as a trader and major creditor have not yet rendered the renminbi a leading currency. The most important factor that is missing in China—a critical element in order for any international currency to be successful—is the maturity of its financial markets. Financial anchors past and present all possessed the most advanced financial systems, along with the deepest and most liquid financial markets. London was the world's foremost financial center prior to World War I. By the time the US supplanted the UK, it, too, had built the world's most advanced financial system. Before World War I, the US dollar ranked behind a number of other currencies, pulled down mainly because of America's underdeveloped financial markets. But founding the Federal Reserve in 1913 had the necessary effect of smoothing out seasonal interest rate spikes, reducing financial volatility, creating a market for trade credits, and solidifying management of the gold standard.[38]

The Federal Reserve also lifted the ban on foreign branches of US banks, which saw a major expansion abroad as a result. The share of the dollar against other currencies subsequently shot up, and between 1918 and 1932, the US dollar moved step by step to overtake the pound sterling. In 1929, the dollar already accounted for about 40 percent of total global public debt, according to historical bond market data. Evidence indicates that the depth of the US financial market—the size of the financial sector relative to the overall economy—was the most important contributor to the rise in the dollar. The UK's declining economic size in relative terms, on the other hand, was the most important factor in the pound sterling's shrinking share of global currencies at the time.[39]

A financial market that has breadth and depth allows investors to access a wide range of financial assets to meet investment needs or to hedge risks. A financial market that is liquid means that investors can buy and sell assets without significantly affecting their price; this requires a large number of buyers and sellers sustaining a high trading volume. International currencies also need to be easily tradable. The ease with which one can sell dollar bonds makes holding dollars attractive for investors. The US Treasury market is the deepest and most liquid in the world, while the Chinese government bond market lags far behind in this regard. In China the majority of government bonds are still held by banks to maturity, instead of being actively traded the way they would be in mature financial markets. Bond trading volume in China is roughly 1 percent of that in the United States and Europe.[40] By contrast, China's stock market turnover is high—not because it is liquid, but because it is dominated by retail investors who are speculating, not long-term investors.

Both in terms of size and depth, China's financial sector trails not just the financial sectors of advanced countries, but also those of many developing countries. Its stock market capitalization as a share of GDP is around 60 percent in 2019, compared with 158 percent in the US, 108 percent in Malaysia, 100 percent in Thailand, and 64.5 percent in Brazil.[41] China's bond market capitalization increased from 35 percent in 2008 to about 110 percent by the end of 2020, but compared with the US at 221 percent of GDP, it still has a lot of catching up to do.[42] And as we have seen, there isn't a wide range of high-quality, safe Chinese assets available to investors, limiting the appetite of foreign institutional investors and central banks to hold renminbi-denominated assets.

A predictable and credible central government is also important. No one wants to hold a currency that runs the risk of depreciating whenever the government finds it expedient to do so, or losing its value whenever the government wants to inflate away real repayments of its debt when debt becomes overbearingly large. A government needs to be transparent about its policies and consistent in enacting them, so that markets are not caught by surprise. This is one important reason why the dollar has maintained its popularity. But so far, China does not score high on these measures. The 2015 stock market swoon was exacerbated by government intervention and miscommunication, the flight of capital prompted by the government's intervention over the exchange rate. Institutional competence and dexterity in handling market volatility may not have been crucial during the high-growth era when the economy was catching up, but they are essential to the next phase of China's development. Allowing market forces to play a larger role in determining the renminbi's value and easing restrictions on the flow of capital accounts would require a complete overhaul of the country's financial system— something the nation does not yet seem to be prepared to do.

If there is anything to be learned from the history of international currency, it is that financial instability can undermine a currency's potential. The US banking crisis in the years following 1929 led to a decline in the share of dollars used in settling international transactions. The Japanese equity and real estate bubble that burst in the late 1980s, followed by an economic and banking crisis, sank the prospects of the rising Japanese yen. Economic instability in the eurozone caused a further decline in the share of euros used internationally.[43] For China, maintaining financial stability and avoiding the financial crisis that some believe is imminent will be essential.

All this is to say that it will be some time before China's currency will serve as a counterweight to the US dollar, despite the weaknesses we observed earlier. Nor are other currencies likely to serve that role. The most likely scenario in the near future is dominant regional currencies: the renminbi in Asia, the euro in Europe, and the dollar everywhere else. However, it is also possible that a fascinating alternative may arise in the form of new payment mechanisms. The desire shared by a number of countries to move out of a dollar-denominated payment and banking system is intensifying due to objections to the use of the dollar as a political weapon and increased skepticism that US Treasury bonds are the safest of all financial assets. We may not have to venture too far into the future before competition between currencies is no longer just a rivalry between sovereign currencies, but a contest between hard currencies and digital currencies, whether these are privately issued like Bitcoin and Ethereum, or sovereign digital currencies like the e-CNY (China became the first major economy to launch a central bank digital currency in 2020), the digital dollar, or the digital euro. Someone in Uruguay, for instance, may well prefer to hold Bitcoins or e-CNY rather than their own hard currency, ravaged by years of inflation and devaluation.

Digital currencies, including decentralized cryptocurrencies, are already making a big splash, which makes perfect sense given how digitized our daily lives have become. Unlike traditional forms of payment, digital currencies are smart: they can collect data and can be programmed so that the money parents give their children, for example, can be used only for parent-sanctioned expenses. Digital currencies can be bundled with particular services so that on some platforms you can access services only by using that platform's digital currency. And of course digital currencies can substantially reduce both the time and the cost associated with most transactions.

For all these reasons and more, governments are racing to establish their own central bank digital currency, or CBDC, before private digital currencies completely capture the market. Arguments on behalf of a sovereign-backed digital currency include safety, cost, convenience, and concern for the consumer. Guaranteed by a particular government, it can enhance the ease of global transactions, while monitoring illicit transactions like laundering money or funding terrorism. CBDC can be used to provide liquidity directly—and almost instantaneously—to large numbers of people during pandemics and other crises. However, if sovereign digital currencies do prevail, one trade-off will be loss of privacy.

How could the rise of digital currency affect China's plans for a global renminbi? Digital currencies may help dislodge the dollar from its dominant position, allowing countries like China to bypass the existing dollar-dominated financial system when conducting business with other countries. This could lead to a future where anyone can send money overseas in whatever currency they choose with the touch of a button. For people living in developing countries the availability of the e-CNY, for example, promises a cheaper way to send and receive remittances that cost people living in sub-Saharan Africa an exorbitant 8 percent of the transaction amount. By moving freely between different national systems—between China and participants in the Belt and Road Initiative, for example—the e-CNY could enjoy a big bump in popularity. The rise of Chinese technology around the world, including the increasing use of Alipay in Africa and the dominance of technological giants such as TikTok, Alibaba, and Tencent, with their already established payment infrastructure, could indirectly enhance the renminbi's cachet. But in the end, whether it is the yuan or the e-CNY, the popularity of China's currency will still depend on economic fundamentals and financial depth, liquidity, and stability. More important, as Niall Ferguson puts it in his book *The Ascent of Money*, "money is trust inscribed." Even the most remarkable technical leaps in making a currency more convenient cannot circumvent the fact that popular perception of an international currency is heavily influenced by that nation's institutions, and by faith in its financial system and government.

What This Means for the World

Although China may not succeed in displacing the dollar anytime soon, a financially more open China would have great consequences for the world's economy. If China's stock and bond markets become comparable in size to those of the US, and foreigners owned 10 percent of China's domestic bonds instead of the current 3 percent, the amount of new capital flowing into China would amount to *trillions* of additional dollars. Even at China's current level of financial integration, which is less than one third that of the US, China's impact on global finance is already pronounced. The 20 percent plunge in the Shanghai Stock Exchange in August 2015 triggered a 10–12 percent drop in the equity markets of Germany, the Netherlands, France, Denmark, and other European economies that same month.[44]

China's continued financial integration is inevitable, thanks to a substantial appetite among investors eager to increase their positions in the second-largest economy in the world. Until recently, global interest rates have been generally low, and Chinese bonds offered attractive returns: ten-year government bonds paid a yield of 3.2 percent in 2021, about 160 basis points higher than the US ten-year Treasury note. Chinese equities and bonds also offer an unusual degree of diversification for global investors, because returns in these markets show little correlation with markets in other economies. For instance, the three-year weekly correlation between American and Chinese government bond returns is 0.14, compared with 0.71 between the UK and the US, or 0.58 between Japan and Germany.[45] The correlation between the Chinese stock market and the largest emerging stock markets is less than 0.5, and the same holds true for correlations with advanced economies.

As China's financial integration progresses, China may provide global liquidity in times of need, to complement the US effort rather than to replace it. The same way that China helped stabilize the international financial system during the 2008 financial crisis, it will continue to do so in the future. Chinese assets will be a welcome addition to any global portfolio both because of their high returns and their low correlation with other major indices.

On the downside lurks the possibility that China's financial integration could trigger an ongoing series of global shocks because the nature of emerging economies is to experience substantial volatility—whether it's due to sharp fluctuations in exchange rates or the stock market, booms and busts in the property sector, or unpredictable monetary policy. Conventional economic thinking organizes economies into two categories: systemic economies, characterized by their substantial spill-over to the rest of world (the US and the EU fit here), and emerging markets, characterized by immature institutions, risk, and nascent capital markets. China is the first case in history where one nation fits into both categories and can be identified as a *systemic-emerging market.* India may also join this exclusive club when it becomes a larger and more financially open economy.

From China's point of view, the question becomes, how quickly should it take on the mantle of financial liberalization? This move could certainly promote the more efficient allocation of capital; rich countries all have open capital markets. It would require China to give up some control over its economic system, which would not be easy, but it could also usher in indirect benefits. China might use this moment as a catalyst to push for much-needed financial reforms at home, much the way China put pressure on SOEs to become more efficient in the run-up to joining the WTO. But if China opens up with too much haste, too widely, and with too little preparation, not only would this be counterproductive for China, it would also create turbulence for everyone else. The fallout from the trade war between the US and China shows us that repercussions from friction between two major powers is never limited to just the two parties. And history demonstrates time and again that one country's tunnel-visioned pursuit of its own national interests without regard for their global implications has disastrous effects.

Following the Paris Peace Conference in 1919–1920, the volume of global trade and commerce fell dramatically after a protectionist US Congress raised tariffs by a whopping 40 percent.[46] In an unanticipated boomerang effect, US imports plummeted 65 percent and the US stock market crashed in 1929, leading to the Great Depression and the long shadow it cast over the next decade, all around the world.[47] A nationalistic, isolationist approach led first to instability and then to open conflict in World War II. Decades later, lack of global collaboration led to the oil price shocks of 1974 and 1979, the petrodollar crisis between 1974 and 1980, the Latin American crises in the 1980s, and then to the raging inflation that swept across the industrialized world. The global financial crisis of 2008 was finally contained when leaders of the G20 committed to coordinating liquid swaps and monetary easing.[48]

I believe that in the future we'll see two major central banks, one in China and one in the US, each with its own mandates and objectives, serving its respective country and exerting its influence on global financial conditions. Because this could easily devolve into vying with each other, coordination between these two major central banks will be paramount. The spirit of collaboration was deeply embedded in the design of the Bretton Woods system, and even after it broke down in 1972, coordination and consultation continued as the prevailing pattern of the international economic order. However, this spirit has been under siege in recent years. The formidable challenge we face is that coordination will need to occur not between like-minded countries, but between two countries that are economically competitive, technologically parallel, and politically divergent. Both sides have much invested in bilateral cooperation, but for the US and other countries in the developed world, understanding China, its system, cultural heritage, social mores, national ambitions, and aspirations will dramatically elevate the likelihood of genuine collaboration in the decades to come.

A New Concept of Economic Leadership

In the end, economic leadership in the world goes beyond possessing a global currency, a powerful central bank, a global financial center, and a key role in the design and maintenance of the international monetary system and financial architecture. Today, the world operates as a network, whether the issue is technology, trade, or the flow of capital. The greatest challenges facing humanity transcend national borders: climate change, the displacement of human workers by AI, and pandemic threats that experts predict will revisit us every ten years or so into the future. In an age based on digital networks, services, and knowledge, economic leadership takes on both new meaning and new relevance.

Networks are more than simply a series of relationships. The more connected the network, the more valuable each link. In global transport, trade, and finance, the more infrastructure there is between nations, the greater the efficiency gains for everyone. In addressing climate change, the more coordination there is among nations, the more likely it is to achieve the desired outcome. Countries that sit at the center of the network, or at critical nodes, may benefit most from it, yet everyone else in the network stands to benefit as well. In its quest to become a global network leader, China launched the ambitious Belt and Road Initiative. It created the Asian Infrastructure Investment Bank, whose guiding principle is "lean, clean, and green." China engaged in multilateral networking through forums like the G20 and Asia-Pacific Economic Cooperation.[49] It became the second-largest financial contributor to the United Nations,[50] and the largest funding provider to African countries for their infrastructure development in recent years.[51] It intends to become the global hub of green finance, establishing international carbon-pricing centers and financial centers focused on green bonds and derivatives. This, in turn, might enable the RMB to become a currency for green finance.

A large economy often takes up a disproportionately large share of public-goods spending in the world; otherwise, these projects might not get funded at all. The US pays much more than its proportional share of NATO's expenses, while China has opted to take up more than its proportional share of infrastructure or climate-related spending around the world, as it has with the Belt and Road Initiative. Of course, China needs to be keenly aware of the potential risks involved, including mounting debt levels in developing countries, environmental damage, and overly extensive engagement with China's own enterprises. One great lesson of the past is that it is easier to conceive projects and lend money than it is to see them successfully through to fruition.

Some argue that China is leading borrowers into a debt trap, whereby they would lose control over important assets should they be unable to repay their loans, or that huge Chinese loans for infrastructure development make their national debt levels unsustainable. But this is misleading. The majority of BRI countries' debt is owed to Western institutions such as hedge funds and asset management companies, or to international organizations, rather than to China. And sovereign debt crises in emerging markets are by no means a novel phenomenon, rather a repeated occurrence since time immemorial.[52] Yet to be fair, China's reluctance to share details of its lending terms and conditions fuels suspicion. Hidden debts—those that are off government balance sheets—raise the question of whether sovereign governments can properly assess and monitor their liabilities. But evidence from a variety of in-depth studies with independently collected data shows that Chinese lending is generally aligned with norms of global development finance,[53] and that lending standards have significantly improved since the inception of the BRI in 2013. The most comprehensive data capturing BRI's 13,427 projects in 145 countries shows that most of its borrowers are not those with high repayment risk, nor the most corrupt. Instead, China lends to a geographically diverse set of countries spanning Asia (29 percent), Africa (23 percent), Latin America (24 percent), and Central and Eastern Europe (18 percent). Most countries are in sound fiscal condition, but a few countries have taken on debts to worrying levels (the Maldives and Laos owe more than 25 percent of their GDP to Chinese lenders, for instance).[54] Not only has China written off a lot of its loans and provided debt relief to borrowers, but asset seizures are extremely rare (there have been none in Africa as of this writing).[55] China bears these risks itself along with its borrowers, especially since many of its loans are large (above US$500 million), and is still navigating its way as a new member of the global lending club. In the spirit of international coordination, it has joined the G20 to endorse debt service suspension related to COVID-19.[56]

The power of the dollar has given the US tremendous political leverage on the global stage. China's pragmatic approach to engaging with developing countries through infrastructure projects, aid, and loans in times of crisis has rallied significant support from many parts of the developing world. Even if these ambitious programs bear geopolitical and strategic interests for China, they also reflect its vision of a world order based on shared economic development. But any nation taking up the torch of leadership will need legitimacy, which extends beyond hard power to include a moral imperative. For a while, the US's commitment to democracy gave it the tacit authority to project power onto the world. But its increasing desire to shift global responsibilities to others, and the economic and technological nationalism pursued in the spirit of "America First," has been gnawing away at that legitimacy.

Threats to the workings of both regional and global networks—in the form of Brexit, trade wars, and pandemics—have served to underscore the need for a new definition of economic leadership. In this new, networked age, the traditional paradigm of competition needs to give way to complementarity, connectivity, and cooperation. As resilient transnational networks supersede sovereign states, the prevailing concept of economic hegemony may itself become obsolete—or at least less relevant. The most central and connected nation enlivens the networks, not with the goal of domination but to ensure its safety, sustainability, and smooth function. The more prominent nodes will need to shape and sustain an architecture that allows others to prosper for the benefit of all.

China flourished beyond its borders because the global system accepted it and encouraged it to flourish. As China becomes ever more integrated into global networks including trade, finance, and infrastructure, it can pay those benefits forward to developing nations as they come online.

TEN

TOWARD A NEW PARADIGM

China, Past and Present

The miracle of China over the past four decades is not the nation's record-breaking span of dizzying GDP growth, but the unimaginable transformation that has taken place for hundreds of millions of Chinese and their children within a single lifetime. This was true for my family and for most families we knew. Had events not taken such a dramatic turn in China, I would have been born in the rural south, where my parents were sent to work as manual laborers during the Cultural Revolution. My father might have settled down in the countryside, working in a slaughterhouse butchering pigs. Instead, he was among the first students to take the national exam reinstated by Deng Xiaoping, part of the resurrection of a national system of higher education abandoned during the Cultural Revolution. Years of blighted hopes ended with one acceptance letter, catapulting my father from the remote countryside to a top-tier university in the nation's capital. I was born there, in Beijing, where our tiny private apartment was regarded as an extraordinary luxury.

In 1978, when China's economic needs finally won the struggle with ideology, the nation was determined to forge a prosperous future, but it possessed little recent experience to draw from. Forty years later, China has reinvented itself as a global power based on a unique melding of politics and economics that incites both ire and admiration from the rest of the world. Having lived through much of this transformation, my generation is proud of what the nation has achieved, although we are also keenly aware of the high price paid along the way. Today we are more sought after by international companies and institutions than any previous generation, which reflects less on our own abilities than it does on what our nation has given us. As China was coming of age, so were we.

One of the most significant shifts over the past forty years has been the way the Chinese view their own country. In the 1960s and 1970s, students who landed an opportunity to go to school in the West usually stayed there, where in general life was better, consumer goods were abundant, and salaries were more than ten times the going rate for a similar position at home. The Chinese were thoroughly impressed by the West, and particularly by America, with its power, technology, and prosperity fueled by an American dream that inspired both its own people and the immigrants it welcomed. But by the time my generation started flowing out of universities abroad with newly minted degrees in the early 2000s, Chinese students had started moving closer to home, parking themselves in cosmopolitan cities like Hong Kong or Singapore, benefiting from opportunities that originated in mainland China but were still a comfortable distance away. By 2013 the mainland had become their prime destination. According to the Chinese Ministry of Education, of the five million students who completed their studies abroad between 2000 and 2019, around 86 percent returned to China. Even my esteemed math professor, Shing-tung Yau, gave up his long-standing position as a tenured professor at Harvard to teach at Peking University.

When Deng Xiaoping decided that young people in China should be allowed to pursue their education overseas, he expected that many would not return home for some time. He took the long view—that eventually most of them would come back, and even those who did not would provide a service to the nation in some way. Yet even he would have been surprised by the strength of the recent trend. Young students tell me that in order to really make it these days, they have to be in China, part of a buoyant start-up scene flush with venture capital from around the world. Scientists and researchers are moving there attracted by high salaries, generous budgets, and large research teams to help advance their work. Even tech professionals with coveted jobs at Facebook, Google, Goldman, and BlackRock are returning home, some to launch firms that will make them billionaires or social media stars.

This growing sense of celebratory homecomings and the nation's appeal bear testimony to China's true success. Living in America, Europe, or Australia is no longer the object of every young Chinese person's desire. Now the dreams that those places once represented can be realized in China.

For those who cling to the belief that Western-style democracy with its full embrace of capitalism is the only system that can generate widespread prosperity, China's global rise poses a perplexing paradox. The state's heavy-handed interventions run counter to free market doctrine. Yet the Chinese playbook has enjoyed phenomenal success, although not without problems. Throughout these pages I have sought to explain how certain mechanisms in China's political economy have come to complement pure market forces, though this approach does not explain all of the factors in play. When we distill the complex mix of China's economy to its essential ingredients, several stand out as we seek to understand the Chinese economic miracle, with all its many puzzles and contradictions.

THE STATE'S UNIQUE DESIGN

The unusual power of the Chinese state is rooted in its ancient bureaucratic structure of *tiaotiao kuaikuai* (lines and blocks)—an elaborate administrative system that makes it possible for authorities at the top to convey instructions all the way down to the smallest administrative unit. Vertical lines of command are combined with horizontal jurisdictions, or blocks, in a network whose reach extends to every corner of the country. This structure, which traces back to imperial times, is still essential to China's ability to build new infrastructure with startling speed, to reap a sudden harvest of Olympic gold medals, or to manage a global pandemic.

For all its effectiveness, the system does not grant China's central authority total control. Power delegated to provinces and municipalities incentivizes local governments to grow their economies, achieve social progress, and maintain order. It's a dynamic balance that sometimes shifts in the direction of the central authority and at other times tilts toward local government, but the central government never fully relinquishes control, and every external shock or crisis tends to shift power back to top leadership.

A strong central government, however, does not guarantee a successful economy. History has made this abundantly clear. China, at least for the last forty years, has been able to succeed in aligning economic incentives for all the key actors in an economy—individuals, households, firms, local governments, and the central authority. Macro-level national strategies get micro-level implementation based on successfully motivating local government officials to take an active role. By delivering striking economic results in their locality, officials ascend the rungs of party hierarchy, wield greater influence, and forge glorious careers. Moreover, competition between regions and the mandatory rotation of leaders at the provincial and municipal levels keep officials from colluding against the central authority and from exploiting local firms for individual gain. Such mechanisms cannot stave off corruption altogether, but they can help keep it in check.

A second aspect of the central government's power lies in its vast resources. It owns the land, its natural resources, and the nation's largest banks. It controls the levers that set GDP growth targets, regulate financial systems, sway property markets, issue licenses and permits, and redistribute wealth. Reform is perhaps its most potent tool, allowing the central government to scrap old laws and impose new ones swiftly, with little political constraint. These resources and abilities explain why the private sector stays close to the state, despite the tension between the former's preference for a free market and the latter's greater comfort with a command economy.

A powerful state is especially effective in an economy's infancy, when market institutions are still a work in progress. A primitive financial system has difficulty underwriting new enterprises of national significance without help from state banks, for instance. And the state picks up the slack when the market fails to deliver, orchestrating suppliers and producers in critical areas that might have taken a long time to come through on their own. But a powerful state is a double-edged sword, and for all the many things that have gone right in China, others have not.

Industrial policies intended to stoke GDP lingered too long after market conditions changed, keeping the Chinese economy pumped up on steroidal easy credit and subsidies. Although some reforms effectively addressed distortions in the economy, new ones were created along the way, leading to poorly allocated capital, human resources, and land.

Where a free market would have weeded out ineffective actors and rewarded capable ones, that cleansing effect was limited. Ultimately, it all comes down to this: China's central leadership, which spurred the most successful economic growth story of our time, could also make choices that might have the opposite effect in the future. The power of the state provides the system's greatest potential and also poses its gravest inherent risk.

COMPETITION, SCALE, AND AN INDUSTRIOUS PEOPLE

Economists use fundamental precepts of modern economic theory to translate an economy into a mathematical framework. As we've been discussing, in China the wild card is the outsize and often unpredictable role of the state. But even if it were possible to factor in this variable, any model constructed with these tools could never do justice to the real thing. Missing would be the life force that animates any economy, the people who bring to the national enterprise their unique traits, including work ethic, competitive fire, and ambition. These qualities help explain why simply giving Chinese workers free choice over their jobs and modest incentives led to hugely successful reforms. They also help explain the later explosion of Chinese trade that took the world by surprise, and the foreign companies that for all their first-rate products, services, and management know-how often found themselves at a loss in the domestic Chinese market, outcompeted by local players who learned fast, copied creatively, and localized diligently.

Even though competition is essential to market economies, maintaining a level playing field is difficult to achieve, which holds true for all economies, including those in the West, where big corporations have unfair advantages and influence that they use to suppress competition. Government subsidies for handpicked sectors, tariffs, and regulatory restrictions all provide speed bumps that affect fair competition. But regardless of the tilt of the playing field, China relies on a labor force whose collective memory includes hunger, deprivation, and working around the clock, first to fill its belly and then to realize its dreams. A Chinese nation intent on its relentless pursuit of a prominent place in the developed world is one of the realities the rest of the world must recognize and come to terms with.

PATERNALISM AND CONTROL

Some ingredients in China's economic brew are difficult to accept based purely on logic and reason. It's not easy to understand why the state takes such an active role in the stock market, the housing market, education, the number of births in a family, and even how much time children can spend playing video games. But this tendency to guide and manage the Chinese people stems from the nation's deep history and culture of paternalism. It is perhaps even more puzzling that the Chinese broadly accept it, although not without grumbling. But the track record so far is that the government has done a good job of maintaining stability and safety even as the nation undergoes a sea change.

The top priority of China's fatherly government is stability. Unfortunately, in market economies volatility is the rule rather than the exception: it's considered commonplace in economic cycles, financial markets, foreign exchange, and capital flows. This leads to state intervention, which inevitably triggers the law of unintended consequences. As we saw in chapter 6, reining in local government debt by banning budget deficits drove those local governments to shadow banking as an alternative, so they could use intermediary companies to borrow whatever they liked. This hidden debt becomes a land mine waiting to explode. And when the central government creates a safety net by diverting huge chunks of capital to bail out companies and investors, or to defend the country's exchange rate, this only serves to encourage greater risk-taking.

One way out of this dilemma is for the government to let companies fail when they cannot meet their obligations. Allow the free market to take its course. However, because deviating from the paternalistic norm can create panic and add fuel to conspiracy theories, government finds itself between Scylla and Charybdis. For our purposes, the cultural trait of paternalism is still the key to understanding many of China's policy decisions and stances. With this in mind, we can assume that state-owned enterprises are in no danger of being sidelined as the vehicles through which the government controls key national assets and provides the so-called national lifeline. SOEs will always remain agents of the Communist Party entrusted with carrying out the nation's goals. They are foot soldiers to be called upon to maintain stability and ultimately to realize China's national dreams, whether they take place in the realms of technology, aviation, outer space, or rapid response to a global pandemic.

Paternalism can also arise in response to what the authorities perceive as undesirable behavior. In feudal times, magistrates appointed by China's emperor viewed their role as *mu min*, tending to the people as if they were sheep. Perversely, this can contribute to a public impulse to play fast and loose with the rules. And it's true that in the early days of reform in China, many did their best to exploit whatever policy loopholes they could find as the nation struggled to establish its footing. This is most evident in the financial system, and explains why the government has heavily regulated fintech and so far banned the crypto industry in China. Going forward, the logic that the government knows what's best for its people, just as parents know what's best for their children, will be challenged. As society evolves, people will express a greater preference for individual self-determination. The grand test of China's system in the future is how a medley of individual preferences can be reflected and aggregated into collective outcomes.

CULTURE AND FUNDAMENTALS

We should always be wary of wholly attributing economic patterns and behaviors to culture, as an explanation for why things "work differently in *our* country." Often, lurking behind these patterns are policies or economic conditions responsible for nudging people to act in certain ways. In China, tradition called for a big family until the one-child policy was enforced in 1980. Forty years later, the government began relaxing the birth control policy, even encouraging young couples to have a third child, but this time the new rules had far less impact. Social mores change, as do practical considerations like the high cost of raising a family and the huge time commitment required from women empowered by prominent roles in business, academia, and government.

Still, culture cannot be categorically written off as a contributing factor. Compliance and paternalism still play major roles in China, as does a long-standing emphasis on education, diligence, and frugality. A tradition of placing community interests above personal interests stands in sharp contrast to a Western emphasis on the individual. As we've seen, multigenerational families often make decisions together and share the burden of housing and caring for older people. Culture also contributes to our understanding of the deference to parents shown by Chinese children who are otherwise independent and may have chosen very different lifestyles. Over the course of the pandemic, we have seen how across and within countries people have made different choices about security and safety versus freedom and liberty. That disparity has been crucial in determining a wide variety of outcomes.

We must also keep in mind that China was once the world's richest nation, with its most advanced technology and infrastructure, supported by a bureaucracy that encouraged the selection of the most competent. China's meritocratic heritage made the transition to modern governance easier, and unleashed its latent capacity to boost modern science and technology in the new era. But this is not a nation that rests on ancient laurels. Its setbacks in recent history serve as a constant reminder of the need to adapt to changing circumstances, to see the world as it is, in a constant state of flux. A glorious history does not necessarily confer upon a nation leadership in the modern world, as countries like Greece, Italy, Portugal, Spain, Britain, and others can testify. Ever since Deng's reforms, China has rebuilt its institutions by learning from advanced economies, picking and choosing, assimilating whatever is suitable to China's unique situation, and rejecting the rest.

China: Toward the Future

What the future holds for China and its evolving role in the world is a key question of our time. It may not be easy to fathom what that looks like. As we have seen throughout these pages, China is constantly changing, adapting its state governance and institutions, and crafting new strategies and policies as the mindset of its people evolves to meet emerging circumstances. China's classic text of divination, the *I Ching*, also known as the *Book of Changes*, elaborates that "all is in a state of flux"; in this world nothing is immutable, and no path is fixed. This dynamism that informs the nation's institutional mechanisms and its rather flexible, pragmatic approach makes the task of foretelling China's future or fortune both daunting and thrilling.

Past is not prologue. What has happened in China offers no reliable indication of what lies ahead. China's political economy system seems sturdy enough to navigate the turbulent and transformative times ahead, but the challenges are daunting. Five significant considerations will shape the course of China's next few decades.

The first, and arguably the most significant, is a return to the "social problem." The sense of urgency to address issues ranging from enlarging the middle-income group, to consumer protection, to the appropriate degree of state provision is becoming increasingly acute. All around the world, labor's share of GDP is declining while capital's share is rising: workers, who have less and less bargaining power, increasingly lose out on the wealth generated by lightly taxed capital. At the same time that it multiplies the fortunes of savvy entrepreneurs, technology is displacing jobs, making room for highly educated and trained tech-savvy workers while increasingly leaving the rest in the lurch. In an era of unprecedented material abundance, social tensions are growing in many developed countries, where an increasing number of people are angry, frustrated, and disillusioned. If nothing is done, the same fate will befall China.

Forty years ago, Deng Xiaoping, leader of a nation guided by Communist ideology, decided that in order for China to rise out of poverty, a certain number of people would have to be allowed to become wealthy first. That rising tide would then lift all boats, eventually bringing about broad-based prosperity. In the ensuing decades, many in China have indeed become wealthy—in fact, *very* wealthy. The country is home to the second-largest number of billionaires in the world. But as the net worth of the privileged few has soared, China's income inequality has widened, from Nordic levels at one point to levels that are fast approaching those of the US.[1] The bottom half of the income distribution in China accounts for only 15 percent of its income share (compared to 12 percent in the US and 22 percent in France). Disparities between the haves and have-nots affect everything from where people live to the quality of their children's education, from their lifetime employment prospects to the length of those lifetimes themselves. A COVID-19 pandemic that affected every country in the world has only served to underscore just how disproportionately that suffering is borne.

Now China's moral mandate is shifting back toward a collective national goal established forty years ago. The concept of "common prosperity," advocated by Deng Xiaoping, has become a signature political goal for President Xi, whose vision for China is a "great modern socialist country." Looking to the West, China sees how the vast divide between rich and poor in advanced economies has stoked divisiveness, distrust, toxicity, and extremism—a scenario that it fervently wishes to avoid. China seeks an olive-shaped income distribution for its people, ample in the middle and narrow at the extremes. It prefers to have its political leaders calling the tune that corporations dance to, rather than the other way around, which has inspired regulatory action against tech platform companies and put pressure on rich entrepreneurs. And although China is not looking to provide a universal basic income (its traditional values encourage hard work as the basis of a meaningful life), the Chinese state does feel duty-bound to provide a basic level of well-being for all its people.

China's priority going forward is to achieve high-quality growth with greater shared prosperity. In the 1980s, Deng Xiaoping encouraged his party cadres not to get bogged down in an ideological debate about socialism versus capitalism; instead, he helped forge a unique system of governance that borrowed features from both. Whether or not it can continue to flourish depends on China's ability to resolve capitalism's biggest dilemma: How can social harmony accompany growing wealth? The goal is formidable. Not only because few nations have achieved even relative success (and they tend to be small, like Denmark), but also because even a fully committed China with its vast resources and unchallenged state power finds solutions elusive. Once again, nearly half a century after Deng Xiaoping's departure from conservative ideology, China is crossing a new river while groping for stones.

By taking its first significant steps to address issues around inequality and fairness, China is tackling capitalism's most intractable problem ahead of the West. Some in the West have told me that the answer to democracy's problem is *more* democracy. China does not believe so, nor does it believe that the answer to free market failures is *freer* markets. It has become increasingly clear that inclusiveness, fairness, and a high quality of life are not fully amenable to market solutions. Capitalism as we know it can no longer be the dominant force for economic improvement if that growth is going to be equitable. Something has to change.

This is especially true in a global economy where market mechanisms no longer serve to maintain equilibrium as they once did in the "widget society," when factory-based production dominated economic activity. Instead, in the information age, markets are more subject to a snowball effect as companies with a disproportionate share of data and technology grow boundlessly, deploying their businesses at unthinkable scale. Monopolies can use their power to charge high prices and stave off competition, to the detriment of consumers everywhere. The seven giants in the AI age—Alphabet, Amazon, Meta, Microsoft, Baidu, Alibaba, and Tencent—dominate AI research. They are applying algorithms to data collected on us, and can nudge us to think and behave so that we make this purchase instead of that one, vote for this candidate instead of the other. Economic beliefs and principles we once cherished need to be challenged, and as the market's invisible hand continues to fail us, some see the case for targeted government intervention as ever more compelling.

In China, the focus on common prosperity is not so much about targeting the top 1 percent, or ferreting out and regulating tax havens where individuals and corporations cache their billions. Nor is it about how to design a progressive tax system that focuses on a narrow definition of inequality based on income. China's first steps have been directed at getting rid of sources of blatantly *illicit* incomes, those made by defrauding, monopolizing, manipulating, or colluding. It is about zeroing in on providing fairer opportunities for people even before earnings become a concern. To this end, it is rolling out affordable housing and prioritizing access to healthcare and efficient infrastructure for everyone. In a dramatic fashion, it has cracked down on various companies, including tutoring companies that took advantage of an overheated environment to peddle an ever-widening array of private tutorials priced for the well-to-do. The sweeping anti-corruption drive, which first started within the confines of the party, has expanded to the SOEs, private companies, financial regulators, and so forth.

Not all income inequality is unjust: some people prefer to work harder than others, and some are more capable or innovative than others. In any economy, including China's, preserving the incentives that drive its private entrepreneurs to create value and jobs is vital. Common prosperity is not to be equated with egalitarianism, but it can be advanced by purging the economy of malfeasance that has formed a not-so-insignificant part of the wealth accumulated over the last few decades.

China's push for common prosperity mandates that Chinese firms be *hefa*, *heli*, and *heqing*—"lawful, reasonable, and empathetic." It is no longer enough to be a big contributor to the mayor economy. In China's changing economic environment, companies have to be disciplined, environmentally conscious, and considerate to their customers. Increasingly they must respect rules and regulations and protect consumer privacy. Monopolies need to be curbed. Discussions about national champions continue, but alongside a greater emphasis on "small is beautiful" as the country moves away from low-end, mass-produced goods and toward more specialized and sophisticated products.[2]

When it comes to curtailing corporate power, China has a distinct advantage over the West, where powerful, well-heeled corporate lobbies manipulate the political system and shape its agendas. After years of prolonged debate over regulating the likes of Facebook and Amazon, the US still has little to show for it. In China, the government has stepped in with immediate effect. In less than a year beginning in 2020, social media and gaming giant Tencent was forced to sell off holdings to reduce its concentration of market power, while regulators also blocked Tencent's proposed merger of the country's top two video-game streaming sites and ordered it to end its exclusive music copyrights. Meituan was fined huge sums for not adequately protecting workers' rights and benefits, and a series of antitrust probes across all sectors targeted the likes of Alibaba and Didi. A sea of regulations swept across the nation, and at the tail end of 2021 the state refused to bail out its deeply indebted real estate giants.

These unexpected and heavy-handed interventions transformed the internet giants' landscape overnight. They also rattled international markets and spooked investors. If common prosperity is pursued with an approach that is too hasty and too draconian, with the same "short, flat, fast" attitude we've seen in the past, China's goal will be turned on its head. Even well-intended policies can backfire if they are poorly designed or implemented. People will lose confidence in business and the government, companies in constant dread of erratic policies will hold back their investment and innovation, and the economic pie will fail to grow, leaving the state with less money at its disposal for responding to contingencies and opportunities. The risk of overzealous regulation is a real one, and could derail the country from its course: to realize its "great rejuvenation." But a measured approach could be a boon to society. A stable society, after all, is itself a critical economic asset.

Many view the interventionist Chinese state with trepidation and skepticism. Some fear that an era of ideological governance could reverse its course of opening up and reform.[3] There is a tendency to interpret every major event in China as both symbolic and permanent, but that is misguided. Some dramatic undertakings are intended to have a "big bang" effect—to arouse awareness and to enforce change. They are often dialed back once the message gets across or if ramifications start to bite. The dramatic regulatory clampdowns on the technology companies in 2020 were eventually followed by their reprieve and even public endorsement in 2022. The Twentieth Party Congress held a few months later underscored the importance of expanding the digital economy. The pendulum sometimes swings to one extreme before it swings back with equal force: isolationism of the 1950s and 1960s followed by all-embracing globalization in the latter half of the twentieth century; a policy environment inimical to the private sector in the 1970s and early 1980s followed by an essentially free rein in the ensuing decades, and a dramatic shift from COVID-19 lockdowns to the nation's reopening in late 2022. However, what is lost in the process cannot be recovered.

The new playbook is but a process to search for a new equilibrium befitting our times. That equilibrium involves striking a balance between greater equality and market incentives, security and growth, self-reliance and continued engagement with the West. Many assume that they are irreconcilable, but they are not. For China, finding that balance will be a constant process of learning, recalibration, and fine-tuning until both means and ends are "fit for purpose." There may be errors and aberrations, twists and turns that may sometimes seriously impinge on the economy. In 2022, China's economy suffered a severe setback: for the first time in forty years, China's GDP growth was lower than that of the US in the second quarter of the year. China's reputation as a reliable, predictable, and stable international business partner was hurt as restricted travel and work disrupted global supply chains.[4]

Sacrifices will be made along the way, and China may risk missing its potential growth in the near term. But I still hold a sanguine view that pragmatism and rationality will eventually prevail—no matter what is thrown in the way, be it a crisis of international relations, more ideology baked into policies, or an epidemiological battle. There is no turning back to a pre-modern and pre-technological society; the Chinese people have fundamentally changed. Having experienced firsthand the virtues of markets and the trappings of modernity, people will loathe an economy of shortage and a lifestyle devoid of diversion, luxuries, travel abroad, and the delights of café culture—whatever mantra rules the day. Having been fully immersed in the age of the internet, with full knowledge of how quickly and widely information spreads, they will not hold back opinions or shy away from remonstrance. Even under heavy scrutiny, censorship, or control, *issues* can be suppressed but not general *sentiment*. Finally, the incoming and incumbent leaders of China today—even the new generation leaders born after the 1980s—are profound beneficiaries of Deng Xiaoping's opening and reform vision. Forty years of reform is hard to reverse, as too many have benefited, and too many interests are entrenched.

On the ground, in late 2022, local officials are still busying themselves with *zhao shang yin zi*, the official terminology for attracting businesses and capital inflows. Fiscal revenues are needed to fill government coffers and the success of private companies is the only thing that will generate sufficient employment. Entrepreneurs, even under greater constraints and scrutiny, are still working on the next big idea to try on a gargantuan market that could make them multimillionaires. Government officials at all levels are fervently trying to lure back foreign interest. Reassuringly, opening up continues, where bond connects, stock connects, and swap connects are slowly but surely prising open China's financial system.

The second force is that China is shedding its status as a young nation as its economy comes of age. The old playbook, based on pioneers bending or breaking rules while the government turned a blind eye, is being replaced by a new one. As a nation becomes wealthier, its priorities shift. As its people become better off, their desire to meet basic needs gives way to longings for work-life balance and access to a wide variety of high-quality goods and services. For society as a whole, *process* becomes as important as *outcomes*. The means must be justified on their own merits, not simply by the ends. China is maturing, and that maturation will accelerate as the state evolves along with its people in an ongoing dynamic, increasingly shaped by a new generation. That generation understands more than any other that as the efficacy of hard power wanes, it will need to build networks, communicate compelling narratives, and work together with other countries to establish international rules, thereby accumulating the soft power that will make China naturally more attractive to the world.

But along with economic maturation comes greater societal complexity. The nation and its people no longer rivet their attention exclusively on their economic prosperity. The local government's performance indicators are no longer solely based on a simple metric around GDP growth. Unless it adapts to the changing conditions, the current system, which was stellar at mobilization and coordination, may not work as well in the new era, without the flexibility and resilience to manage a more complex society, and the right set of governance mechanisms to prevent deeply entrenched interests from standing in the way of further reforms. To encourage indigenous innovation and technology breakthroughs, the state, including local governments, will need to recede to the background while letting markets and entrepreneurs do the work. To reflect what the people want, rather than what the states think they should want, paternalism must give way to greater political representation for all. New mechanisms will need to supplant old ones, but they are not yet part of the new playbook. And thus, in an age of unprecedented challenges, the ultimate test is whether China's political economy system can continue to adapt to the shifting landscape.

The third powerful influence on China's future is based on two goals it has set for itself. The first is to become the preeminent economic power as measured by GDP. Even though it will take decades to be ranked among the richest economies in per capita terms, China is only a few years away from overtaking the US in overall economic size. Yet this can happen only if China succeeds in navigating a course that widens and deepens its connections with the global economy while at the same time establishing its independence and leadership when it comes to cutting-edge technologies and energy supply. Fortunately for China's economic ambitions, there are still major sources of growth left to tap at home, including investment in urbanization to accommodate internal migration, breaking down the remaining barriers to internal trade, and accommodating the rise of the service sector.

Right alongside its goal of achieving the world's largest GDP, China nurtures a desire to influence global rules and norms and to build a vast number of economic linkages where they are welcomed. In recent decades, China has ramped up efforts to provide capital, technology, and expertise in infrastructure development to many developing countries, prompting Europe and the US to do more than they have in the past. It may still be a novice when it comes to undertaking large, potentially risky global development projects, and there may be strategic agendas. But shared prosperity through economic development and cooperation is an important part of China's world vision. In this context, it is stepping up to fill in the gaping holes left by rich countries and international institutions in developing countries.

The fourth factor at work shaping China's future is a need that it shares with the United States—that the world's two economic superpowers peacefully and cooperatively accommodate each other. For China, competition with the US is not just about trade, but also about Chinese aspirations, the right model of development and governance, and the future of technology. Once considered America's strategic partner during the Clinton era, more recently China has been dubbed its chief rival. We can only hope that China and the US, for all their political differences and competitiveness, will actively seek space for collaboration. This is especially true where their need for each other is obvious, as it is in the arenas of climate crisis mitigation and the advancement of peaceful resolution to disputes between nations. Both countries will have to figure out not only what the other wants but also what is realistically possible to achieve. For China, it would be unrealistic to seek to displace the US as the world's sole superpower. For the US, it would be fanciful to assume that its economic and military hegemony will extend into the indefinite future.

It is unlikely that China will actively seek conflict. Nor will it seek convergence, knowing full well that the gulf that divides these two nations in terms of values, beliefs, and systems will never fully close. It does not aspire to be the world's "shining city on a hill," nor do its ambitions include exporting its ideology or foisting its development model on the rest of the world, knowing full well that its experience and formula can inspire but not be duplicated. This has been a historical tradition: even at the height of its preeminence in the world up until the Industrial Revolution, China did not seek to spread values or make efforts to proselytize the relevance of its culture and institutions. In the words of Henry Kissinger in his book *On China*, "China did not export its ideas but let others come to seek them."

Today, a sensible approach would call for both nations to look after their own security while respecting each other's needs and desires, and for an ongoing dialogue about shared global challenges that will gradually bring the two nations closer together. This is a model for coexistence to which China also aspires, if more cannot be achieved. Frost in the bilateral relationship may have set in, and it may chill the air for a time. However, forty-plus years of mutual investment, trade, personal exchanges, and official cooperation would, I hope, make it impractical to dismantle such deep and well-established bonds.

When it comes to war, we tend to focus on the price paid by the vanquished, but it's easy to overlook the cost to the victors—in human lives lost, years of diminished expectations, and colossal amounts of money that could have been diverted from military spending to social programs, or to eradicating disease around the world. What is not visible is no less significant. Kissinger once warned against conflict between two major countries with comparable military and technical power by saying that "a victor is not possible without a risk of destroying humanity."

Lastly, for all that China is unlikely to evolve into a Western-style democracy, its people are increasingly becoming attuned to a social and legal environment that considers and protects their legitimate rights. They are holding their local governments more and more accountable for their roles in people's daily lives, using social media, public postings on government websites, and civil court cases to express their views and press for change. Under the Administrative Procedure Law, the people can sue governmental institutions for infringement on their personal rights, and they do win civil court cases. The version of the law codified in 2021 marks a new milestone in improving the rule of law. In that ongoing dynamic of the state evolving with its people, the people will take on an increasingly assertive role.

This book began with the stated objective of reading China in the original. It ends by examining what it means for the rest of the world if we do and if we don't. For readers outside of China keen to learn about the nation and its economy, I have tried to provide a view from an angle otherwise not easy to locate. As for the Chinese themselves, it's not always easy to achieve perspective when you, yourself, are immersed. Su Shi, a famous poet from the Song dynasty, described the difficulty of conveying the haunting beauty of Mount Lushan in Jiangxi Province this way: "Why can't I tell the true shape of Lushan? Because I myself am in the mountain." Sensitive to these challenges given my dual identity as someone educated in both China and the US who is now an educator dividing her time between Beijing and London, I have tried to shed light by delving into Chinese society, traditions, culture, economics, and political systems both as a local and as an outside observer.

However, understanding Chinese thinking does not mean endorsing it in its entirety. There is room for debate about the wisdom of China's strategy as well as its approach to achieving those ends. But understanding where these differences come from, and why, will help each of us suspend our suspicions of the other. Even when governments cannot see eye to eye, their people can. And in the end, most exchanges take place between individuals rather than between states, as we see in the active collaboration between businesses and universities, in the sciences, in the open flow of students. It's far less likely that one nation has all the answers than that the best answers will come from a variety of sources. Having experience in both countries, I appreciate the Chinese education system with its emphasis on discipline and competition, and I have also been inspired by an American education that encourages taking initiative and pursuing your passions.

Alongside the geopolitical benefits of reading China's playbook come enormous financial rewards. Deeper understanding leads to better predictions about the economy, which allows informed decisions to replace hunches. Firms selling to Chinese consumers can benefit from understanding the staggering generational shifts under way. For foreign companies going toe-to-toe with Chinese companies, understanding their competitors will encourage them to find their own successful niches. For investors who have direct and indirect exposure to Chinese stocks and bonds, understanding the power of state intervention and the network of state backers behind China's entrepreneurial boom, and recognizing the system's fragilities, will help them to reap more profit in good times and to lose less when things turn down. For those negotiating with Chinese policy makers, understanding their thinking can only be advantageous. Chinese reasoning is circular rather than linear; it's informed by logic, but also actively shaped by context and a complex system of relationships.

Future generations must overcome a mounting number of challenges left for them by previous generations, including crippling debt, geopolitical tensions, and existential threats to the environment. There are those who are creating a more dangerous world by promulgating a transactional world view of winners and losers, pitting people and nations against each other. On the brighter side, our fears and prejudices hide a deeper truth: we the people have much more in common than we realize. For one, we all want a brighter future for our children. But to make that possible, our nations will have to adapt to and harmonize with new realities—together. Perhaps, with the help of the new generation stepping into positions of leadership around the world, we can find ways to depict these realities not as a perpetual threat to humankind, but as part of an ongoing cycle of change and renewal. And if less energy ends up being spent on vying for dominance and more on shaping the future, that would be a success in any playbook.

ACKNOWLEDGMENTS

This long journey began in 1997, when Bill Cloherty, the late American lobbyist and educator, brought me from China to America as a Chinese exchange student. He and Dr. Lawrence Weiss, headmaster of the Horace Mann School at the time, gave me a once-in-a-lifetime opportunity to see the world through a multidimensional lens in my formative years, kindling an interest in me to recount the tale of China. This American generosity included the Horace Mann community and my host family, the Koppells, all of whom took me in warmly. I was the lucky beneficiary of America's openness and magnanimity, extended to a young student from the remote land of Communist China. At Harvard, my advisers, in particular Kenneth Rogoff and the late Emmanuel Farhi, were a constant source of support and inspiration.

My hope is that through this book another side of the Chinese story can be told. My views are based on my multicultural education and life experience, building on a myriad of excellent works from scholars, as well as my personal observations derived from everyday living and working in China and beyond. In writing it, I want to thank Patrizia van Daalen, who initiated this opportunity. She, with great enthusiasm, proposed that I write a book about China after listening in on a presentation about "Chinese puzzles" that I gave for Bertelsmann a few years ago. She connected me to my editor at Penguin, Patrick Nolan, to whom I owe my deepest gratitude for his unwavering support right from the beginning, when the project was only a scribbled page of ideas from a first-time author. His faith in me was crucial in the process, along with the contribution of his incisive team members Matt Klise and Annika Karody, who meticulously gave excellent comments and suggestions along the way.

I am enormously grateful to my agent, Sylvie Carr, whose guidance and commitment have been invaluable, and to Peter Guzzardi, who went beyond the call of duty, pouring his heart and soul into helping me improve and refine the manuscript. He did a phenomenal job in making the manuscript sparkle, and I have learned a great deal from Peter throughout the process. All errors remain my own. My excellent research assistants, Bingyan Gu, Hu Mian, Nachiket Shah, Buyuan Yang, and Jianding Zhang, helped me collect data and valuable scholarly resources. Wentao Xiong read through some of the earlier chapters and provided valuable feedback.

Lastly, everything I have and put into this book comes from my family, the guiding star to my wandering barque.

NOTES

CHAPTER ONE: THE CHINA PUZZLE

1. Thomas Piketty, Li Yang, and Gabriel Zucman, "Capital Accumulation, Private Property, and Rising Inequality in China, 1978–2015," *American Economic Review* 109, no. 7 (July 2019): 2469–96, https://doi.org/10.1257/aer.20170973.
2. Christian Haerpfer et al., eds., *World Values Survey: Round Seven–Country-Pooled Datafile Version 3.0* (Madrid and Vienna: JD Systems Institute & WVSA Secretariat, 2020), https://doi.org/10.14281/18241.16. See survey question 150.
3. Edward Cunningham, Tony Saich, and Jesse Turiel, "Understanding CCP Resilience: Surveying Chinese Public Opinion through Time," Ash Center for Democratic Governance and Innovation, Harvard Kennedy School, July 2020, https://ash.harvard.edu/files/ash/files/final_policy_brief_7.6.2020.pdf.
4. Haerpfer et al., *World Values Survey.* See survey question 71.
5. Deborah Lehr, "Trust in China," Edelman, January 18, 2022, https://www.edelman.com/trust/2022-trust-barometer/trust-china. See also Cary Wu et al., "Chinese Citizen Satisfaction with Government Performance during COVID-19," *Journal of Contemporary China 30*, no. 132 (March 17, 2021): 930–44, https://doi.org/10.1080/10670564.2021.1893558.
6. The online *zuobiao* survey asked more than 460,000 respondents whether they agreed that Western multiparty systems are unsuitable for China in its current state. About 38 percent of the respondents born after 1985 were in favor of this view while only around 16 percent of those born thirty years earlier agreed with this view. The

survey data comes from Jennifer Pan and Yiqing Xu, "China's Ideological Spectrum," *Journal of Politics* 80, no. 1 (January 2018): 254–73, https://doi.org/10.1086/694255.

7. Li and Shi, *Experience, Attitudes and Social Transition*, 338–61.

CHAPTER TWO: CHINA'S ECONOMIC MIRACLE

1. Angus Maddison, Maddison Database 2010, www.rug.nl/ggdc/historicaldevelopment/maddison/releases/maddison-database-2010.

2. Singapore had an annual growth rate above 8 percent for forty-two years, and Hong Kong sustained it for thirty-one years. Japan witnessed two decades of rapid growth, but its early decades were postwar catch-up—the rapid rebuilding and reconstruction of previously destroyed stocks of capital.

3. Robert E. Lucas Jr., "Making a Miracle," *Econometrica* 61, no. 2 (March 1993): 251–72, https://doi.org/10.2307/2951551.

4. Nicholas R. Lardy, *Markets over Mao: The Rise of Private Business in China* (Washington, DC: Peterson Institute for International Economics, 2014).

5. The World Values Survey is a comprehensive database covering over ninety countries. It has more than a quarter million participants answering more than a thousand questions on topics regarding values and beliefs.

6. Christian Haerpfer et al., eds, *World Values Survey: Round Seven–Country-Pooled Datafile Version 3.0* (Madrid and Vienna: JD Systems Institute & WVSA Secretariat, 2020), questions 7–17, https://doi.org/10.14281/18241.16.

7. Works include Tu Wei-ming, "The Rise of Industrial East Asia: The Role of Confucian Values," *Copenhagen Journal of Asian Studies* 4 (1989): 81–97, https://doi.org/10.22439/cjas.v4i1.1767; and Christian Jochim, "Confucius and Capitalism: Views of Confucianism in Works on Confucianism and Economic Development," *Journal of Chinese Religions* 20, no. 1 (1992): 135–71, https://doi.org/10.1179/073776992805307539.

8. Tan Kong Yam, "Pattern of Asia Pacific Economic Growth and Implications for China," paper presented at the Symposium on Economic Trade Cooperation between China and Asian Pacific Region, Beijing, October 28–31, 1989, 11–12, quoted in Tu Wei-Ming, "The Rise of Industrial East Asia: The Role sf Confucian Values," *Copenhagen Papers in East and Southeast Asian Studies* 4 (1989): 90–91.

9. Loren Brandt, Debin Ma, and Thomas G. Rawski, "From Divergence to Convergence: Reevaluating the History behind China's Economic Boom," *Journal of Economic Literature* 52, no. 1 (March 2014): 45–123, https://doi.org/10.1257/jel.52.1.45.

10. Loren Brandt and Thomas G. Rawski, eds., *China's Great Economic Transformation* (Cambridge: Cambridge University Press, 2010), 5.

11. Wei Li and Dennis Tao Yang, "The Great Leap Forward: Anatomy of a Central Planning Disaster," *Journal of Political Economy* 113, no. 4 (August 2005): 840–77, https://doi.org/10.1086/430804.

12. Brandt and Rawski, *China's Great Economic Transformation*, 170.

13. Ross Garnaut, Ligang Song, and Cai Fang, eds., *China's 40 Years of Reform and Development: 1978–2018* (Acton, Australia: Australian National University, 2018), 11.

14. Zeping Ren, Jiajin Ma, and Zhiheng Luo, *Report on China's Private Economy: 2019*, Evergrande Research Institute. 2019, http://pdf.dfcfw.com/pdf/H3_AP201910161368 844678_1.pdf.

15. Barry Bosworth, and Susan M. Collins, "Accounting for Growth: Comparing China and India," *Journal of Economic Perspectives* 22, no. 1 (Winter 2008): 45–66, https://doi.org/10.1257/jep.22.1.45.

16. Dwight H. Perkins and Thomas G. Rawski, "Forecasting China's Economic Growth to 2025," in *China's Great Economic Transformation*, eds. Loren Brandt and Thomas G. Rawski (Cambridge: Cambridge University Press, 2008), 829–86.

17. Jinghai Zheng, Arne Bigsten, and Angang Hu, "Can China's Growth Be Sustained? A Productivity Perspective," *World Development* 37, no. 4 (April 2009): 874–88, https://doi.org/10.1016/j.worlddev.2008.07.008.

18. Loren Brandt and Xiaodong Zhu, "Accounting for China's Growth," IZA Discussion Paper No. 4764, Institute for the Study of Labor, Bonn, Germany, February 2010, http://dx.doi.org/10.2139/ssrn.1556552.

19. Shekhar Aiyar, Romain Duval, Damien Puy, Yiqun Wu, and Longmei Zhang, "Growth Slowdowns and the Middle-Income Trap," *Japan and the World Economy* 48 (December 2018): 22–37, https://doi.org/10.1016/j.japwor.2018.07.001. Differences in estimates arise from different assumptions about the capital share and production functions.

20. Xiaodong Zhu, "Understanding China's Growth: Past, Present, and Future," *Journal of Economic Perspectives* 26, no. 4 (Fall 2012): 103–24, https://doi.org/10.1257/jep.26.4.103.

21. Loren Brandt et al., "China's Productivity Slowdown and Future Growth Potential," Policy Research Working Paper, 9298, World Bank, Washington, DC, June 2020, https://openknowledge.worldbank.org/handle/10986/33993.

22. Brandt and Zhu, "Accounting for China's Growth."

23. Data comes from the National Income and Product Accounts published by the Bureau of Economic Analysis, https://apps.bea.gov/iTable/iTable.cfm?reqid=19&step= 2#reqid=19&step=2&isuri=1&1921=survey.

24. Abhijit V. Banerjee and Esther Duflo, *Good Economics for Hard Times* (New York: PublicAffairs, 2021), 189.

25. Loren Brandt, Chang-Tai Hsieh, and Xiaodong Zhu, "Growth and Structural Transformation in China," in *China's Great Economic Transformation*, eds. Loren Brandt and Thomas G. Rawski (New York: Cambridge University Press, 2008), 683–728.

26. Zhu, "Understanding China's Growth."

27. Chong-En Bai, Chang-Tai Hsieh, and Yingyi Qian, "The Return to Capital in China," NBER Working Paper 12755, National Bureau of Economic Research, Cambridge, MA, December 2006, https://doi.org/10.3386/w12755.

28. Keyu Jin, "China's Steroids Model of Growth," in *Meeting Globalization's Challenges*, eds. Luís Catão and Maurice Obstfeld (Princeton, NJ: Princeton University Press, 2019), 77–93.

29. According to the World Justice Project Rule of Law Index 2019, China placed 82 out of 126 countries worldwide. The World Bank's doing business study placed China at 31 in 2019, up from 90 in 2015. *The Global Competitiveness Report 2019* by the World Economic Forum ranked China 72 out of 141 countries surveyed in terms of the index component called "Institution: Corporate governance."

30. Data comes from China Institute for Income Distribution, "Chinese Household Income Project (CHIP) Dataset," accessed October 1, 2022, http://www.ciidbnu.org/chip/index.asp; also see Qiaoyi Li, "600m with $140 Monthly Income Worries Top," *Global Times*, May 29, 2020, https://www.globaltimes.cn/content/1189968.shtml.

31. Hongbin Li, Prashant Loyalka, Scott Rozelle, and Binzhen Wu, "Human Capital and China's Future Growth," *Journal of Economic Perspectives* 31, no. 1 (Winter 2017): 25–48, https://doi.org/10.1257/jep.31.1.25.

32. Trevor Tombe and Xiaodong Zhu, "Trade, Migration, and Productivity: A Quantitative Analysis of China," *American Economic Review* 109, no. 5 (May 2019): 1843–72, https://doi.org/10.1257/aer.20150811.

CHAPTER THREE: CHINA'S CONSUMERS AND THE NEW GENERATION

1. Martin King Whyte, Wang Feng, and Yong Cai, "Challenging Myths about China's One-Child Policy," *China Journal* 74 (July 2015): 144–59, https://doi.org/10.1086/681664.

2. The 2005 One-Percent Population Survey, which provides data on 1 percent of the Chinese population across all provinces, showed that family support is the main source of income for almost half of the elderly urban population (ages sixty-five and older). And CHARLS (2011) made it clear that people in their forties and fifties expect this pattern to continue and count on having their children provide at least half of their income in their old age. It asked the whole sample of adults between forty-five and sixty-five in urban areas the question, "Whom do you think you can rely on for old-age support?" In addition, CHARLS (2008) showed that 45 percent of the elderly in urban households lived with their children. More information can be found in Taha Choukhmane, Nicolas Coeurdacier, and Keyu Jin, "The One-Child Policy and Household Saving," Working paper, July 2017, https://personal.lse.ac.uk/jink/pdf/onechildpolicy_ccj.pdf.

3. According to "A Decision on Establishing a Unified Basic Pension System for Enterprise Workers," State Council Document, 1997, 26. In 1997–98, the State Council established the urban employees' basic pension and medical insurance systems. By 2002, 58 percent of urban workers were covered by basic pension insurance. In 2006, the Sixth Plenary Session of the Sixteenth Central Committee of the Communist Party of China proposed to establish and improve a social security system covering both urban and rural residents, after which a series of measures were introduced between 2009 and 2015. By 2020, about 84 percent of rural and urban adults were covered by basic pension schemes. See also Li Yang, "Towards Equity and Sustainability? China's Pension System Reform Moves Center Stage," SSRN, June 2021, https://doi.org/10.2139/ssrn.3879895.

4. Gary S. Becker and H. Gregg Lewis, "On the Interaction between the Quantity and Quality of Children," *Journal of Political Economy* 81, no. 2 (1973): S279–88, http://www.jstor.org/stable/1840425.

5. Tencent, *Aggressive Post-00s 2019 Tencent Post-00s Research Report*.

6. Quanbao Jiang, Shuzhuo Li, and Marcus W. Feldman, "China's Missing Girls in the Three Decades from 1980 to 2010," *Asian Women* 28, no. 3 (September 2012): 53–73.

7. Avraham Ebenstein, "The 'Missing Girls' of China and the Unintended Consequences of the One Child Policy," *Journal of Human Resources* 45, no. 1 (Winter 2010): 87–115, https://doi.org/10.1353/jhr.2010.0003.

8. Wei Huang, Xiaoyan Lei, and Ang Sun, "Fertility Restrictions and Life Cycle Outcomes: Evidence from the One-Child Policy in China," *Review of Economics and Statistics* 103, no. 4 (October 2021): 694–710, https://doi.org/10.1162/rest_a_00921. The study finds that exposure to the policy's fertility restrictions leads to a 4.5 percentage point (35 percent of the mean) increase in the high school completion rate for women and a 3.1 percentage point (13 percent) higher completion rate for men.

9. Emily Hannum, Yuping Zhang, and Meiyan Wang, "Why Are Returns to Education Higher for Women Than for Men in Urban China?," *China Quarterly* 215 (September 2013): 616–40, https://doi.org/10.1017/s0305741013000696.

10. Huang, Lei, and Sun, "Fertility Restrictions and Life Cycle Outcomes."

11. Erica Field and Attila Ambrus, "Early Marriage, Age of Menarche, and Female Schooling Attainment in Bangladesh," *Journal of Political Economy* 116, no. 5 (October 2008): 881–930, https://doi.org/10.1086/593333.

12. Vanessa L. Fong, "China's One-Child Policy and the Empowerment of Urban Daughters," *American Anthropologist* 104, no. 4 (December 2002): 1098–109, https://doi.org/10.1525/aa.2002.104.4.1098.

13. Claudia Goldin and Lawrence F. Katz, "The Power of the Pill: Oral Contraceptives and Women's Career and Marriage Decisions," *Journal of Political Economy* 110, no. 4 (August 2002): 730–70, https://doi.org/10.1086/340778.

14. According to estimates by Huang, Lei, and Sun, "Fertility Restrictions and Life Cycle Outcomes," the availability of the pill increased college attainment 2 to 3 percent among young women in the United States. But the study's estimates suggest that China's one-child policy increased the female college completion rate by 34 percent. See also Elizabeth Oltmans Ananat and Daniel M. Hungerman, "The Power of the Pill for the Next Generation: Oral Contraception's Effects on Fertility, Abortion, and Maternal and Child Characteristics," *Review of Economics and Statistics* 94, no. 1 (February 2012): 37–51, https://doi.org/10.1162/rest_a_00230.

15. Shang-Jin Wei and Xiaobo Zhang, "The Competitive Saving Motive: Evidence from Rising Sex Ratios and Savings Rates in China," *Journal of Political Economy* 119, no. 3 (June 2011): 511–64, https://doi.org/10.1086/660887.

16. CEIC data, "CN: Disposable Income per Capita: Ytd: Urban," accessed April 28, 2022, https://insights.ceicdata.com/series/5049701_SR526054. Also "Disposable Income per Capita: Ytd: Rural," accessed April 28, 2022, https://insights.ceicdata.com/series/3653 59527_SR88609007.

17. Yang Du, "Changes of College Student Employment and Policy Suggestions," *People's Daily*, September 16, 2022, http://finance.people.com.cn/n1/2022/0916/c444648-3252 7858.html.

CHAPTER FOUR: PARADISE AND JUNGLE, THE STORY OF CHINESE FIRMS

1. Mao Yarong, "Private Enterprises Contribute More Than 60% of GDP and More Than 50% of National Tax Revenue," Yicai (December 23, 2019), https://www.yicai.com/news/100444934.html.

2. Chong-En Bai, Chang-Tai Hsieh, and Zheng Song, "Special Deals with Chinese Characteristics," *NBER Macroeconomics Annual* 34, no. 1 (2020): 341–79, https://doi.org/10.1086/707189.

3. National Bureau of Statistics, *Statistics Yearbook 2001: Employment by Urban and Rural Areas at Year-End* (2002), www.stats.gov.cn/tjsj/ndsj/zgnj/2000/E04c.htm.

4. TVEs were largely dismantled between 1989 and 1996. With increased market integration and competition, official discrimination against TVEs, and official preference for foreign-owned enterprises, TVEs lost their competitive position. See Yasheng Huang, "How Did China Take Off?," *Journal of Economic Perspectives* 26, no. 4 (Fall 2012): 147–70, https://doi.org/10.1257/jep.26.4.147.

5. From a survey on firms in Wenzhou and Kunshan. See Figure 4 in Franklin Allen, Jun Qian, and Meijun Qian, "Law, Finance, and Economic Growth in China," *Journal of Financial Economics* 77, no. 1 (July 2005): 57–116, https://doi.org/10.1016/j.jfineco.2004.06.010.

6. Chang-Tai Hsieh and Zheng (Michael) Song, "Grasp the Large, Let Go of the Small: The Transformation of the State Sector in China," Brookings Papers on Economic Activity, Spring 2015, 295–366, https://doi.org/10.1353/eca.2016.0005

7. The average asset size of industrial SOEs increased from RMB 134 million in 1999 to 923 million in 2008. See Gao Xu, "State-Owned Enterprises in China: How Big Are They?," *East Asia & Pacific on the Rise* (blog), World Bank, January 19, 2010, https://blogs.worldbank.org/eastasiapacific/state-owned-enterprises-in-china-how-big-are-they.

8. Subnational governments were endowed with lawmaking power since the PRC's founding in 1949. See Chenggang Xu, "The Fundamental Institutions of China's Reforms and Development," *Journal of Economic Literature* 49, no. 4 (December 2011): 1076–151, https://doi.org/10.1257/jel.49.4.1076.

9. Di Guo, Kun Jiang, Byung-Yeon Kim, and Chenggang Xu, "Political Economy of Private Firms in China," in "Economic Systems in the Pacific Rim Region Symposium," ed. Josef C. Brada, special issue, *Journal of Comparative Economics* 42, no. 2 (May 2014): 286–303, https://doi.org/10.1016/j.jce.2014.03.006.

10. Bai, Hsieh, and Song, "Special Deals with Chinese Characteristics."

11. Qiaomei Du, "7 Billion: Why Did NIO Headquarters Finally Land in Hefei," NetEase News (May 6, 2020), https://auto.163.com/20/0506/07/FBU6IPRI000884MR.html.

12. Chong-En Bai, Chang-Tai Hsieh, Zheng Song, and Xin Wang, "The Rise of State-Connected Private Owners in China," NBER Working Paper 28170, National Bureau of Economic Research, Cambridge, MA, December 2020, www.nber.org/system/files/working_papers/w28170/w28170.pdf. The data set used is the firm registration data of the State Administration for Industry and Commerce.

13. Foreign investors would normally use three major types of business forms for incorporating foreign-invested entities in China: equity joint ventures, cooperative joint ventures, and wholly foreign-owned enterprises.

14. Data based on Chinese firms are from an annual survey of manufacturing enterprises collected by the Chinese National Bureau of Statistics. The data set includes nonstate firms with sales over RMB 5 million (about US$600,000) and all the state firms for the 1998–2007 period. These results come from Yan Bai, Keyu Jin, and Dan Lu, "Misallocation under Trade Liberalization," NBER Working Paper 26188, National Bureau of Economic Research, Cambridge, MA, August 2019, https://doi.org/10.3386/w26188, who measure distortions at the firm level and interpret them as taxes and subsidies.

15. Yasheng Huang and Heiwai Tang, "Are Foreign Firms Favored in China? Firm-Level Evidence on the Collection of Value-Added Taxes," *Journal of International Business Policy* 1, no. 1–2 (June 2018): 71–91, https://doi.org/10.1057/s42214-018-0006-z.

16. Feng Li, "Why Western Digital Firms Have Failed in China," *Harvard Business Review*, August 14, 2018, https://hbr.org/2018/08/why-western-digital-firms-have-failed-in-china.

17. David Greenaway, Alessandra Guariglia, and Zhihong Yu, "The More the Better? Foreign Ownership and Corporate Performance in China," *European Journal of Finance* 20, no. 7–9 (2014): 681–702, https://doi.org/10.1080/1351847X.2012.671785.

18. Chunling Li and Yunqing Shi, *Experience, Attitudes and Social Transition: A Sociological Study of the Post-1980 Generation* (Beijing: Social Sciences Academic Press, 2013), 350–52.

CHAPTER FIVE: THE STATE AND THE MAYOR ECONOMY

1. Rana Mitter and Elsbeth Johnson, "What the West Gets Wrong about China," *Harvard Business Review*, May 1, 2021, https://hbr.org/2021/05/what-the-west-gets-wrong-about-china.

2. Pierre F. Landry, Xiaobo Lü, and Haiyan Duan, "Does Performance Matter? Evaluating Political Selection along the Chinese Administrative Ladder," *Comparative Political Studies* 51, no. 8 (2018): 1074–105, https://doi.org/10.1177/0010414017730078.

3. Charlotte Gao, "China's Anti-Graft Campaign: 527,000 People Punished in 2017," *The Diplomat*, January 12, 2018, https://thediplomat.com/2018/01/chinas-anti-graft-campaign-527000-people-punished-in-2017.

4. Trevor Tombe and Xiaodong Zhu, "Trade, Migration, and Productivity: A Quantitative Analysis of China," *American Economic Review* 109, no. 5 (May 2019): 1843–72, https://doi.org/10.1257/aer.20150811.

5. Wei Chen et al., "A Forensic Examination of China's National Accounts," Brookings Papers on Economic Activity, Spring 2019, 77–141, https://www.jstor.org/stable/90000434.

6. The notorious scandal of Sanlu formula milk laced with melamine in 2008 cast a long shadow over food security and in particular parents' confidence in Chinese local-made infant formula. While it was the local dairy producers who put melamine in the

milk to boost protein levels so as to pass nutritional testing, Sanlu's management did not stop the production and sale of the tainted milk, even after they were aware of the health hazard of their products. The tainted formula milk took the lives of six infants and sickened three hundred thousand, leaving many to depend on kidney dialysis for the rest of their lives. Sanlu's chairwoman got a life sentence, and this state-owned company went bankrupt. A total of twenty-two companies were involved in this tragedy. This incident led to infant formula being among the most heavily regulated foodstuffs in China.

7. Gene M. Grossman and Alan B. Krueger, "Economic Growth and the Environment," *Quarterly Journal of Economics* 110, no. 2 (May 1995): 353–77, https://doi.org/10.2307/2118443.

8. Ruxin Wu and Piao Hu, "Does the 'Miracle Drug' of Environmental Governance Really Improve Air Quality? Evidence from China's System of Central Environmental Protection Inspections," *International Journal of Environmental Research and Public Health* 16, no. 5 (March 2019): 850, https://doi.org/10.3390/ijerph16050850.

9. Bei Qin, David Strömberg, and Yanhui Wu, "Why Does China Allow Freer Social Media? Protests versus Surveillance and Propaganda," *Journal of Economic Perspectives* 31, no. 1 (Winter 2017): 117–40, https://doi.org/10.1257/jep.31.1.117.

10. Markus K. Brunnermeier, *The Resilient Society* (Colorado Springs, CO: Endeavor Literary Press, 2021), 13–19.

CHAPTER SIX: THE FINANCIAL SYSTEM

1. Franklin Allen, Jun "QJ" Qian, Chenyu Shan, and Julie Zhu, "Dissecting the Long-Term Performance of the Chinese Stock Market," SSRN 2880021, November 2021, https://doi.org/10.2139/ssrn.2880021; Franklin Allen, Jun Q. J. Qian, Chenyu Shan, and Julie Lei Zhu, "The Development of the Chinese Stock Market," in *The Handbook of China's Financial System*, eds. Marlene Amstad, Guofeng Sun, and Wei Xiong (Princeton, NJ: Princeton University Press, 2020), 283–313, https://doi.org/10.2307/j.ctv11vcdpc.15.

2. Edward Glaeser, Wei Huang, Yueran Ma, and Andrei Shleifer, "A Real Estate Boom with Chinese Characteristics," *Journal of Economic Perspectives* 31, no. 1 (Winter 2017): 93–116, https://doi.org/10.1257/jep.31.1.93.

3. Nargiza Salidjanova, "China's Stock Market Meltdown Shakes the World, Again," U.S.-China Economic and Security Review Commission, January 14, 2016, www.uscc.gov/sites/default/files/Research/Issue%20brief%20-%20China%27s%20Stocks%20Fall%20Again.pdf.

4. "The Causes and Consequences of China's Market Crash," *The Economist*, August 24, 2015, https://www.economist.com/news/2015/08/24/the-causes-and-consequences-of-chinas-market-crash.

5. World Bank data, "Domestic Credit to Private Sector by Banks (% of GDP)–China," accessed April 28, 2022, https://data.worldbank.org/indicator/FD.AST.PRVT.GD.ZS?locations=CN; "Domestic Credit to Private Sector by Banks (% of GDP)–United States," accessed April 28, 2022, https://data.worldbank.org/indicator/FD.AST.PRVT.GD.ZS?locations=US.

6. CEIC, "China Market Capitalization: % of GDP," accessed April 28, 2022, https://www .ceicdata.com/en/indicator/china/market-capitalization--nominal-gdp; CEIC, "United States Market Capitalization: % of GDP," accessed April 28, 2022, https://www.ceic data.com/en/indicator/united-states/market-capitalization--nominal-gdp; and Marlene Amstad and Zhiguo He, "Chinese Bond Markets and Interbank Market," in *The Handbook of China's Financial System*, eds. Amstad, Sun, and Xiong, 105–48.

7. Zhiguo He and Wei, "China's Financial System and Economy," NBER Working Paper 30324, National Bureau of Economic Research, Cambridge, MA, August 2022, https://doi.org/10.3386/w30324.

8. Data from St. Louis Fed FRED. "Mutual Fund Assets to GDP for China," accessed April 28, 2022, https://fred.stlouisfed.org/series/DDDI07CNA156NWDB; "Mutual Fund Assets to GDP for United States," accessed April 28, 2022, https://fred.stlouis fed.org/series/DDDI07USA156NWDB.

9. Nicholas Borst and Nicholas Lardy, "Maintaining Financial Stability in the People's Republic of China during Financial Liberalization," Working Paper No. 15-4, Peterson Institute for International Economics, Washington, DC, March 2015, https://doi .org/10.2139/ssrn.2588543.

10. Franklin Allen et al., "The Development of the Chinese Stock Market," in *The Handbook of China's Financial System*, eds. Amstad, Sun, and Xiong.

11. Franklin Allen, Jun Q. J. Qian, Chenyu Shan, and Julie Zhu, "Dissecting the Long-Term Performance of the Chinese Stock Market," SSRN 2880021, November 2021, https://doi.org/10.2139/ssrn.2880021.

12. U.S.-China Economic and Security Review Commission, "Chinese Companies Listed on Major U.S. Stock Exchanges," March 31, 2022, https://www.uscc.gov/research/chi nese-companies-listed-major-us-stock-exchanges.

13. These numbers are computed by Allen, Qian, Shan, and Zhu in "Dissecting the Long-Term Performance of the Chinese Stock Market."

14. Alexandra Stevenson, Michael Forsythe, and Cao Li, "China and Evergrande Ascended Together. Now One Is About to Fall," *New York Times*, September 28, 2021, https://www.nytimes.com/2021/09/28/business/china-evergrande-economy.html.

15. Grace Xing Hu, Jun Pan, and Jiang Wang, "Chinese Capital Market: An Empirical Overview," NBER Working Paper 24346, National Bureau of Economic Research, Cambridge, MA, February 2018, https://doi.org/10.3386/w24346; and Charles M. Jones, Donghui Shi, Xiaoyan Zhang, and Xinran Zhang, "Understanding Retail Investors: Evidence from China," SSRN 3628809, October 2021, https://doi.org/10.2139/ssrn.3628809.

16. Jeremy C. Stein and Adi Sunderam, "The Fed, the Bond Market, and Gradualism in Monetary Policy," *Journal of Finance* 73, no. 3 (June 2018): 1015–60, https://doi.org /10.1111/jofi.12614.

17. Glaeser, Huang, Ma, and Shleifer, "A Real Estate Boom with Chinese Characteristics."

18. Bin Zhang et al., "New Citizens and New Models: The Real Estate Market for the Future," China Finance 40 Forum, June 1, 2022, http://www.cf40.org.cn/Uploads /Picture/2022/06/01/u6297090ccd409.pdf.

19. Kenneth S. Rogoff and Yuanchen Yang, "Peak China Housing," NBER Working Paper 27697, National Bureau of Economic Research, Cambridge, MA, August 2020, https://doi.org/10.3386/w27697.

20. Rogoff and Yang, "Peak China Housing."

21. Hanming Fang, Quanlin Gu, Wei Xiong, and Li An Zhou, "Demystifying the Chinese Housing Boom," *NBER Macroeconomics Annual* 30, no. 1 (2016): 105–66, https://doi.org/10.1086/685953; and Chang Liu and Wei Xiong, "China's Real Estate Market," in *The Handbook of China's Financial System*, eds. Amstad, Sun, and Xiong.

22. For the period 2003–2013, the mortgage data is used. The seventy-city index, which covers the later period of 2013–2017, was provided by the National Bureau of Statistics, and adjusts for housing quality.

23. Liu and Xiong, "China's Real Estate Market."

24. Ting Chen, Laura Xiaolei Liu, Wei Xiong, and Li-An Zhou, "Real Estate Boom and Misallocation of Capital in China," Working Paper, Princeton University, Princeton, NJ, December 2017, https://editorialexpress.com/cgi-bin/conference/download.cgi?db_name=CICF2018&paper_id=915.

25. Listed property companies from China have an average of 80 percent debt to asset ratio, compared to 57 percent in the US and 37 percent in the UK. See CEIC, "CN: Listed Company: Debt to Asset Ratio," accessed April 28, 2022, https://insights.ceicdata.com/series/234354101_SR2937736.

26. Institute of Social Science Survey (ISSS) of Peking University, "China Family Panel Studies (CFPS)," accessed October 1, 2022, https://www.isss.pku.edu.cn/cfps/en.

27. A discussion of the transformation of former ghost cities can be found in the Chinese source www.sohu.com/a/133489588_141721.

28. An insightful study on this is Kinda Hachem and Zheng Song, "Liquidity Rules and Credit Booms," *Journal of Political Economy* 129, no. 10 (October 2021): 2721–65, https://doi.org/10.1086/715074.

29. Zhuo Chen, Zhiguo He, and Chun Liu, "The Financing of Local Government in China: Stimulus Loan Wanes and Shadow Banking Waxes," *Journal of Financial Economics* 137, no. 1 (July 2020): 42–71, https://doi.org/10.1016/j.jfineco.2019.07.009; Zheng Michael Song and Wei Xiong, "Risks in China's Financial System," NBER Working Paper 24230, National Bureau of Economic Research, Cambridge, MA, January 2018, https://doi.org/10.3386/w24230; China Banking Wealth Management Registration and Custody Center, *China Wealth Management Products Market Annual Report (2016)*, May 19, 2017, http://www.efnchina.com/uploadfile/2017/0531/20170531032656799.pdf.

30. Entrusted loans are firm-to-firm loans that use banks as a trustee. Banks earn a fee by administering the loan, given that nonfinancial firms in China are prohibited from lending to each other.

31. Zhiwu Chen, "China's Dangerous Debt: Why the Economy Could Be Headed for Trouble," *Foreign Affairs* 94, no. 3 (May/June 2015): 13–18, www.jstor.org/stable/24483658.

32. "Development and Reform Commission: The Composition of 4 Trillion Yuan Investment and Latest Progress of Investment Projects," http://www.gov.cn/gzdt/2009-05/21/content_1321149.htm.

33. Chong-En Bai, Chang-Tai Hsieh, Zheng Song, and Xin Wang, "The Rise of State-Connected Private Owners in China," NBER Working Paper 28170, National Bureau

of Economic Research, Cambridge, MA, December 2020, https://doi.org/10.3386/w28170.

34. Chen, He, and Liu, "The Financing of Local Government in China."

35. Andrew Ang, Jennie Bai, and Hao Zhou, "The Great Wall of Debt: Real Estate, Political Risk, and Chinese Local Government Financing Cost," Georgetown McDonough School of Business Research Paper No. 2603022, July 2018, https://papers.ssrn.com/sol3/papers.cfm?abstract_id=2603022.

36. Chen, He, and Liu, "The Financing of Local Government in China."

37. Fitch Ratings, "Rating Report: China Evergrande Group," July 5, 2021, https://www.fitchratings.com/research/corporate-finance/china-evergrande-group-05-07-2021.

38. Song and Xiong, "Risks in China's Financial System."

39. See discussion in Song and Xiong, "Risks in China's Financial System."

40. Zhiyong Yang, Cin Zhang, and Linmin Tang, "Chinese Academy of Social Sciences: How Risky Is Local Government Debt," *The Paper*, December 2, 2019, https://www.thepaper.cn/newsDetail_forward_5119321.

41. One can make a simple calculation based on the flow of saving every year divided by the amount of interest payments serviced annually. That ratio is as large as eight times the number the US had leading up to its 2007 housing bust.

CHAPTER SEVEN: THE TECHNOLOGY RACE

1. Kai-Fu Lee, "Kai-Fu Lee on How Covid Spurs China's Great Robotic Leap Forward," *The Economist*, June 25, 2020, https://www.economist.com/by-invitation/2020/06/25/kai-fu-lee-on-how-covid-spurs-chinas-great-robotic-leap-forward.

2. Graham Allison, Kevin Klyman, Karina Barbesino, and Hugo Yen, "The Great Tech Rivalry: China vs. the U.S.," Belfer Center for Science and International Affairs, Harvard Kennedy School, Cambridge, MA, December 2021, www.belfercenter.org/sites/default/files/GreatTechRivalry_ChinavsUS_211207.pdf.

3. W. Brian Arthur, *The Nature of Technology: What It Is and How It Evolves* (New York: Free Press, 2009), 24.

4. Christina Larson, "From Imitation to Innovation: How China Became a Tech Superpower," *Wired*, February 13, 2018, https://www.wired.co.uk/article/how-china-became-tech-superpower-took-over-the-west.

5. Yu Zhou, William Lazonick, and Yifei Sun, eds., *China as an Innovation Nation* (Oxford: Oxford University Press, 2016), 133–162.

6. Scott Malcomson, "How China Became the World's Leader in Green Energy: And What Decoupling Could Cost the Environment," *Foreign Affairs*, February 28, 2020, https://www.foreignaffairs.com/articles/china/2020-02-28/how-china-became-worlds-leader-green-energy.

7. Kai-Fu Lee, *AI Superpowers: China, Silicon Valley, and the New World Order* (Boston: Houghton Mifflin, 2018), 30–42.

8. Hal Varian, "Artificial Intelligence, Economics, and Industrial Organization," in *The Economics of Artificial Intelligence: An Agenda*, eds. Ajay Agrawal, Joshua Gans, and Avi Goldfarb (Chicago, London: University of Chicago Press, 2018), 399–419.

9. Sheena Chestnut Greitens, *Dealing with Demand for China's Global Surveillance Exports*, Brookings Institution, April 2020, www.brookings.edu/research/dealing-with-demand-for-chinas-global-surveillance-exports.

10. Aaron Klein, China's Digital Payments Revolution, Brookings Institution, April 2020, www.brookings.edu/wp-content/uploads/2020/04/FP_20200427_china_digital_payments_klein.pdf.

11. Harald Hau, Yi Huang, Hongzhe Shan, and Zixia Sheng, "How FinTech Enters China's Credit Market," *AEA Papers and Proceedings* 109 (May 2019): 60–64, https://doi.org/10.1257/pandp.20191012; Lili Dai, Jianlei Han, Jing Shi, and Bohui Zhang, "Debt Collection through Digital Footprints," SSRN 4135159, August 2022, https://doi.org/10.2139/ssrn.4135159.

12. Jianwei Xing, Eric Zou, Zhentao Yin, Yong Wang, and Zhenhua Li, "'Quick Response' Economic Stimulus: The Effect of Small-Value Digital Coupons on Spending," NBER Working Paper 27596, National Bureau of Economic Research, Cambridge, MA, July 2020, https://doi.org/10.3386/w27596; Qiao Liu, Qiaowei Shen, Zhenghua Li, and Shu Chen, "Stimulating Consumption at Low Budget: Evidence from a Large-Scale Policy Experiment amid the COVID-19 Pandemic," *Management Science* 67, no. 12 (December 2021): 7291–7307, https://doi.org/10.1287/mnsc.2021.4119.

13. Keyu Jin, Tao Jin, and Yifei Ren, "Fiscal Policy through Fintech Platforms," Working Paper, London School of Economics and Political Science, October 2022.

14. Allison, Klyman, Barbesino, and Yen, "The Great Tech Rivalry."

15. Michelle Tang, "Ride-Hailing in Latin America: A Race between Uber and Didi's 99," *Measurable AI* (blog), August 18, 2022, https://blog.measurable.ai/2022/08/18/ride-hailing-in-latin-america-a-race-between-uber-and-didis-99.

16. Clive Thompson, "Inside the Machine That Saved Moore's Law," *MIT Technology Review*, October 27, 2021, https://www.technologyreview.com/2021/10/27/1037118/moores-law-computer-chips.

17. Che Pan, "China's Top Chip Maker SMIC Achieves 7-Nm Tech Breakthrough on Par with Intel, TSMC and Samsung, Analysts Say," *South China Morning Post*, August 29, 2022, https://www.scmp.com/tech/big-tech/article/3190590/chinas-top-chip-maker-smic-achieves-7-nm-tech-breakthrough-par-intel.

18. Mariana Mazzucato, "The Entrepreneurial State," *Soundings* 49 (Winter 2011): 131–42, https://doi.org/10.3898/136266211798411183.

19. Elsa B. Kania, "China's Quantum Future," *Foreign Affairs*, September 26, 2018, https://www.foreignaffairs.com/articles/china/2018-09-26/chinas-quantum-future.

20. Keyu Jin, "How China Is Fighting the Chip War with America," *New York Times*, October 27, 2022, https://www.nytimes.com/2022/10/27/opinion/china-america-chip-tech-war.html.

21. Jon Schmid and Fei-Ling Wang, "Beyond National Innovation Systems: Incentives and China's Innovation Performance," *Journal of Contemporary China* 26, no. 104 (2017): 280–96, https://doi.org/10.1080/10670564.2016.1223108.

22. This analogy is from a conversation between the American political scientist Graham Allison and Xue Lan, professor and dean of the School of Public Policy and Management, Tsinghua University.

CHAPTER EIGHT: CHINA'S ROLE IN GLOBAL TRADE

1. Pol Antràs, "De-Globalisation? Global Value Chains in the Post-COVID-19 Age," NBER Working Paper 28115, National Bureau of Economic Research, Cambridge, MA, November 2020, https://doi.org/10.3386/w28115.

2. Xiaohua Li and Wenxuan Li, "The Transformation of China's Manufacturing Competitive Advantage in the 40 Years of Reform and Opening-Up," *Southeast Academic Research* 5 (2018): 12.

3. Fang Cai and Meiyan Wang, "A Counterfactual Analysis on Unlimited Surplus Labor in Rural China," *China and World Economy* 16, no. 1 (January–February 2008): 51–65, https://doi.org/10.1111/j.1749-124X.2008.00099.x.

4. Pol Antràs, "Conceptual Aspects of Global Value Chains," *World Bank Economic Review* 34, no. 3 (October 2020): 551–74, http://hdl.handle.net/10986/33228.

5. World Trade Organization, *Global Value Chain Development Report 2019: Technological Innovation, Supply Chain Trade, and Workers in a Globalized World* (Geneva: World Trade Organization, 2019), https://documents.worldbank.org/curated/en/384161555079173489.

6. Accenture, "Globality and Complexity of the Semiconductor Ecosystem," Accenture, February 21, 2020, https://www.accenture.com/cz-en/insights/high-tech/semiconductor-ecosystem.

7. Yuqing Xing, "How the iPhone Widens the U.S. Trade Deficit with China: The Case of the iPhone X," *Frontiers of Economics in China* 15, no. 4 (2020): 642–58, https://doi.org/10.3868/s060-011-020-0026-8.

8. Xin Li, Bo Meng, and Zhi Wang, "Recent Patterns of Global Production and GVC Participation," in *Global Value Chain Development Report 2019* (Washington, DC: World Bank Group, 2019), 9–44.

9. Mary Amiti, Stephen J. Redding, and David E. Weinstein, "The Impact of the 2018 Tariffs on Prices and Welfare," *Journal of Economic Perspectives* 33, no. 4 (Fall 2019): 187–210, https://doi.org/10.1257/jep.33.4.187.

10. US Bureau of Labor Statistics, "Workforce Statistics in Manufacturing: Employment (in Thousands)," accessed April 28, 2022, https://www.bls.gov/iag/tgs/iag31-33.htm#workforce.

11. Bob Davis and Jon Hilsenrath, "How the China Shock, Deep and Swift, Spurred the Rise of Trump," *Wall Street Journal*, August 11, 2016.

12. Daron Acemoglu, David Autor, David Dorn, Gordon H. Hanson, and Brendan Price, "Import Competition and the Great US Employment Sag of the 2000s," in "Labor Markets in the Aftermath of the Great Recession," eds. David Card and Alexandre Mas, supplement, *Journal of Labor Economics* 34, no. S1 (January 2016): S141–98, https://doi.org/10.1086/682384; David H. Autor, David Dorn, and Gordon H. Hanson, "The China Syndrome: Local Labor Market Effects of Import Competition in the United States," *American Economic Review* 103, no. 6 (October 2013): 2121–68, https://doi.org/10.1257/aer.103.6.2121; David H. Autor, David Dorn, and Gordon H. Hanson, "The China Shock: Learning from Labor-Market Adjustment to Large Changes in Trade," *Annual Review of Economics* 8, no. 1 (October 31, 2016): 205–40, https://doi.org/10.1146/annurev-economics-080315-015041.

13. Daron Acemoglu and Pascual Restrepo, "Robots and Jobs: Evidence from US Labor Markets," *Journal of Political Economy* 128, no. 6 (June 2020): 2188–244, https://doi .org/10.1086/705716.

14. Teresa C. Fort, Justin R. Pierce, and Peter K. Schott, "New Perspectives on the Decline of US Manufacturing Employment," *Journal of Economic Perspectives* 32, no. 2 (Spring 2018): 47–72, https://doi.org/10.1257/jep.32.2.47.

15. Kerwin Kofi Charles, Erik Hurst, and Mariel Schwartz, "The Transformation of Manufacturing and the Decline in US Employment," *NBER Macroeconomics Annual* 33, no. 1 (2019): 307–72, https://doi.org/10.1086/700896.

16. Katherine Eriksson, Katheryn N. Russ, Jay C. Shambaugh, and Minfei Xu, "Reprint: Trade Shocks and the Shifting Landscape of U.S. Manufacturing," *Journal of International Money and Finance* 111 (March 2021): 102–254, https://doi.org/10.1016 /j.jimonfin.2021.102407.

17. Anne Case and Angus Deaton, *Deaths of Despair and the Future of Capitalism* (Princeton, NJ: Princeton University Press, 2020), 9–10.

18. "U.S.-China Trade War Has Cost up to 245,000 U.S. Jobs: Business Group Study," Reuters, January 14, 2021, https://www.reuters.com/article/us-usa-trade-china-jobs -idUSKBN29J2O9.

19. Zhi Wang, Shang-Jin Wei, Xinding Yu, and Kunfu Zhu, "Re-examining the Effects of Trading with China on Local Labor Markets: A Supply Chain Perspective," NBER Working Paper 24886, National Bureau of Economic Research, Cambridge, MA, August 2018, https://www.nber.org/papers/w24886; Robert Feenstra, Hong Ma, Akira Sasahara, and Yuan Xu, "Reconsidering the 'China Shock' in Trade," Center for Economic Policy Research, January 18, 2018, https://cepr.org/voxeu/columns/reconsider ing-china-shock-trade.

20. Teresa Fort, Justin Pierce, and Peter Schott, "The Evolution of US Manufacturing," Center for Economic Policy Research, August 18, 2020, https://cepr.org/voxeu/columns /evolution-us-manufacturing.

21. Gene M. Grossman and Elhanan Helpman, "Protection for Sale," *American Economic Review* 84, no. 4 (September 1994): 833–50, https://www.jstor.org/stable/2118033.

22. Between 2000 and 2010, the share of Chinese imports in total imports increased by 25 percentage points in the US. In the UK and the Netherlands, that number was 16 percentage points, and in Spain, Italy, and Germany, 14 percentage points. France and Sweden were least exposed, with a 13-percentage-point increase in the import share. The numbers come from Dalia Marin, "The China Shock: Why Germany Is Different," Center for Economic Policy Research, September 7, 2017, https://cepr.org /voxeu/columns/china-shock-why-germany-different. And the China shock is estimated to explain about 10 percent of Norway's decline in manufacturing employment; see Ragnhild Balsvik, Sissel Jensen, and Kjell G. Salvanes, "Made in China, Sold in Norway: Local Labor Market Effects of an Import Shock," *Journal of Public Economics* 127 (July 2015): 137–44, https://doi.org/10.1016/j.jpubeco.2014.08.006.

23. Wolfgang Dauth, Sebastian Findeisen, and Jens Suedekum, "The Rise of the East and the Far East: German Labor Markets and Trade Integration," *Journal of the European Economic Association* 12, no. 6 (July 2014): 1643–75, https://doi.org/10.1111/jeea .12092.

24. Kyle Handley and Nuno Limão, "Policy Uncertainty, Trade, and Welfare: Theory and Evidence for China and the United States," *American Economic Review* 107, no. 9 (September 2017): 2731–83, https://doi.org/10.1257/aer.20141419.

25. Pablo D. Fajgelbaum and Amit K. Khandelwal, "Measuring the Unequal Gains from Trade," *Quarterly Journal of Economics* 131, no. 3 (March 2016): 1113–80, https://doi .org/10.1093/qje/qjw013.

26. Johan Hombert, Adrien Matray, and Daniel Brown, "Yes, You Can Outmuscle Chinese Imports through Innovation and R&D," *Forbes*, April 25, 2018, https://www .forbes.com/sites/hecparis/2018/04/25/how-us-manufacturers-can-outmuscle -chinese-imports-through-innovation-and-rd.

27. Daniel Michaels, "Foreign Robots Invade American Factory Floors," *Wall Street Journal*, March 26, 2017, https://www.wsj.com/articles/powering-americas-manufacturing -renaissance-foreign-robots-1490549611.

28. Nicholas Bloom, Miko Draca, and John Van Reenen, "Trade Induced Technical Change? The Impact of Chinese Imports on Innovation, IT, and Productivity," *Review of Economic Studies* 83, no. 1 (January 2016): 87–117, https://doi.org/10.1093/re stud/rdv039.

29. Johan Hombert and Adrien Matray, "Can Innovation Help U.S. Manufacturing Firms Escape Import Competition from China?," *Journal of Finance* 73, no. 5 (October 2018): 2003–39, https://doi.org/10.1111/jofi.12691.

30. Dani Rodrik, *The Globalization Paradox: Why Global Markets, States, and Democracy Can't Coexist* (Oxford: Oxford University Press, 2012), 67–88.

31. Ha-Joon Chang, *Bad Samaritans: The Guilty Secrets of Rich Nations and the Threat to Global Prosperity* (London: Random House, 2008), 19–39.

32. Shang-Jin Wei, "Misreading China's WTO Record Hurts Global Trade," Project Syndicate, December 11, 2021, https://www.project-syndicate.org/commentary/misread ing-china-wto-record-hurts-global-trade-by-shang-jin-wei-2021-12.

33. Fareed Zakaria, *Ten Lessons for a Post-Pandemic World* (New York: W. W. Norton, 2021).

34. Lili Yan Ing, Miaojie Yu, and Rui Zhang, "The Evolution of Export Quality: China and Indonesia," in *World Trade Evolution*, eds. Lili Yan Ing and Miaojie Yu (London: Routledge, 2018), 261–302.

35. Daisuke Wakabayashi and Tripp Mickle, "Tech Companies Slowly Shift Production Away from China," *New York Times*, September 1, 2022, sec. Business, https://www .nytimes.com/2022/09/01/business/tech-companies-china.html.

36. Siqi Ji, "How China, Japan's Hot Trade and Economic Relationship Is Being Tested by Cold Politics," *South China Morning Post*, August 18, 2022, https://www.scmp.com /economy/china-economy/article/3189234/how-china-japans-hot-trade-and -economic-relationship-being; and Jeffrey Kucik and Rajan Menon, "Can the United States Really Decouple from China?," *Foreign Policy*, January 11, 2022, https://for eignpolicy.com/2022/01/11/us-china-economic-decoupling-trump-biden.

37. Stephen Ross Yeaple, "The Multinational Firm," *Annual Review of Economics* 5, no. 1 (August 2013): 193–217, https://doi.org/10.1146/annurev-economics-081612-071350.

38. State Council of the People's Republic of China, "China and the World in the New Era," September 27, 2019, http://www.gov.cn/zhengce/2019-09/27/content_5433889.htm.

CHAPTER NINE: ON THE WORLD'S FINANCIAL STAGE

1. Robert E. Lipsey, "Foreign Direct Investment and the Operations of Multinational Firms: Concepts, History, and Data," NBER Working Paper 8665, National Bureau of Economic Research, Cambridge, MA, December 2001, https://doi.org/10.3386/w8665.

2. Saleem Bahaj and Ricardo Reis, "Jumpstarting an International Currency," HKIMR Working Paper No.19/2020, Hong Kong Institute for Monetary and Financial Research, December 2020, https://doi.org/10.2139/ssrn.3757279.

3. Ramon Moreno, Dubravko Mihaljek, Agustin Villar, and Előd Takáts, "The Global Crisis and Financial Intermediation in Emerging Market Economies: An Overview," BIS Papers, No. 54, Bank for International Settlements, December 2010, https://www.bis.org/publ/bppdf/bispap54.pdf.

4. Tarek El-Tablawy, "Egypt Moves Closer to IMF Loan with China Currency Swap Deal," Bloomberg.com, October 30, 2016, https://www.bloomberg.com/news/articles/2016-10-30/egypt-moves-closer-to-imf-loan-with-china-currency-swap-deal.

5. Emmanuel Farhi and Matteo Maggiori, "A Model of the International Monetary System," Quarterly Journal of Economics 133, no. 1 (2018): 295–355, https://doi.org/10.1093/qje/qjx031.

6. As measured by the sum of financial assets and liabilities as a share of GDP. Data is from International Monetary Fund, "Balance of Payments and International Investment Position," accessed April 28, 2022, https://data.imf.org/?sk=7A51304B-6426-40C0-83DD-CA473CA1FD52; World Bank, "GDP (Current US$): China, United States," accessed April 28, 2022, https://data.worldbank.org/indicator/NY.GDP.MKTP.CD.

7. Trade openness is measured as the sum of exports and imports as a share of GDP, and financial openness is measured by the sum of foreign assets and liabilities as a share of GDP. Source: IMF Balance of Payments and International Investment Position Statistics, World Bank.

8. WIND, "Statistics on Mainland Stocks: Statistics on Foreign Ownership," accessed April 28, 2022, via WIND Financial Terminal; Evelyn Cheng, "Overseas Investors Are Snapping Up Mainland Chinese Bonds," CNBC, May 21, 2021, https://www.cnbc.com/2021/05/21/overseas-investors-buy-up-mainland-chinese-bonds-in-a-search-for-yield.html; analysis by Bloomberg News, "China's Finance World Opens Up to Foreigners, Sort Of," Washington Post, September 24, 2020, https://www.washingtonpost.com/business/chinas-finance-world-opens-up-to-foreigners-sort-of/2020/09/24/e168d5c8-fee0-11ea-b0e4-350e4e60cc91_story.html; Federal Reserve, "Assets and Liabilities of U.S. Branches and Agencies of Foreign Banks," March 2022, https://www.federalreserve.gov/data/assetliab/current.htm.

9. International Monetary Fund, "Coordinated Portfolio Investment Survey," April 22, 2022, https://data.imf.org/?sk=B981B4E3-4E58-467E-9B90-9DE0C3367363.

10. Yanliang Miao and Tuo Deng, "China's Capital Account Liberalization: A Ruby Jubilee and Beyond," China Economic Journal 12, no. 3 (2019): 245–71, https://doi.org/10.1080/17538963.2019.1670472.

11. Ana Maria Santacreu and Heting Zhu, "China's Foreign Reserves Are Declining. Why, and What Effects Could This Have?," On the Economy (blog), Federal Reserve

Bank of St. Louis, October 3, 2017, https://www.stlouisfed.org/on-the-economy/2017/october/china-foreign-reserves-declining-effects.

12. Robert Peston, "China Devalues Yuan Currency to Three-Year Low," BBC News, August 11, 2015, https://www.bbc.com/news/business-33858433.

13. "China Capital Outflows Rise to Estimated $1 Trillion in 2015," Bloomberg News, January 25, 2016, https://www.bloomberg.com/news/articles/2016-01-25/china-capital-outflows-climb-to-estimated-1-trillion-in-2015.

14. "The Causes and Consequences of China's Market Crash," *The Economist*, August 24, 2015, https://www.economist.com/news/2015/08/24/the-causes-and-consequences-of-chinas-market-crash.

15. Gita Gopinath and Jeremy C. Stein, "Banking, Trade, and the Making of a Dominant Currency," *Quarterly Journal of Economics* 136, no. 2 (May 2021): 783–830, https://doi.org/10.1093/qje/qjaa036.

16. David M. Andrews, ed., *International Monetary Power* (Ithaca, NY: Cornell University Press, 2006), 7–28.

17. Benjamin J. Cohen, *The Future of Money* (Princeton, NJ: Princeton University Press, 2006).

18. Rachelle Younglai and Roberta Rampton, "U.S. Pushes EU, SWIFT to Eject Iran Banks," Reuters, February 15, 2012, https://www.reuters.com/article/us-iran-usa-swift/u-s-pushes-eu-swift-to-eject-iran-banks-idUSTRE81F00I20120216.

19. "The Search to Find an Alternative to the Dollar," *The Economist*, January 18, 2020, https://www.economist.com/leaders/2020/01/18/the-search-to-find-an-alternative-to-the-dollar.

20. "America's Aggressive Use of Sanctions Endangers the Dollar's Reign," *The Economist*, January 18, 2020, https://www.economist.com/briefing/2020/01/18/americas-aggressive-use-of-sanctions-endangers-the-dollars-reign.

21. Zhitao Lin, Wenjie Zhan, and Yin Wong Cheung, "China's Bilateral Currency Swap Lines," *China and World Economy* 24, no. 6 (November–December 2016): 19–42, https://doi.org/10.1111/cwe.12179.

22. Naohiko Baba and Frank Packer, "From Turmoil to Crisis: Dislocations in the FX Swap Market before and after the Failure of Lehman Brothers," in "The Global Financial Crisis: Causes, Threats and Opportunities," ed. Mark P. Taylor, special issue, *Journal of International Money and Finance* 28, no. 8 (December 2009): 1350–74, https://doi.org/10.1016/j.jimonfin.2009.08.003; and Cho Hoi Hui, Hans Genberg, and Tsz-Kin Chung, "Funding Liquidity Risk and Deviations from Interest-Rate Parity during the Financial Crisis of 2007–2009," *International Journal of Finance and Economics* 16, no. 4 (October 2011): 307–23, https://doi.org/10.1002/ijfe.427.

23. Scott O'Malia, "Action Needed to Address EM Dollar Shortfall," ISDA (International Swaps and Derivatives Association), April 14, 2020, https://www.isda.org/2020/04/14/action-needed-to-address-em-dollar-shortfall.

24. J. Lawrence Broz, Zhiwen Zhang, and Gaoyang Wang, "Explaining Foreign Support for China's Global Economic Leadership," *International Organization* 74, no. 3 (June 2020): 417–52, https://doi.org/10.1017/S0020818320000120.

25. Gerard Baker, Carol E. Lee, and Michael C. Bender, "Trump Says Dollar 'Getting Too Strong,' Won't Label China a Currency Manipulator," *Wall Street Journal*, April 12,

2017, https://www.wsj.com/articles/trump-says-dollar-getting-too-strong-wont-label-china-currency-manipulator-1492024312.

26. Barry Eichengreen, "Ragnar Nurkse and the International Financial Architecture," *Baltic Journal of Economics* 18, no. 2 (2018): 118–28, https://doi.org/10.1080/1406099X.2018.1540186.

27. Ethan Ilzetzki, Carmen M. Reinhart, and Kenneth S. Rogoff, "The Country Chronologies to Exchange Rate Arrangements into the 21st Century: Will the Anchor Currency Hold?," NBER Working Paper 23135, National Bureau of Economic Research, Cambridge, MA, February 2017, https://doi.org/10.3386/w23135.

28. Data comes from the IMF's Currency Composition of Official Foreign Exchange Reserves (COFER) database, available at https://data.imf.org/?sk=E6A5F467-C14B-4AA8-9F6D-5A09EC4E62A4.

29. International Monetary Fund, "Review of the Method of Valuation of the SDR—Initial Considerations," Policy Papers 2015, no. 41 (July 16, 2015), https://doi.org/10.5089/9781498344319.007.

30. Data comes from BIS Triennial Central Bank Survey 2019. Measures used by Matteo Maggiori, Brent Neiman, and Jesse Schreger in "International Currencies and Capital Allocation," NBER Working Paper 24673, National Bureau of Economic Research, Cambridge, MA, May 2018, https://doi.org/10.3386/w24673; and Matteo Maggiori, Brent Neiman, and Jesse Schreger, "The Rise of the Dollar and Fall of the Euro as International Currencies," *AEA Papers and Proceedings* 109 (May 2019): 521–26, https://doi.org/10.1257/pandp.20191007.

31. International Monetary Fund, "Review of the Method of Valuation of the SDR."

32. Maurice Obstfeld and Alan M Taylor, "Globalization and Capital Markets," in *Globalization in Historical Perspective*, eds. Michael D. Bordo, Alan M. Taylor, and Jeffrey G. Williamson (Chicago: University of Chicago Press, 2003), 121–88.

33. Muge Adalet and Barry Eichengreen, "Current Account Reversals: Always a Problem?," in *G7 Current Account Imbalances: Sustainability and Adjustment*, ed. Richard H. Clarida (Chicago: University of Chicago Press, 2007), 205–46.

34. Thomas Piketty and Gabriel Zucman, "Capital Is Back: Wealth-Income Ratios in Rich Countries 1700–2010," *Quarterly Journal of Economics* 129, no. 3 (August 2014): 1255–310, https://doi.org/10.1093/qje/qju018.

35. Barry Eichengreen, Arnaud Mehl, and Livia Chiṭu, *How Global Currencies Work: Past, Present, and Future* (Princeton, NJ: Princeton University Press, 2018), 164.

36. Sebastian Horn, Carmen M. Reinhart, and Christoph Trebesch, "China's Overseas Lending," *Journal of International Economics* 133 (November 2021), https://doi.org/10.1016/j.jinteco.2021.103539.

37. Bahaj and Reis, "Jumpstarting an International Currency."

38. Eichengreen, Mehl, and Chiṭu, *How Global Currencies Work*, 30–41.

39. Livia Chiṭu, Barry Eichengreen, and Arnaud Mehl, "When Did the Dollar Overtake Sterling as the Leading International Currency? Evidence from the Bond Markets," *Journal of Development Economics* 111 (November 2014): 225–45, https://doi.org/10.1016/j.jdeveco.2013.09.008.

40. Barry Eichengreen, *Exorbitant Privilege: The Rise and Fall of the Dollar* (Oxford: Oxford University Press, 2012).

41. CEIC Data. CEIC, "China Market Capitalization: % of GDP," accessed April 28, 2022, https://www.ceicdata.com/en/indicator/china/market-capitalization--nominal-gdp; CEIC, "United States Market Capitalization: % of GDP," accessed April 28, 2022, https://www.ceicdata.com/en/indicator/united-states/market-capitalization -nominal-gdp; CEIC, "Malaysia Market Capitalization: % of GDP," accessed April 28, 2022, https://www.ceicdata.com/en/indicator/malaysia/market-capitalization -nominal-gdp; CEIC, "Thailand Market Capitalization: % of GDP," accessed April 28, 2022, https://www.ceicdata.com/en/indicator/thailand/market-capitalization -nominal-gdp; CEIC, "Brazil Market Capitalization: % of GDP," accessed April 28, 2022, https://www.ceicdata.com/en/indicator/brazil/market-capitalization–nominal -gdp.[aa]

42. Marlene Amstad and Zhiguo He, "Chinese Bond Markets and Interbank Market," in *The Handbook of China's Financial System*, eds. Marlene Amstad, Guofeng Sun, and Wei Xiong (Princeton, NJ: Princeton University Press, 2020), 105–48, https://doi.org /10.2307/j.ctv11vcdpc; "China's Bond Market—the Last Great Frontier," S&P Global Ratings, April 15, 2021, https://www.spglobal.com/ratings/en/research/articles/210415 -china-s-bond-market-the-last-great-frontier-11888676.

43. Maggiori, Neiman, and Schreger, "International Currencies and Capital Allocation."

44. Guntram B. Wolff and Thomas Walsh, "The Dragon Sneezes, Europe Catches a Cold," *Bruegel* (blog), August 26, 2015, https://www.bruegel.org/2015/08/china-stock -market.

45. BlackRock, "Investors Can Benefit from Diversifying into Chinese Bonds," May 2020, accessed April 28, 2022, https://www.blackrock.com/hk/en/insights/invest ment-inspiration/investors-can-benefit-from-diversifying-into-chinese-bonds. Cor-relations reflect three-year weekly correlations of five-year government bonds. Over a ten-year period, the average correlation of month-to-month total returns with global developed market government bonds is 0.2 (S&P calculation).

46. In 1922, Congress had enacted the Fordney-McCumber Act, which was among the most punitive protectionist tariffs passed in the country's history, raising the average import tax to some 40 percent.

47. United Nations Statistics Division, "International Trade Statistics: 1900–1960," May 1962, https://unstats.un.org/unsd/trade/imts/Historical%20data%201900-1960.pdf.

48. Edwin M. Truman, "International Coordination of Economic Policies in the Global Financial Crisis: Successes, Failures, and Consequences," Working Paper No. 19-11, Peterson Institute for International Economics, Washington, DC, July 2019, https:// doi.org/10.2139/ssrn.3417234.

49. Organisation for Economic Co-operation and Development, *Active with the People's Republic of China* (Paris: OECD, March 2018), 6–7, www.oecd.org/china/active-with -china.pdf.

50. Huaxia, "China Pays in Full Its UN Regular Budget Dues for 2021," Xinhuanet, April 14, 2021, http://www.xinhuanet.com/english/2021-04/14/c_139878726.htm.

51. Infrastructure Consortium for Africa, *Infrastructure Financing Trends in Africa– 2018* (Abidjan, Côte d'Ivoire: Infrastructure Consortium for Africa, 2018), https:// www.icafrica.org/fileadmin/documents/IFT_2018/ICA_Infrastructure_Financing _in_Africa_Report_2018_En.pdf.

52. Carmen M. Reinhart and Kenneth S. Rogoff, "Serial Default and the 'Paradox' of Rich-to-Poor Capital Flows," *American Economic Review* 94, no. 2 (May 2004): 53–58, https://doi.org/10.1257/0002828041302370.

53. David Dollar, Yiping Huang, and Yang Yao, eds., *Economic Challenges of a Rising Global Power* (Washington, DC: Brookings Institution Press, 2020), 285–386, www.jstor.org/stable/10.7864/j.ctvktrz58.

54. Dollar, Huang, and Yao, *Economic Challenges*.

55. Agatha Kratz, Allen Feng, and Logan Wright, "New Data on the 'Debt Trap' Question," Rhodium Group, April 29, 2019, https://rhg.com/research/new-data-on-the-debt-trap-question.

56. Kevin Acker, Deborah Brautigam, and Yufan Huang, "Debt Relief with Chinese Characteristics," CARI Working Paper Series, no. 39, China Africa Research Initiative, School of Advanced International Studies, Johns Hopkins University, Baltimore, MD, June 2020, https://ssrn.com/abstract=3745021.

CHAPTER TEN: TOWARD A NEW PARADIGM

1. Thomas Piketty, Li Yang, and Gabriel Zucman, "Capital Accumulation, Private Property, and Rising Inequality in China, 1978–2015," *American Economic Review* 109, no. 7 (July 2019): 2469–96, https://doi.org/10.1257/aer.20170973.

2. State Council of the People's Republic of China, "The State Council Adopted Various Measures to Support Small Enterprise Development," May 27, 2021, http://www.gov.cn/zhengce/2021-05/27/content_5612867.htm.

3. Kevin Rudd, "The World According to Xi Jinping," *Foreign Affairs*, October 10, 2022, https://www.foreignaffairs.com/china/world-according-xi-jinping-china-ideologue-kevin-rudd.

4. European Chamber, "European Business in China Position Paper 2022/2023," September 21, 2022, https://www.europeanchamber.com.cn/en/publications-archive/1068/European_Business_in_China_Position_Paper_2022_2023.

BIBLIOGRAPHY

Acemoglu, Daron, David Autor, David Dorn, Gordon H. Hanson, and Brendan Price. "Import Competition and the Great US Employment Sag of the 2000s." In "Labor Markets in the Aftermath of the Great Recession," edited by David Card and Alexandre Mas. Supplement, *Journal of Labor Economics* 34, no. S1 (January 2016): S141–98. https://doi.org/10.1086/682384.

Acemoglu, Daron, and Pascual Restrepo. "Robots and Jobs: Evidence from US Labor Markets." *Journal of Political Economy* 128, no. 6 (June 2020): 2188–244. https://doi.org /10.1086/705716.

Acker, Kevin, Deborah Brautigam, and Yufan Huang. "Debt Relief with Chinese Characteristics." CARI Working Paper Series, no. 39, China Africa Research Initiative, School of Advanced International Studies, Johns Hopkins University, Baltimore, MD, June 2020.

Adalet, Muge, and Barry Eichengreen. "Current Account Reversals: Always a Problem?" In *G7 Current Account Imbalances: Sustainability and Adjustment*, edited by Richard H. Clarida, 205–46. Chicago: University of Chicago Press, 2007.

Aiyar, Shekhar, Romain Duval, Damien Puy, Yiqun Wu, and Longmei Zhang. "Growth Slowdowns and the Middle-Income Trap." *Japan and the World Economy* 48 (December 2018): 22–37. https://doi.org/10.1016/j.japwor.2018.07.001.

Allen, Franklin, Jun Qian, and Meijun Qian. "Law, Finance, and Economic Growth in China." *Journal of Financial Economics* 77, no. 1 (July 2005): 57–116. https://doi.org /10.1016/j.jfineco.2004.06.010.

Allen, Franklin, Jun Q. J. Qian, Chenyu Shan, and Julie Lei Zhu. "The Development of the Chinese Stock Market." In *The Handbook of China's Financial System*, edited by

Marlene Amstad, Guofeng Sun, and Wei Xiong, 283–313. Princeton, NJ: Princeton University Press, 2020. https://doi.org/10.2307/j.ctv11vcdpc.15.

———. "Dissecting the Long-Term Performance of the Chinese Stock Market." SSRN 2880021, November 2021. https://doi.org/10.2139/ssrn.2880021.

Allison, Graham, Kevin Klyman, Karina Barbesino, and Hugo Yen. "The Great Tech Rivalry: China vs. the U.S." Belfer Center for Science and International Affairs, Harvard Kennedy School, Cambridge, MA, December 2021. www.belfercenter.org/sites/default/files/GreatTechRivalry_ChinavsUS_211207.pdf.

Amiti, Mary, Stephen J. Redding, and David E. Weinstein. "The Impact of the 2018 Tariffs on Prices and Welfare." *Journal of Economic Perspectives* 33, no. 4 (Fall 2019): 187–210. https://doi.org/10.1257/jep.33.4.187.

Amstad, Marlene, and Zhiguo He. "Chinese Bond Markets and Interbank Market." In *The Handbook of China's Financial System*, edited by Marlene Amstad, Guofeng Sun, and Wei Xiong, 105–48. Princeton, NJ: Princeton University Press, 2020. https://doi.org/10.2307/j.ctv11vcdpc.9.

Amstad, Marlene, Guofeng Sun, and Wei Xiong, eds. *The Handbook of China's Financial System*. Princeton, NJ: Princeton University Press, 2020.

Ananat, Elizabeth Oltmans, and Daniel M. Hungerman. "The Power of the Pill for the Next Generation: Oral Contraception's Effects on Fertility, Abortion, and Maternal and Child Characteristics." *Review of Economics and Statistics* 94, no. 1 (February 2012): 37–51. https://doi.org/10.1162/rest_a_00230.

Andrews, David M., ed. *International Monetary Power*. Ithaca, NY: Cornell University Press, 2006.

Ang, Andrew, Jennie Bai, and Hao Zhou. "The Great Wall of Debt: Real Estate, Political Risk, and Chinese Local Government Financing Cost." Georgetown McDonough School of Business Research Paper No. 2603022, July 2018. https://papers.ssrn.com/sol3/papers.cfm?abstract_id=2603022.

Antràs, Pol. "Conceptual Aspects of Global Value Chains." *World Bank Economic Review* 34, no. 3 (October 2020): 551–74. http://hdl.handle.net/10986/33228.

———. "De-Globalisation? Global Value Chains in the Post-COVID-19 Age." NBER Working Paper 28115, National Bureau of Economic Research, Cambridge, MA, November 2020. https://doi.org/10.3386/w28115.

———. *Global Production: Firms, Contracts, and Trade Structure*. Princeton, NJ: Princeton University Press, 2020.

Arthur, W. Brian. *The Nature of Technology: What It Is and How It Evolves*. New York: Free Press, 2009.

Autor, David H., David Dorn, and Gordon H. Hanson. "The China Syndrome: Local Labor Market Effects of Import Competition in the United States." *American Economic Review* 103, no. 6 (October 2013): 2121–68. https://doi.org/10.1257/aer.103.6.2121.

———. "The China Shock: Learning from Labor-Market Adjustment to Large Changes in Trade." *Annual Review of Economics* 8, no. 1 (October 31, 2016): 205–40. https://doi.org/10.1146/annurev-economics-080315-015041.

Baba, Naohiko, and Frank Packer. "From Turmoil to Crisis: Dislocations in the FX Swap Market before and after the Failure of Lehman Brothers." In "The Global Financial

Crisis: Causes, Threats and Opportunities," edited by Mark P. Taylor. Special issue, *Journal of International Money and Finance* 28, no. 8 (December 2009): 1350–74. https://doi.org/10.1016/j.jimonfin.2009.08.003.

Bahaj, Saleem, and Ricardo Reis. "Jumpstarting an International Currency." HKIMR Working Paper No.19/2020, Hong Kong Institute for Monetary and Financial Research, December 2020. https://doi.org/10.2139/ssrn.3757279.

Bai, Chong-En, Chang-Tai Hsieh, and Zheng Song. "Special Deals with Chinese Characteristics." *NBER Macroeconomics Annual* 34, no. 1 (2020): 341–79. https://doi.org/10.1086/707189.

Bai, Chong-En, Chang-Tai Hsieh, Zheng Song, and Xin Wang. "The Rise of State-Connected Private Owners in China." NBER Working Paper 28170, National Bureau of Economic Research, Cambridge, MA, December 2020. https://doi.org/10.3386/w28170.

Bai, Yan, Keyu Jin, and Dan Lu. "Misallocation under Trade Liberalization." NBER Working Paper 26188, National Bureau of Economic Research, Cambridge, MA, August 2019. https://doi.org/10.3386/w26188.

Balsvik, Ragnhild, Sissel Jensen, and Kjell G. Salvanes. "Made in China, Sold in Norway: Local Labor Market Effects of an Import Shock." *Journal of Public Economics* 127 (July 2015): 137–44. https://doi.org/10.1016/j.jpubeco.2014.08.006.

Becker, Gary S., and H. Gregg Lewis. "On the Interaction between the Quantity and Quality of Children." *Journal of Political Economy* 81, no. 2 (1973): S279-88. http://www.jstor.org/stable/1840425.

Borst, Nicholas, and Nicholas Lardy. "Maintaining Financial Stability in the People's Republic of China during Financial Liberalization." Working Paper No. 15-4, Peterson Institute for International Economics, Washington, DC, March 2015. https://doi.org/10.2139/ssrn.2588543.

Bosworth, Barry, and Susan M. Collins. "Accounting for Growth: Comparing China and India." *Journal of Economic Perspectives* 22, no. 1 (Winter 2008): 45–66. https://doi.org/10.1257/jep.22.1.45.

Brandt, Loren, Chang-Tai Hsieh, and Xiaodong Zhu. "Growth and Structural Transformation in China." In *China's Great Economic Transformation*, edited by Loren Brandt and Thomas G. Rawski, 683–728. Cambridge: Cambridge University Press, 2008.

Brandt, Loren, Debin Ma, and Thomas G. Rawski. "From Divergence to Convergence: Reevaluating the History behind China's Economic Boom." *Journal of Economic Literature* 52, no. 1 (March 2014): 45–123. https://doi.org/10.1257/jel.52.1.45.

Brandt, Loren, John Litwack, Elitza Mileva, Luhang Wang, Yifan Zhang, and Luan Zhao. "China's Productivity Slowdown and Future Growth Potential." Policy Research Working Paper 9298, World Bank, Washington, DC, June 2020. https://openknowledge.worldbank.org/handle/10986/33993.

Brandt, Loren, and Thomas G. Rawski, eds. *China's Great Economic Transformation*. Cambridge: Cambridge University Press, 2010.

Brandt, Loren, and Xiaodong Zhu. "Accounting for China's Growth." IZA Discussion Paper No. 4764, Institute for the Study of Labor, Bonn, Germany, February 2010. http://dx.doi.org/10.2139/ssrn.1556552.

Broz, J. Lawrence, Zhiwen Zhang, and Gaoyang Wang. "Explaining Foreign Support for China's Global Economic Leadership." *International Organization* 74, no. 3 (June 2020): 417–52. https://doi.org/10.1017/S0020818320000120.

Brunnermeier, Markus Konrad. *The Resilient Society.* Colorado Springs, CO: Endeavor Literary Press, 2021.

Cai, Fang, and Meiyan Wang. "A Counterfactual Analysis on Unlimited Surplus Labor in Rural China." *China and World Economy* 16, no. 1 (January–February 2008): 51–65. https://doi.org/10.1111/j.1749-124X.2008.00099.x.

Campbell, Douglas L., and Karsten Mau. "On 'Trade Induced Technical Change: The Impact of Chinese Imports on Innovation, IT, and Productivity.'" *Review of Economic Studies* 88, no. 5 (October 2021): 2555–59. https://doi.org/10.1093/restud/rdab037.

Case, Anne, and Angus Deaton. *Deaths of Despair and the Future of Capitalism.* Princeton, NJ: Princeton University Press, 2020.

Chang, Ha-Joon. *Bad Samaritans: The Guilty Secrets of Rich Nations and the Threat to Global Prosperity.* London: Random House, 2008.

Charles, Kerwin Kofi, Erik Hurst, and Mariel Schwartz. "The Transformation of Manufacturing and the Decline in US Employment." *NBER Macroeconomics Annual* 33, no. 1 (2019): 307–72. https://doi.org/10.1086/700896.

Chen, Ting, and James Kai-sing Kung. "Busting the 'Princelings': The Campaign against Corruption in China's Primary Land Market." *Quarterly Journal of Economics* 134, no. 1 (February 2019): 185–226. https://doi.org/https:/doi.org/10.1093/qje/qjy027.

Chen, Ting, Laura Xiaolei Liu, Wei Xiong, and Li-An Zhou. "Real Estate Boom and Misallocation of Capital in China." Working paper, Princeton University, Princeton, NJ, December 2017. https://editorialexpress.com/cgi-bin/conference/download.cgi?db_name =CICF2018&paper_id=915.

Chen, Wei, Xilu Chen, Chang-Tai Hsieh, and Zheng Song. "A Forensic Examination of China's National Accounts." Brookings Papers on Economic Activity, Spring 2019, 77–141. https://www.jstor.org/stable/90000434.

Chen, Zhiwu. "China's Dangerous Debt: Why the Economy Could Be Headed for Trouble." *Foreign Affairs* 94, no. 3 (May/June 2015): 13–18. www.jstor.org/stable/24483658.

Chen, Zhuo, Zhiguo He, and Chun Liu. "The Financing of Local Government in China: Stimulus Loan Wanes and Shadow Banking Waxes." *Journal of Financial Economics* 137, no. 1 (July 2020): 42–71. https://doi.org/10.1016/j.jfineco.2019.07.009.

Chiţu, Livia, Barry Eichengreen, and Arnaud Mehl. "When Did the Dollar Overtake Sterling as the Leading International Currency? Evidence from the Bond Markets." *Journal of Development Economics* 111 (November 2014): 225–45. https://doi.org/10.1016/j.jdeveco.2013.09.008.

China Banking Wealth Management Registration and Custody Center. *China Wealth Management Products Market Annual Report (2016),* May 19, 2017. http://www.efnchina.com/uploadfile/2017/0531/20170531032656799.pdf.

Choukhmane, Taha, Nicolas Coeurdacier, and Keyu Jin. "The One-Child Policy and Household Saving." Working paper, July 2017. https://personal.lse.ac.uk/jink/pdf/onechildpolicy_ccj.pdf.

Clemens, Michael A., and Jeffrey G. Williamson. "Why Did the Tariff–Growth Correlation Change after 1950?" *Journal of Economic Growth* 9, no. 1 (March 2004): 5–46. https://doi.org/10.1023/B:JOEG.0000023015.44856.a9.

Cohen, Benjamin J. *The Future of Money*. Princeton, NJ: Princeton University Press, 2006.

Cui, Xiaomin, and Miaojie Yu. "Exchange Rate and Domestic Value Added in Processing Exports: Evidence from Chinese Firms." Working Paper Series, E2018017. Beijing: China Center for Economic Research, National School of Economic Development, Peking University, August 2018. https://en.nsd.pku.edu.cn/docs/20181027004756364270.pdf.

Cunningham, Edward, Tony Saich, and Jesse Turiel. "Understanding CCP Resilience: Surveying Chinese Public Opinion through Time." Ash Center for Democratic Governance and Innovation, Harvard Kennedy School, Cambridge, MA, July 2020. https://ash.harvard.edu/files/ash/files/final_policy_brief_7.6.2020.pdf.

Dai, Lili, Jianlei Han, Jing Shi, and Bohui Zhang. "Digital Footprints as Collateral for Debt Collection." SSRN 4135159, August 2022. https://doi.org/10.2139/ssrn.4135159.

Dauth, Wolfgang, Sebastian Findeisen, and Jens Suedekum. "The Rise of the East and the Far East: German Labor Markets and Trade Integration." *Journal of the European Economic Association* 12, no. 6 (July 2014): 1643–75. https://doi.org/10.1111/jeea.12092.

Davis, Bob, and Jon Hilsenrath. "How the China Shock, Deep and Swift, Spurred the Rise of Trump." *Wall Street Journal*, August 11, 2016.

Dollar, David, Yiping Huang, and Yang Yao, eds. *Economic Challenges of a Rising Global Power*. Washington, DC: Brookings Institution Press, 2020. www.jstor.org/stable/10.7864/j.ctvktrz58.

Du, Yang. "Changes of College Student Employment and Policy Suggestions." *People's Daily*, September 16, 2022. http://finance.people.com.cn/n1/2022/0916/c444648-32527858.html.

Ebenstein, Avraham. "The 'Missing Girls' of China and the Unintended Consequences of the One Child Policy." *Journal of Human Resources* 45, no. 1 (Winter 2010): 87–115. https://doi.org/10.1353/jhr.2010.0003.

Eichengreen, Barry. *Exorbitant Privilege: The Rise and Fall of the Dollar*. Oxford: Oxford University Press, 2012.

———. "Ragnar Nurkse and the International Financial Architecture." *Baltic Journal of Economics* 18, no. 2 (2018): 118–28. https://doi.org/10.1080/1406099X.2018.1540186.

Eichengreen, Barry, Arnaud Mehl, and Livia Chiţu. *How Global Currencies Work: Past, Present, and Future*. Princeton, NJ: Princeton University Press, 2018.

El-Tablawy, Tarek. "Egypt Moves Closer to IMF Loan with China Currency Swap Deal." Bloomberg.com, October 30, 2016. https://www.bloomberg.com/news/articles/2016-10-30/egypt-moves-closer-to-imf-loan-with-china-currency-swap-deal.

Eriksson, Katherine, Katheryn N. Russ, Jay C. Shambaugh, and Minfei Xu. "Trade Shocks and the Shifting Landscape of U.S. Manufacturing." In "2019 Asia Economic Policy Conference (AEPC): Monetary Policy under Global Uncertainty," edited by Zheng Liu and Mark M. Spiegel. *Journal of International Money and Finance* 114 (June 2021): 102407. https://doi.org/10.1016/j.jimonfin.2021.102407.

European Chamber. "European Business in China Position Paper 2022/2023," September 21, 2022. https://www.europeanchamber.com.cn/en/publications-archive/1068/European_Business_in_China_Position_Paper_2022_2023.

European Commission. "Reforming the WTO towards a Sustainable and Effective Multilateral Trading System." European Commission, March 25, 2022. https://knowledge4policy.ec.europa.eu/publication/reforming-wto-towards-sustainable-effective-multilateral-trading-system_en.

Fajgelbaum, Pablo D., and Amit K. Khandelwal. "Measuring the Unequal Gains from Trade." *Quarterly Journal of Economics* 131, no. 3 (March 2016): 1113–80. https://doi.org/10.1093/qje/qjw013.

Fang, Hanming, Quanlin Gu, Wei Xiong, and Li An Zhou. "Demystifying the Chinese Housing Boom." *NBER Macroeconomics Annual* 30, no. 1 (2016): 105–66. https://doi.org/10.1086/685953.

Feenstra, Robert, Hong Ma, Akira Sasahara, and Yuan Xu. "Reconsidering the 'China Shock' in Trade." Center for Economic Policy Research, January 18, 2018. https://cepr.org/voxeu/columns/reconsidering-china-shock-trade.

Feenstra, Robert C., and Akira Sasahara. "The 'China Shock,' Exports and U.S. Employment: A Global Input-Output Analysis." *Review of International Economics* 26, no. 5 (2018): 1053–83. https://doi.org/10.1111/roie.12370.

Field, Erica, and Attila Ambrus. "Early Marriage, Age of Menarche, and Female Schooling Attainment in Bangladesh." *Journal of Political Economy* 116, no. 5 (October 2008): 881–930. https://doi.org/10.1086/593333.

Fitch Ratings. "Rating Report: China Evergrande Group." Fitch Ratings, July 5, 2021. https://www.fitchratings.com/research/corporate-finance/china-evergrande-group-05-07-2021.

Flaaen, Aaron, Ali Hortaçsu, and Felix Tintelnot. "The Production Relocation and Price Effects of US Trade Policy: The Case of Washing Machines." *American Economic Review* 110, no. 7 (July 2020): 2103–27. https://doi.org/10.1257/aer.20190611.

Fong, Vanessa L. "China's One-Child Policy and the Empowerment of Urban Daughters." *American Anthropologist* 104, no. 4 (December 2002): 1098–109. https://doi.org/10.1525/aa.2002.104.4.1098.

Fort, Teresa C., Justin R. Pierce, and Peter K. Schott. "New Perspectives on the Decline of US Manufacturing Employment." *Journal of Economic Perspectives* 32, no. 2 (Spring 2018): 47–72. https://doi.org/10.1257/jep.32.2.47.

Garnaut, Ross, Ligang Song, and Cai Fang, eds. *China's 40 Years of Reform and Development: 1978–2018.* Acton, Australia: Australian National University Press, 2018.

Glaeser, Edward, Wei Huang, Yueran Ma, and Andrei Shleifer. "A Real Estate Boom with Chinese Characteristics." *Journal of Economic Perspectives* 31, no. 1 (Winter 2017): 93–116. https://doi.org/10.1257/jep.31.1.93.

Goldin, Claudia, and Lawrence F. Katz. "The Power of the Pill: Oral Contraceptives and Women's Career and Marriage Decisions." *Journal of Political Economy* 110, no. 4 (August 2002): 730–70. https://doi.org/10.1086/340778.

Gopinath, Gita, and Jeremy C. Stein. "Banking, Trade, and the Making of a Dominant Currency." *Quarterly Journal of Economics* 136, no. 2 (May 2021): 783–830. https://doi.org/10.1093/qje/qjaa036.

Greenaway, David, Alessandra Guariglia, and Zhihong Yu. "The More the Better? Foreign Ownership and Corporate Performance in China." *European Journal of Finance* 20, no. 7–9 (2014): 681–702. https://doi.org/10.1080/1351847X.2012.671785.

Greitens, Sheena Chestnut. *Dealing with Demand for China's Global Surveillance Exports.* Brookings Institution, April 2020. www.brookings.edu/research/dealing-with-demand -for-chinas-global-surveillance-exports.

Grossman, Gene M., and Alan B. Krueger. "Economic Growth and the Environment." *Quarterly Journal of Economics* 110, no. 2 (May 1995): 353–77. https://doi.org/10.2307 /2118443.

Grossman, Gene M., and Elhanan Helpman. "Protection for Sale." *American Economic Review* 84, no. 4 (September 1994): 833–50. https://www.jstor.org/stable/2118033.

Guo, Di, Kun Jiang, Byung-Yeon Kim, and Chenggang Xu. "Political Economy of Private Firms in China." In "Economic Systems in the Pacific Rim Region Symposium," edited by Josef C. Brada. Special issue, *Journal of Comparative Economics* 42, no. 2 (May 2014): 286–303. https://doi.org/10.1016/j.jce.2014.03.006.

Hachem, Kinda, and Zheng Song. "Liquidity Rules and Credit Booms." *Journal of Political Economy* 129, no. 10 (October 2021): 2721–65. https://doi.org/10.1086/715074.

Haerpfer, Christian, Ronald Inglehart, Alejandro Moreno, Christian Welzel, Kseniya Kizilova, Jaime Diez-Medrano, Marta Lagos et al., eds. *World Values Survey: Round Seven–Country-Pooled Datafile Version 3.0.* Madrid and Vienna: JD Systems Institute & WVSA Secretariat, 2020. https://doi.org/ 10.14281/18241.16.

Handley, Kyle, and Nuno Limão. "Policy Uncertainty, Trade, and Welfare: Theory and Evidence for China and the United States." *American Economic Review* 107, no. 9 (September 2017): 2731–83. https://doi.org/10.1257/aer.20141419.

Hannum, Emily, Yuping Zhang, and Meiyan Wang. "Why Are Returns to Education Higher for Women Than for Men in Urban China?" *China Quarterly* 215 (September 2013): 616–40. https://doi.org/10.1017/s0305741013000696.

Hau, Harald, Yi Huang, Hongzhe Shan, and Zixia Sheng. "How FinTech Enters China's Credit Market." *AEA Papers and Proceedings* 109 (May 2019): 60–64. https://doi.org /10.1257/pandp.20191012.

He, Zhiguo, and Wei. "China's Financial System and Economy." NBER Working Paper 30324, National Bureau of Economic Research, Cambridge, MA, August 2022. https:// doi.org/10.3386/w30324.

Hombert, Johan, and Adrien Matray. "Can Innovation Help U.S. Manufacturing Firms Escape Import Competition from China?" *Journal of Finance* 73, no. 5 (October 2018): 2003–39. https://doi.org/10.1111/jofi.12691.

Horn, Sebastian, Carmen M. Reinhart, and Christoph Trebesch. "China's Overseas Lending." *Journal of International Economics* 133 (November 2021): 103539. https://doi.org /10.1016/j.jinteco.2021.103539.

Hsieh, Chang-Tai, and Zheng (Michael) Song. "Grasp the Large, Let Go of the Small: The Transformation of the State Sector in China." Brookings Papers on Economic Activity, Spring 2015, 295–366. https://doi.org/10.1353/eca.2016.0005.

Hu, Grace Xing, Jun Pan, and Jiang Wang. "Chinese Capital Market: An Empirical Overview." NBER Working Paper 24346, National Bureau of Economic Research, Cambridge, MA, February 2018. https://doi.org/10.3386/w24346.

Huang, Wei, Xiaoyan Lei, and Ang Sun. "Fertility Restrictions and Life Cycle Outcomes: Evidence from the One-Child Policy in China." *Review of Economics and Statistics* 103, no. 4 (October 2021): 694–710. https://doi.org/10.1162/rest_a_00921.

Huang, Yasheng. "How Did China Take Off?" *Journal of Economic Perspectives* 26, no. 4 (Fall 2012): 147–70. https://doi.org/10.1257/jep.26.4.147.

Huang, Yasheng, and Heiwai Tang. "Are Foreign Firms Favored in China? Firm-Level Evidence on the Collection of Value-Added Taxes." *Journal of International Business Policy* 1, no. 1–2 (June 2018): 71–91. https://doi.org/10.1057/s42214-018-0006-z.

Hui, Cho Hoi, Hans Genberg, and Tsz-Kin Chung. "Funding Liquidity Risk and Deviations from Interest-Rate Parity during the Financial Crisis of 2007–2009." *International Journal of Finance and Economics* 16, no. 4 (October 2011): 307–23. https://doi.org/10.1002/ijfe.427.

Ilzetzki, Ethan, Carmen M. Reinhart, and Kenneth S. Rogoff. "The Country Chronologies to Exchange Rate Arrangements into the 21st Century: Will the Anchor Currency Hold?," NBER Working Paper 23135, National Bureau of Economic Research, Cambridge, MA, February 2017. https://doi.org/10.3386/w23135.

IMF (International Monetary Fund). "Review of the Method of Valuation of the SDR— Initial Considerations." *Policy Papers* 2015, no. 41 (Washington, DC: International Monetary Fund, July 16, 2015). https://doi.org/10.5089/9781498344319.007.

Infrastructure Consortium for Africa. *Infrastructure Financing Trends in Africa–2018.* Abidjan, Côte d'Ivoire: Infrastructure Consortium for Africa, 2018. https://www.icafrica.org/fileadmin/documents/IFT_2018/ICA_Infrastructure_Financing_in_Africa_Report_2018_En.pdf.

Ing, Lili Yan, Miaojie Yu, and Rui Zhang. "The Evolution of Export Quality: China and Indonesia." In *World Trade Evolution*, edited by Lili Yan Ing and Miaojie Yu, 261–302. London: Routledge, 2018.

Jiang, Quanbao, Shuzhuo Li, and Marcus W. Feldman. "China's Missing Girls in the Three Decades from 1980 to 2010." *Asian Women* 28, no. 3 (September 2012): 53–73.

Ji, Siqi. "How China, Japan's Hot Trade and Economic Relationship Is Being Tested by Cold Politics." *South China Morning Post*, August 18, 2022.

Jin, Keyu. "China's Steroids Model of Growth." In *Meeting Globalization's Challenges*, edited by Luís Catão and Maurice Obstfeld, 77–93. Princeton, NJ: Princeton University Press, 2019.

Jin, Keyu, Tao Jin, and Yifei Ren. "Fiscal Policy through Fintech Platforms." Working Paper, London School of Economics and Political Science, October 2022.

Jochim, Christian. "Confucius and Capitalism: Views of Confucianism in Works on Confucianism and Economic Development." *Journal of Chinese Religions* 20, no. 1 (1992): 135–71. https://doi.org/10.1179/073776992805307539.

Jones, Charles I., and Christopher Tonetti. "Nonrivalry and the Economics of Data." *American Economic Review* 110, no. 9 (September 2020): 2819–58. https://doi.org/10.1257/aer.20191330.

Jones, Charles M., Donghui Shi, Xiaoyan Zhang, and Xinran Zhang. "Understanding Retail Investors: Evidence from China." SSRN 3628809, October 2021. https://papers.ssrn.com/sol3/Delivery.cfm/SSRN_ID3935426_code3168539.pdf?abstractid=3628809&mirid=1.

Kania, Elsa B. "China's Quantum Future." *Foreign Affairs*, September 26, 2018. https:// www.foreignaffairs.com/articles/china/2018-09-26/chinas-quantum-future.

Kenen, Peter B. "The Role of the Dollar as the International Currency." *Group of Thirty Occasional Papers* 13 (1983). https://group30.org/images/uploads/publications/G30 _RoleDollarIntlCurrency.pdf.

Kissinger, Henry. *On China*. New York: Penguin Press, 2011.

Klein, Aaron. *China's Digital Payments Revolution*. Brookings Institution, April 2020. www.brookings.edu/wp-content/uploads/2020/04/FP_20200427_china_digital_pay ments_klein.pdf.

Kucik, Jeffrey, and Rajan Menon. "Can the United States Really Decouple from China?" *Foreign Policy*, January 11, 2022. https://foreignpolicy.com/2022/01/11/us-china-economic -decoupling-trump-biden.

Landry, Pierre F., Xiaobo Lü, and Haiyan Duan. "Does Performance Matter? Evaluating Political Selection along the Chinese Administrative Ladder." *Comparative Political Studies* 51, no. 8 (2018): 1074–105. https://doi.org/10.1177/0010414017730078.

Lardy, Nicholas R. *Markets over Mao: The Rise of Private Business in China*. Washington, DC: Peterson Institute for International Economics, 2014.

Lee, Kai-Fu. *AI Superpowers: China, Silicon Valley, and the New World Order*. Boston: Houghton Mifflin, 2018.

Lehr, Deborah. "Trust in China." Edelman, January 18, 2022. https://www.edelman.com /trust/2022-trust-barometer/trust-china.

Li, Chunling, and Yunqing Shi. *Experience, Attitudes and Social Transition: A Sociological Study of the Post-1980 Generation*. Beijing: Social Sciences Academic Press, 2013.

Li, Hongbin, Prashant Loyalka, Scott Rozelle, and Binzhen Wu. "Human Capital and China's Future Growth." *Journal of Economic Perspectives* 31, no. 1 (Winter 2017): 25–48. https://doi.org/https://doi.org/10.1257/jep.31.1.25.

Li, Qiaoyi. "600m with $140 Monthly Income Worries Top." *Global Times*, May 29, 2020. https://www.globaltimes.cn/content/1189968.shtml.

Li, Wei, and Dennis Tao Yang. "The Great Leap Forward: Anatomy of a Central Planning Disaster." *Journal of Political Economy* 113, no. 4 (August 2005): 840–77. https://doi .org/10.1086/430804.

Li, Xiaohua, and Wenxuan Li. "The Transformation of China's Manufacturing Competitive Advantage in the 40 Years of Reform and Opening-Up." *Southeast Academic Research* 5 (2018): 92–103.

Li, Xin, Bo Meng, and Zhi Wang. "Recent Patterns of Global Production and GVC Participation." In *Global Value Chain Development Report 2019*, 9–44. Washington, DC: World Bank Group, 2019.

Li, Yang, Xiaojing Zhang, and Xin Chang. *China's National Balance Sheet 2013*. Beijing: China Social Sciences Press, 2013.

Lin, Zhitao, Wenjie Zhan, and Yin Wong Cheung. "China's Bilateral Currency Swap Lines." *China and World Economy* 24, no. 6 (November–December 2016): 19–42. https://doi.org/10.1111/cwe.12179.

Lipsey, Robert E. "Foreign Direct Investment and the Operations of Multinational Firms: Concepts, History, and Data." NBER Working Paper 8665, National Bureau of Economic Research, Cambridge, MA, December 2001. https://doi.org/10.3386/w8665.

Liu, Chang, and Wei Xiong. "China's Real Estate Market." In *The Handbook of China's Financial System*, edited by Marlene Amstad, Guofeng Sun, and Wei Xiong, 183–207. Princeton, NJ: Princeton University Press, 2020. https://doi.org/10.2307/j.ctv11vcd pc.11.

Liu, Qiao, Qiaowei Shen, Zhenghua Li, and Shu Chen. "Stimulating Consumption at Low Budget: Evidence from a Large-Scale Policy Experiment amid the COVID-19 Pandemic." *Management Science* 67, no. 12 (December 2021): 7291–7307. https://doi.org/10.1287/mnsc.2021.4119.

Lucas, Robert E., Jr. "Making a Miracle." *Econometrica* 61, no. 2 (March 1993): 251–72. https://doi.org/10.2307/2951551.

Ma, Deyong, and Shuxia Zhang. "'The Left' And 'the Right' of Chinese Netizens." *Twenty-First Century*, no. 142 (April 2014): 86–103. http://www.cuhk.edu.hk/ics/21c/media/articles/c142-201309061.pdf.

Ma, Jun, Xiaorong Zhang, and Zhiguo Li. *A Study of China's National Balance Sheet*. Beijing: Social Sciences Press, 2012.

Maddison, Angus. Maddison Database 2010. Groningen Growth and Development Centre. www.rug.nl/ggdc/historicaldevelopment/maddison/releases/maddison-database-2010.

Maggiori, Matteo, Brent Neiman, and Jesse Schreger. "International Currencies and Capital Allocation." NBER Working Paper 24673, National Bureau of Economic Research, Cambridge, MA, May 2018. https://doi.org/10.3386/w24673.

———. "The Rise of the Dollar and Fall of the Euro as International Currencies." *AEA Papers and Proceedings* 109 (May 2019): 521–26. https://doi.org/10.1257/pandp.2019 1007.

Malik, Ammar A., Bradley Parks, Brooke Russell, Joyce Jiahui Lin, Katherine Walsh, Kyra Solomon, Sheng Zhang et al. *Banking on the Belt and Road: Insights from a New Global Dataset of 13,427 Chinese Development Projects*. AidData at William & Mary, Williamsburg, VA, September 2021.

Mao, Yarong. "Private Enterprises Contribute More than 60% of GDP and More than 50% of National Tax Revenue." Yicai, December 23, 2019. https://www.yicai.com/news/10 0444934.html.

Marin, Dalia. "The China Shock: Why Germany Is Different." Center for Economic and Policy Research, September 7, 2017. https://cepr.org/voxeu/columns/china-shock-why-germany-different.

Mazzucato, Mariana. "The Entrepreneurial State." *Soundings* 49 (Winter 2011): 131–42. https://doi.org/10.3898/136266211798411183.

Menzie, Chinn, and Jeffrey Frankel. "Will the Euro Eventually Surpass the Dollar as Leading International Reserve Currency?" NBER Working Paper 11510, National Bureau of Economic Research, Cambridge, MA, August 2005. https://doi.org/10.3386/w11510.

Miao, Yanliang, and Tuo Deng. "China's Capital Account Liberalization: A Ruby Jubilee and Beyond." *China Economic Journal* 12, no. 3 (2019): 245–71. https://doi.org/10.1080/17538963.2019.1670472.

Mitter, Rana, and Elsbeth Johnson. "What the West Gets Wrong about China." *Harvard Business Review*, May 1, 2021. https://hbr.org/2021/05/what-the-west-gets-wrong-about-china.

Moreno, Ramon, Dubravko Mihaljek, Agustin Villar, and Előd Takáts. "The Global Crisis and Financial Intermediation in Emerging Market Economies: An Overview." BIS Papers, No. 54, Bank for International Settlements, December 2010. https://www.bis.org/publ/bppdf/bispap54.pdf.

National Bureau of Statistics. *Statistics Yearbook 2001: Employment by Urban and Rural Areas at Year-End*. 2002. www.stats.gov.cn/tjsj/ndsj/zgnj/2000/E04c.htm.

Obstfeld, Maurice, and Alan M. Taylor. "Globalization and Capital Markets." In *Globalization in Historical Perspective*, edited by Michael D. Bordo, Alan M. Taylor, and Jeffrey G. Williamson, 121–88. Chicago: University of Chicago Press, 2003.

OECD (Organisation for Economic Co-operation and Development). *Active with the People's Republic of China*. Paris: OECD, March 2018. https://www.oecd.org/china/active-with-china.pdf.

Pan, Che. "China's Top Chip Maker SMIC Achieves 7-Nm Tech Breakthrough on Par with Intel, TSMC and Samsung, Analysts Say." *South China Morning Post*, August 29, 2022. https://www.scmp.com/tech/big-tech/article/3190590/chinas-top-chip-maker-smic-achieves-7-nm-tech-breakthrough-par-intel.

Pan, Jennifer, and Yiqing Xu. "China's Ideological Spectrum." *Journal of Politics* 80, no. 1 (January 2018): 254–73. https://doi.org/10.1086/694255.

Perkins, Dwight H., and Thomas G. Rawski. "Forecasting China's Economic Growth to 2025." In *China's Great Economic Transformation*, edited by Loren Brandt and Thomas G. Rawski, 829–86. Cambridge: Cambridge University Press, 2008.

Piketty, Thomas, Li Yang, and Gabriel Zucman. "Capital Accumulation, Private Property, and Rising Inequality in China, 1978–2015." *American Economic Review* 109, no. 7 (July 2019): 2469–96. https://doi.org/10.1257/aer.20170973.

Piketty, Thomas, and Gabriel Zucman. "Capital Is Back: Wealth-Income Ratios in Rich Countries 1700–2010." *Quarterly Journal of Economics* 129, no. 3 (August 2014): 1255–310. https://doi.org/10.1093/qje/qju018.

Qiao, Jie, Yuanyuan Wang, Xiaohong Li, Fan Jiang, Yunting Zhang, Jun Ma, Yi Song et al. "A *Lancet* Commission on 70 Years of Women's Reproductive, Maternal, Newborn, Child, and Adolescent Health in China." *The Lancet* 397, no. 10293 (June 2021): 2497–536. https://doi.org/10.1016/s0140-6736(20)32708-2.

Qin, Bei, David Strömberg, and Yanhui Wu. "Why Does China Allow Freer Social Media? Protests versus Surveillance and Propaganda." *Journal of Economic Perspectives* 31, no. 1 (Winter 2017): 117–40. https://doi.org/10.1257/jep.31.1.117.

Reinhart, Carmen M., and Kenneth S. Rogoff. "Serial Default and the 'Paradox' of Rich-to-Poor Capital Flows." *American Economic Review* 94, no. 2 (May 2004): 53–58. https://doi.org/10.1257/0002828041302370.

Ren, Zeping, Jiajin Ma, and Zhiheng Luo. *Report on China's Private Economy: 2019*. Evergrande Research Institute, 2019. http://pdf.dfcfw.com/pdf/H3_AP201910161368844678_1.pdf.

Rodrik, Dani. *The Globalization Paradox: Why Global Markets, States, and Democracy Can't Coexist*. Oxford: Oxford University Press, 2012.

Rogoff, Kenneth S, and Yuanchen Yang. "Peak China Housing." NBER Working Paper 27697. National Bureau of Economic Research, Cambridge, MA, August 2020. https://doi.org/10.3386/w27697.

Rudd, Kevin. "The World according to Xi Jinping." *Foreign Affairs*, October 10, 2022. https://www.foreignaffairs.com/china/world-according-xi-jinping-china-ideologue -kevin-rudd.

Salidjanova, Nargiza. "China's Stock Market Meltdown Shakes the World, Again." Washington, DC: U.S.-China Economic and Security Review Commission, January 14, 2016. https://www.uscc.gov/sites/default/files/Research/Issue%20brief%20-%20China%27 s%20Stocks%20Fall%20Again.pdf.]

Schmid, Jon, and Fei-Ling Wang. "Beyond National Innovation Systems: Incentives and China's Innovation Performance." *Journal of Contemporary China* 26, no. 104 (2017): 280–96. https://doi.org/10.1080/10670564.2016.1223108.

Song, Zheng Michael, and Wei Xiong. "Risks in China's Financial System." NBER Working Paper 24230, National Bureau of Economic Research, Cambridge, MA, January 2018. https://doi.org/10.3386/w24230.

State Council of the People's Republic of China. "China and the World in the New Era." Gov. cn, September 27, 2019. http://www.gov.cn/zhengce/2019-09/27/content_5433889.htm.

———. "The State Council Adopted Various Measures to Support Small Enterprise Development." Gov.cn, May 27, 2021. http://www.gov.cn/zhengce/2021-05/27/content_5612 867.htm.

Stein, Jeremy C., and Adi Sunderam. "The Fed, the Bond Market, and Gradualism in Monetary Policy." *Journal of Finance* 73, no. 3 (June 2018): 1015–60. https://doi.org/10.1111 /jofi.12614.

Stevenson, Alexandra, Michael Forsythe, and Cao Li. "China and Evergrande Ascended Together. Now One Is About to Fall." *New York Times*, September 28, 2021. https:// www.nytimes.com/2021/09/28/business/china-evergrande-economy.html.

Storesletten, Kjetil, and Fabrizio Zilibotti. "China's Great Convergence and Beyond." *Annual Review of Economics* 6, no. 1 (August 2014): 333–62. https://doi.org/10.1146/annurev -economics-080213-041050.

Su, Zhenhua, Yanyu Ye, Jingkai He, and Waibin Huang. "Constructed Hierarchical Government Trust in China: Formation Mechanism and Political Effects." *Pacific Affairs* 89, no. 4 (December 2016): 771–94. https://doi.org/10.5509/2016894771.

Tang, Michelle. "Ride-Hailing in Latin America: A Race between Uber and Didi's 99." *Measurable AI*, August 18, 2022. https://blog.measurable.ai/2022/08/18/ride-hailing -in-latin-america-a-race-between-uber-and-didis-99.

Tencent. *Aggressive Post-00s 2019 Tencent Post-00s Research Report*, 2019.

Thompson, Clive. "Inside the Machine That Saved Moore's Law." *MIT Technology Review*, October 27, 2021. https://www.technologyreview.com/2021/10/27/1037118/moores-law -computer-chips.

Tombe, Trevor, and Xiaodong Zhu. "Trade, Migration, and Productivity: A Quantitative Analysis of China." *American Economic Review* 109, no. 5 (May 2019): 1843–72. https:// doi.org/10.1257/aer.20150811.

Truman, Edwin M. "International Coordination of Economic Policies in the Global Financial Crisis: Successes, Failures, and Consequences." Working Paper No. 19-11. Peterson Institute for International Economics, Washington, DC, July 2019. https://doi .org/10.2139/ssrn.3417234.

Tu, Wei-ming. "The Rise of Industrial East Asia: The Role of Confucian Values." *Copenhagen Journal of Asian Studies* 4 (1989): 81–97. https://doi.org/10.22439/cjas.v4i1.1767.

United Nations Statistics Division. International Trade Statistics: 1900–1960, May 1962. https://unstats.un.org/unsd/trade/imts/Historical%20data%201900-1960.pdf.

US-China Business Council. *China's 2017 Communist Party Leadership Structure & Transition*. Washington, DC: US-China Business Council, 2017. https://www.uschina.org /reports/chinas-2017-communist-party-leadership-structure-transition.

Varian, Hal. "Artificial Intelligence, Economics, and Industrial Organization." In *The Economics of Artificial Intelligence: An Agenda*, edited by Ajay Agrawal, Joshua Gans, and Avi Goldfarb, 399–419. Chicago, London: University of Chicago Press, 2018.

Wakabayashi, Daisuke, and Tripp Mickle. "Tech Companies Slowly Shift Production Away from China." *New York Times*, September 1, 2022. https://www.nytimes.com /2022/09/01/business/tech-companies-china.html.

Wang, Zhi, Shang-Jin Wei, Xinding Yu, and Kunfu Zhu. "Re-examining the Effects of Trading with China on Local Labor Markets: A Supply Chain Perspective." NBER Working Paper 24886, National Bureau of Economic Research, Cambridge, MA, August 2018. https://www.nber.org/papers/w24886.

Wei, Shang-Jin. "Misreading China's WTO Record Hurts Global Trade." Project Syndicate, December 11, 2021. https://www.project-syndicate.org/commentary/misreading -china-wto-record-hurts-global-trade-by-shang-jin-wei-2021-12.

Wei, Shang-Jin, and Xiaobo Zhang. "The Competitive Saving Motive: Evidence from Rising Sex Ratios and Savings Rates in China." *Journal of Political Economy* 119, no. 3 (June 2011): 511–64. https://doi.org/10.1086/660887.

Whyte, Martin King, Wang Feng, and Yong Cai. "Challenging Myths about China's One-Child Policy." *China Journal* 74 (July 2015): 144–59. https://doi.org/10.1086/681664.

World Trade Organization. *Global Value Chain Development Report 2019: Technological Innovation, Supply Chain Trade, and Workers in a Globalized World*. Geneva: World Trade Organization, 2019. https://documents.worldbank.org/curated/en/384161555079 173489.

Wu, Cary, Zhilei Shi, Rima Wilkes, Jiaji Wu, Zhiwen Gong, Nengkun He, Zang Xiao et al. "Chinese Citizen Satisfaction with Government Performance during COVID-19." *Journal of Contemporary China* 30, no. 132 (March 17, 2021): 930–44. https://doi.org /10.1080/10670564.2021.1893558.

Wu, Ruxin, and Piao Hu. "Does the 'Miracle Drug' of Environmental Governance Really Improve Air Quality? Evidence from China's System of Central Environmental Protection Inspections." *International Journal of Environmental Research and Public Health* 16, no. 5 (March 2019): 850–879. https://doi.org/10.3390/ijerph16050850.

Xing, Jianwei, Eric Zou, Zhentao Yin, Yong Wang, and Zhenhua Li. "'Quick Response' Economic Stimulus: The Effect of Small-Value Digital Coupons on Spending." NBER Working Paper 27596, National Bureau of Economic Research, Cambridge, MA, July 2020. https://doi.org/10.3386/w27596.

Xing, Yuqing. "How the iPhone Widens the U.S. Trade Deficit with China: The Case of the iPhone X." *Frontiers of Economics in China* 15, no. 4 (2020): 642–58. https://doi.org /10.3868/s060-011-020-0026-8.

Xu, Chenggang. "Capitalism and Socialism: A Review of Kornai's *Dynamism, Rivalry, and the Surplus Economy.*" *Journal of Economic Literature* 55, no. 1 (March 2017): 191–208. https://doi.org/10.1257/jel.20151282.

———. "The Fundamental Institutions of China's Reforms and Development." *Journal of Economic Literature* 49, no. 4 (December 2011): 1076–151. https://doi.org/10.1257/jel .49.4.1076.

Yang, Li. "Towards Equity and Sustainability? China's Pension System Reform Moves Center Stage." SSRN 3879895, June 2021. https://doi.org/10.2139/ssrn.3879895.

Yang, Zhiyong, Cin Zhang, and Linmin Tang. "Chinese Academy of Social Sciences: How Risky Is Local Government Debt." *The Paper*, December 2, 2019. https://www.thepa per.cn/newsDetail_forward_5119321.

Yeaple, Stephen Ross. "The Multinational Firm." *Annual Review of Economics* 5, no. 1 (August 2013): 193–217. https://doi.org/10.1146/annurev-economics-081612-071350.

Zakaria, Fareed. *Ten Lessons for a Post-Pandemic World.* New York: W. W. Norton, 2021.

Zhang, Bin, He Zhu, Yi Zhong, Zhongming Sheng, and Zihan Sun. "New Citizens and New Models: The Real Estate Market for the Future." China Finance 40 Forum, June 1, 2022. http://www.cf40.org.cn/Uploads/Picture/2022/06/01/u6297090ccd409.pdf.

Zhao, Yaohui, John Strauss, Albert Park, and Yan Sun. *2008 CHARLS (China Health and Retirement Longitudinal Study, Pilot).* Beijing: School of Development, Peking University, 2009. https://charls.charlsdata.com/pages/Data/2008-charls-pilot/en.html.

Zhao, Yaohui, John Strauss, Gonghuan Yang, John Giles, Peifeng (Perry) Hu, Yisong Hu, Xiaoyan Lei et al. *2011 CHARLS (China Health and Retirement Longitudinal Study) Wave 1 (Baseline).* Beijing: National School of Development, 2013. https://charls.charls data.com/pages/Data/2011-charls-wave1/en.html.

Zheng, Jinghai, Arne Bigsten, and Angang Hu. "Can China's Growth Be Sustained? A Productivity Perspective." *World Development* 37, no. 4 (April 2009): 874–88. https:// doi.org/10.1016/j.worlddev.2008.07.008.

Zhou, Yu, William Lazonick, and Yifei Sun, eds. *China as an Innovation Nation.* Oxford: Oxford University Press, 2016.

Zhu, Xiaodong. "Understanding China's Growth: Past, Present, and Future." *Journal of Economic Perspectives* 26, no. 4 (Fall 2012): 103–24. https://doi.org/10.1257/jep.26.4.103.

INDEX